Materials & Components of Interior Design

J. Rosemary Riggs

A RESTON BOOK
PRENTICE-HALL, INC., Englewood Cliffs, New Jersey 07632

Library of Congress Cataloging in Publication Data
Riggs, J. Rosemary.
  Materials and components of interior design.
  Bibliography: p.
  1. Building materials.   2. Household appliances.
3. Plumbing—Equipment and supplies.   4. Interior
decoration.   I. Title.
TA403.R524 1985   690'.028   84-17800
ISBN 0-8359-4290-2

CONTENTS

WALLS

CEILINGS

OTHER COMPONENTS

FOREWORD

Benjamin Thompson said, "Search implies a struggle with no absolute end and no fixed in-betweens. For those who search, the struggle is more important than the end and, once that end is reached, the search begins anew, somewhere else."

To the serious design student, the obligation to understand the processes of design and the combination of materials, colors, and textures is an immense undertaking.

Since interior design is a search of these various combinations to satisfactorily solve the program requirements, then a reference book of the many materials available is a critical part of a student's education.

Rosemary Riggs' book is such a resource. Many hours have been spent in objectively presenting various materials and their attributes to the serious student.

One's search should not end, however, at the conclusion of this or any other book, in that there are new materials coming out daily and the continual

contribution of designers and producers is vast. It is, therefore, required that designers continue their search throughout their professional lives.

This reference book offers a substantial base for the students' search. It allows the students to see and understand some of the combinations of materials that may be used. However, students should be allowed and willing to do their own research, make their own combinations.

In reading this or any reference book, one should remember that the creative ability of individuals and what they can bring to bear to the design profession is of the utmost importance. One is not made into a great designer simply by reading one book or many books, but by the process of trial and error, and by learning from experience.

Therefore this book is recommended to you for enjoyment and to stimulate your own creative combinations and ingenuity.

Joseph Linton

PREFACE

While teaching an introductory class in interior design, I noticed that the students usually chose paint or wallpaper for the walls and always used carpeting on the floor, as though these were the only suitable treatments for walls and floors. I felt I needed to break the cycle and expose students to the fascinating world of materials—and so this book started to take shape.

I was unable to find a book that fully covered the exciting materials available to the interior designer. Some authors concentrated on historical aspects of the home, both in architecture and furniture. Some emphasized upholstered furniture, draperies, and carpets, while still others stressed the principles and elements of design and color and the aesthetic values that make up a home. However, no one concentrated on the "nuts and bolts" of interior design. Some books purporting to cover all types of flooring did not even mention wood floors, while others had only one or two paragraphs on the subject.

In the past, the interior design profession has dealt mainly with the more decorative aspects of design. Today it has become increasingly necessary for interior designers to be knowledgeable, not only about the finishing materials used in the design field, but about some of the structural materials as well. Many interior designers are working for, or with, architects, so it is important that they understand the properties and uses of all materials. Thus the "raison d'être" of this textbook.

Most sales representatives realize that the interior design student of today is the customer of tomorrow, but there are still some who do not understand the scope of the interior design field. Many interior designers are female, and I have found that the ability to talk knowledgeably about materials earns the respect of a male in the profession more than any other ability.

All disciplines have their own jargon and, in order for one to communicate properly with contractors and architects, it is necessary to be able to understand their language. When designers or prospective builders have read and studied *Materials and Components of Interior Design,* they will be able to talk knowledgeably with architects and contractors about the uses of materials and their methods of installation. This understanding will also enable them to decide for themselves which materials and methods are best suited for their purposes, without being unduly influenced by personal bias or ease of installation.

This book can also serve as a reference for designers who are already practicing. A contractor who read the book said that, from his point of view, contractors would also benefit from using this book as a reference.

In arranging the subject matter, I placed the chapter on paint first, since all types of surfaces—floors, walls, and ceilings—may be painted. Then, starting from the bottom up, the logical progression was floors, walls, and ceilings. Chapter 5 covers all the other components that make up a well-designed room, including mouldings, doors, hardware, hinges, fireplaces, and stoves. Chapter 6 is, with the assistance of the Architectural Woodwork Institute, an explanation of what goes into the structure and design of fine cabinetry. Chapter 7 covers kitchen cabinets and, with the background of the previous chapter, enables the reader to make an intelligent selection. This chapter also covers the various appliances used in kitchens. Chapter 8 covers bathrooms, both residential and institutional. In the future, designers will be called on more and more to assist in the renovation of homes, and a knowledge of kitchens and bathrooms will be very useful.

A glossary made up of words that are boldfaced in the text is placed at the end of each chapter. They have been broken down by chapter to make it easier to relate to other words from the same subject matter. Appendix A is a listing of manufacturers and associations who sell or represent the products mentioned in the chapters. Appendix B lists the names and addresses of the manufacturers previously named. Every effort has been made to make this list as up-to-date as possible, but businesses do change names and locations.

I am indebted to the many manufacturers and trade organizations who have so willingly provided me with technical information and brochures, from which I have been able to compile an up-to-date summary. I have found the trade organizations to be very helpful and particularly wish to thank the Architectural Woodwork Institute for its many drawings and information. Other trade organizations that have assisted me with preparation of the text were the Marble Institute of America and the Door and Hardware Institute.

In order to be as accurate and current as possible with the information contained in the text, I was assisted by many professionals. Those who were especially helpful include Craig Flint of Sherwin-Williams, Dale Ottley of Ottley Floors, David Stanley of State Stone, Gary Sandburg of Granite Mill, American Olean, and Buehner Concrete. The Eljer Plumbingware Company also gave invlauable assistance in the chapter on bathrooms.

Five individuals deserve my special thanks: Glenna Peterson, who read my book from the layman's point of view, made sure that I avoided the technical and sometimes foreign jargon that is present in so many design books, and made corrections in presentation methods; Pattie Heaton, a fellow faculty member at Brigham Young University, who reviewed the text from the professional interior design aspect; Richard Springgate, the photographer, who knew exactly what I wanted to emphasize in a photograph without it looking like an advertisement for that product; Joseph Linton, an architect and friend, who wrote the foreword, read the text, and provided many useful additions and explanations. (His home is shown on the cover.) Most of all, I wish to thank my husband, sculptor Frank Riggs, for his support and encouragement, and for many of the line drawings in the text. I am also grateful to him for not complaining about meals served at odd times during the writing of this book.

INTRODUCTION

For too many years, the fields of architecture and interior design have been treated as two separate areas involved in creating a pleasant living environment. The architect planned the exterior and interior of the home, often with little attention to where the furniture was to be placed. The interior designer had to contend with such things as walls that were not long enough to allow placement of furniture, or heating vents being placed directly under the bed or some other piece of furniture.

On the other hand, designers would ruin the architect's designs by using the incorrect style furniture, thereby spoiling the whole concept of the building.

Today, these problems are gradually being resolved because many architects have interior designers on their staffs. The result is that both disciplines cooperate from the very beginning of the project.

From the interior designer's point of view, this cooperation involves learning and appreciating the language and problems associated with architecture. The American Institute of Architects is a professional organization that accredits architects, and the American Society of Interior Designers acts in the same capacity for interior designers. It is because of the professionalism of these organizations that the fields of architecture and interior design have gradually become aware of the necessity for closer cooperation.

This book is dedicated to fostering that cooperation.

PAINTS AND FINISHES

CONTENTS

It is only since 1867 that prepared paints have been available on the American market. Originally, paint was used to decorate a home, as in the frescoes at Pompeii, and it is still used for that purpose today. However, modern technology has now made paint both a decorative and a protective finish.

The colors used are also of great psychological importance. A study done at Johns Hopkins University showed that planned color environments greatly improved scholastic achievement. Many major paint companies now have color consultants who can work with their customers on selection of colors for schools, hospitals, and other commercial and industrial buildings. Today, paint is the most inexpensive method of changing the environment.

Paint is commonly defined as a substance that can be put on a surface to make a film, whether white, black, or colored. This definition has now been expanded to include clear films.

CLASSIFICATION OF PAINTS

Most paints are classified according to their **vehicles** or **binders**—in other words, whether the contents of the vehicle or liquid portion is water, oil, varnish, or dissolved synthetic **resins**.

Oil Paints

Oil-based paints consist of a pigment suspended in linseed oil, a drier, and mineral spirits or other types of thinners. Until the development of alkyds, oil paints were considered the traditional house paint. Today, however, most oil-based paints are alkyds. Due to the lesser durability of oil-based paints and the strong odor, alkyds have now replaced oil-base paints.

Alkyds

Alkyds are oil-modified resins that dry faster and are much harder than ordinary oils. Drying results both from evaporation of the **solvent** and **oxidation** of the oil. The more oil there is in the formula, the longer it takes to dry, the better the wetting properties and the better the elasticity. Alkyds are used for both interior and exterior paints. They dry quickly and evenly, are durable for both interior and exterior application, have good color and color retention, are easy to apply, and are moderately priced.

Freshly made alkaline surfaces such as concrete, masonry, or plaster must be treated with an alkali-resistant primer before an alkyd is applied. Fumes of some alkyd paints are odorless but are toxic and flammable until the surface has dried. Therefore, the area should be thoroughly ventilated. Alkyd paint is the most durable of the common finishing paints.

Latex Emulsion

Latex binders are synthetic materials that can be varied in hardness, **flexibility,** development, and **gloss** of retention. There are several types of latex binders including styrene butadiene, polyvinyl acetate, acrylics, and vinyl acetate-acrylics, with the pure acrylics being the preferable choice. Drying results from **coalescence** of latex particles as the water evaporates from the film. Advantages of latex paint over oils or alkyds include the ease of application, freedom from solvent odor, fast drying and recoating, minimal fire hazard, blister and peel resistance, and ease of cleanup (requires soap and water only). In exterior applications, latex paints are durable, **chalk resistant,** and have good color and gloss retention. The main disadvantage is that they must be protected from freezing and applied at above-freezing temperatures—usually 50°F is recommended and, because of ease of application, the temptation may be to make the paint go further—

thus, coverage may not be as heavy as needed for a good paint job.

There are several finishes or **lusters** available in both alkyds and latex:

Flat. Velvety, with a rich, soft-looking surface for walls requiring little washing.

Eggshell or Satin. Slightly higher gloss/sheen for walls in residential areas where finger marks need removing.

Flat or Eggshell Enamel. Dull luster for washable surfaces.

Semigloss. Just enough sheen for contrast with flat-finished surfaces. Used in kitchens, bathrooms, nurseries, and school rooms in order to give greater resistance to wear and washing.

Gloss or High Gloss Enamel. Very shiny surface giving easy washability. However, the higher the gloss, the more likely it is to show surface discrepancies. This is true with both walls and woodwork, and demonstrates the importance of proper surface preparation.

The classification of paints according to gloss ratings depends on the ability of the surface to bounce back varying amounts of light beamed on it, and these readings show the relative reflectability of the coated surface as compared with a smooth flat mirror (see Table 1-1). The ratings in Table 1-1 measure the light reflectance of the surface only. Table 1-2 shows the

Table 1-1
Standard Gloss Range for Architectural and Special Coatings

Name	Gloss Range	Test Method (ASTM D-523)
Flat	Below 15	85° meter*
Eggshell	5–20	60° meter
Satin	15–35	60° meter
Semigloss	30–65	60° meter
Gloss	Over 65	60° meter

*Angle at which light is reflected.

Source. Consumerism Subcommittee of the N.P.C.A. Scientific Committee acting with the Subcommittee D01.13 of the American Society for Testing and Materials (ASTM).

Table 1-2
Percentage of Light Reflected by Colors

Color	Percentage of Light Reflected
White	89%
Ivory	77
Canary yellow	77
Cream	77
Orchid	67
Cream gray	66
Sky blue	65
Buff	63
Pale green	59
Shell pink	55
Olive tan	43
Forest green	22
Coconut brown	16
Black	2

percentage of light reflected by different hues and their different values.

Enamels

Enamels are pigmented paints that produce a hard, glossy, durable surface. In the standard architectural coatings, the highest sheen is produced by an alkyd enamel, but many lacquers and urethanes can achieve higher sheens. Enamels come in semigloss and gloss, but a flat appearance can be produced by adding a **flatting** agent, though this addition can affect some performance properties.

There are also water-based enamels on the market but, according to *Consumer Reports*, October 1980, water-based enamels are not as good as oil-based enamels because few dry to a truly glossy and hard finish. These problems may be overcome by future technology. Enamels and other paints should be applied to a properly prepared surface. A glossy surface will not have **tooth** and should be sanded with sandpaper or a liquid sanding material before application of another coat of paint.

Pigments

Pigments are the minute solid coloring parts of paints, and different pigments have different purposes. **Titanium dioxide** is the best white pigment for **hiding power.** Other pigments, whether organic or inorganic, merely add color to the paint. The third type, such as **calcium carbonate** is inert, acts mainly as a filler, and is used in masonry paints.

Stains

Stains are pigments applied to bare or sealed wood and may be transparent or opaque, depending upon requirements. Medium to light hues enhance the wood surface. There are several different types of stains. Probably the most common for interior use is the oil-based type where the oil penetrates to a measurable depth, thereby giving a more durable colored base. The oil-based stains should be covered with a urethane varnish on doors and window sills in order to provide a protective, durable surface for the wood. Due to the higher cost of urethane varnish, other wood surfaces not subject to heavy traffic or abuse may be coated with an oil or alkyd varnish.

Water-based stains have a water vehicle and have a tendency to penetrate the surface rapidly but not always evenly. Because water raises the grain of the wood, sanding is necessary, whereas it is not needed with oil-based stains. Alcohol stains have an alcohol base and they dry extremely quickly due to the rapid evaporation of the solvent. They are mainly used under lacquer and are applied by spraying.

Non-grain–raising (NGR) stains are more of a surface type of stain, rather than a penetrating one, but they do not require sanding before application of the final coat. Both alcohol stains and NGR's are used industrially due to ease of application and fast drying qualities.

Varnish stains are pigmented and give a very superficial colored protective surface to the wood. These are used when a cheap, fast finish is desired, but they never have the depth of color obtained with other stains. When the surface of a varnish stain is scratched, the natural wood color may show through.

Stain waxes do the staining and waxing in one process, penetrating the pores of the wood and allowing the natural grain to show, while providing the protective finish of a wax. Real wood paneling may be finished with a stain wax provided the surface of the wood will not be soiled.

Danish oil finish is used on wood; there are two types—clear and stain. The clear gives a natural finish while the stained contains a wood stain to achieve the stained effect. Danish oil finish has as its main components tung oil and boiled linseed oil, and gives the wood a rich, penetrating oil surface, while sealing the pores.

Primer

A *primer* is the first coat applied to the **substrate** to prepare for subsequent finishing coats and may have an oil, alkyd, or latex base. Some primers also serve as sealers and function on porous substrates such as some woods, but more especially on the paper used on **gypsum wallboard.** These nonpenetrating sealers prevent the waste of paint caused by absorption of the porous materials and provide a good base for the final coats. Other primers are specially formulated for use on wood surfaces where the natural dyes might cause unsightly stains. Some finish coats are self-priming, while others require a separate primer. The manufacturers' specifications will give this information.

Varnish

Varnish is a transparent or pigmentless film applied to stained or unstained wood. Varnish dries and hardens by evaporation of the volatile solvents, oxidation of the oil, or both.

Where a hard, glossy finish that is impervious to moisture is desired, spar varnish is recommended for both outdoor and indoor use. In areas where moisture is not present, an alkyd varnish provides a slightly longer lasting finish. Polyurethane is a synthetic resin used to make varnish resistant to water and alcohol, thus making it usable as a finish on wood floors and table tops. This type of varnish does not yellow or change color as much as conventional varnishes. The moisture-cured urethane varnishes are more durable but are also more expensive. **Humidity** must be rigidly controlled because less than 30 percent humidity will cause too slow a curing time and too high humidity will cause too fast a curing time, resulting in a bubbly surface.

Where a satin finish is desired, the gloss varnish surface may be rubbed down with steel wool, or a "satin" varnish may be used. Names of finishes do not seem to vary as much in opaque paints as they do in varnishes. One manufacturer will label varnish "dull" and another will call it "flat." Semigloss may also be called "satin" or "medium rubbed effect" and high gloss may simply be called "gloss." It should be remembered that the paired names are synonymous.

Shellac

Shellac is a resinous substance that is secreted by the lac bug and dissolved in alcohol. It is available in clear, orange, and pigmented white. Shellac was the original glossy, transparent surface finish for furniture and is the finish on most antiques. The urethane and oil varnishes have replaced shellac because they are not as quickly affected by heat and water. On a piece of furniture shellac will turn white when exposed to water and/or heat. Shellac is an inexpensive finish. Old shellac should never be used, as the surface will not dry thoroughly. If there is any doubt about the age of a particular shellac, it should be tried before it is used on a project. If the surface remains tacky, the shellac should be thrown away as it will never harden.

Lacquer

Lacquer is a paint that dries by solvent evaporation only and is applied by a spray gun. Lacquer may or may not contain pigments and is used commercially in the finishing of wood furniture and cabinets. A fine built-up finish may be achieved by many coats of lacquer, each of which is finely sanded before the subsequent coats.

Flame-Retardant Paints

Flame-retardant paints differ from conventional paints in that they are able to slow down the rate of combustion. Some of these fire-retardant paints are *intumescent*, which means that they form blisters and bubbles—thus forming an insulating layer—while others give off a gas that excludes air from the surface, thereby extinguishing the flames.

Flame-retardant paints are specified for public buildings, especially offices and hotels. After the tragic hotel fires of the early 1980's, it may become necessary to seriously consider these paints which, while not fireproof, do reduce the flammability of the substrate.

For many commercial painting contracts, a Class A fire rating is required by law, which means a **0-25 flame spread.** Included in some technical data are the amounts of smoke developed and fuel contributed. As more people die in fires due to smoke inhalation, perhaps the smoke development figure is more important than the flame spread figure. All major paint companies have flame-retardant paints and these manufacturers should be contacted for more specific information.

There is a great deal of misunderstanding about flame ratings and flame-retardant paints. The flame ratings are based on paints applied to either a wood surface (fir) or a noncombustible surface (cement-asbestos board). A paint applied to a cement-asbestos board will have a lower flame rating than the same one applied in the same manner to the wood surface because of the difference in combustibility of the substrate materials.

Solvents

Solvents, when used in paints, are liquids that dissolve the resins or **gums** or other binder constituents. These liquids are mineral spirits in the case of alkyds and oil paints, water for latex emulsions, alcohol for shellac, and lacquer thinner for lacquers. These solvents are used as thinners and for cleanup of the products in which they are used. Turpentine was used as a solvent before mineral spirits came on the market, but is not used as much today due to toxicity, high cost, and strong odor.

HOW TO BUY PAINTS

The specifier should learn how to read the technical part of the product guide, or find the same information on the label of the can. Some manufacturers state in the product description that it is a short, medium, or long oil coating. A long oil paint has a longer drying period and is usually more expensive. One of the properties of a long oil product is that it coats the surface better than a short oil product because of its wetting ability. The volume of solids is expressed as a percentage per gallon of paint and this percentage can vary from the 40's to the high teens. If, for the sake of comparison, a uniform thickness of 1 1/2 **mils** is used, the higher percentage volume paint would cover 453 square feet and the lower percentage only 199 square feet. This, of course, means that more than twice as much paint of the lower volume would have to be purchased when compared to the higher volume. Thus, the paint that seems to be a bargain may turn out to cost more in order to achieve the same result.

APPLICATION METHODS

There are four methods of applying paints—brush, roller, pad, and spray, either airless or conventional. The best available equipment should be used as poor quality tools will result in a poor quality paint job.

Regardless of the material used for the bristles (hog hair or synthetic), brushes should have **flagged bristles** (which help load the brush with more paint while assisting the paint to flow more smoothly). Cheap brushes have little or no flagging, which causes the paint to flow unevenly. Brushes are used for woodwork and for uneven surfaces, while rollers are used for walls and flat areas.

PPG Industries suggests that the rule for selecting and using almost all paint roller covers is: The smoother the surface, the shorter the nap and the rougher the surface, the longer the nap. Hence, the texture of the painted surface can be easily regulated.

A *pad applicator* is a foam pad covered with mohair or napped fabric. It gives a smoother and more even paint film and there is no spattering such as occurs with the use of a roller.

Spray guns are used to cover large areas, especially in commercial interiors. Airless spraying uses fluid pressure and conventional spraying uses air pressure. Most airless spraying uses undiluted paint, thus providing better coverage but also using more paint. The operation of a conventional spray gun requires a solvent-reduced paint.

All surrounding areas must be covered or masked off to avoid overspray, and this masking time is always included in the painting contractor's estimates.

Spraying is eight to ten times faster than other methods of application. These figures refer to flat walls, but spraying is an easier and more economical method of coating uneven or irregular surfaces than brushing, since it enables the paint to penetrate into the crevices. When spraying walls, the use of a roller immediately after spraying will even out the coat of paint.

Spraying is also the method used for finishing furniture and kitchen cabinets. For a clear finish on furniture and cabinets, a heated lacquer is used, which dries quickly, cures to a very hard film with heat, and produces fewer toxic emissions. Heated lacquer is formulated to be used without **reduction,** thus giving a better finished surface.

SURFACE PREPARATION

Mildew is a major cause of paint failure. It is not produced by the paint itself, but is a fungus whose spores will thrive in any damp, warm place—exterior or interior. There are several mildew cleaning solutions available, the simplest of which is bleach and water. Other remedies have additional ingredients and may be purchased premixed, but caution should be used with these products as they are extremely irritating to the eyes and skin. Instructions should be read and followed very carefully.

Wood

Moisture is the major problem when painting wood. Five to ten percent moisture content is the proper range. Today most wood is **kiln-dried,** but exposure to high humidity may change that moisture content. While knots in the wood are not technically a moisture problem, they also cause difficulties when the surface is to be painted, as the resin in the knots may bleed through the surface of the paint; therefore, a special knot sealer or shellac must be used. The shellac should be sanded to give tooth and to prevent a shiny surface from showing when covered by a flat paint.

All cracks and nail holes must be filled with a suitable wood putty or filler. This may be applied before or after priming according to instructions on the can or in the paint guides. Some woods with open pores require the use of a paste wood filler (see Table 1-3). If a natural or painted finish is desired, the filler is diluted with a thinner but, if the surface is to be stained, the filler is diluted with the stain.

If coarse sanding is required, it may be done at an angle to the grain; medium or fine sanding grits should always be used with the grain. Awkward places should never be sanded across the grain because the

Table 1-3
Wood Classification According to Openness of Pores

Name	Soft	Hard	Open Pore	Closed Pore	Notes
Ash		X	X		Needs filler
Alder	X			X	Stains well
Aspen		X		X	Paints well
Basswood		X		X	Paints well
Beech		X		X	Varnishes well, paints poorly
Birch		X		X	Paints and varnishes well
Cedar	X			X	Paints and varnishes well
Cherry		X		X	Varnishes well
Chestnut		X	X		Requires filler, paints poorly
Cottonwood		X		X	Paints well
Cypress		X		X	Paints and varnishes well
Elm		X	X		Requires filler, paints poorly
Fir	X			X	Paints poorly
Gum		X		X	Varnishes well
Hemlock	X			X	Paints fairly well
Hickory		X	X		Needs filler
Mahogany		X	X		Needs filler
Maple		X		X	Varnishes well
Oak		X	X		Needs filler
Pine	X			X	Variable
Redwood	X			X	Paints well
Teak		X	X		Needs filler
Walnut		X	X		Needs filler

Source. Abel Banov, *Paintings & Coatings Handbook.* Torstar Corporation, 1973, p. 127.

sanding marks will show up when the surface is stained.

Plaster

When preparing a plaster wall for painting, it is necessary to be sure that the plaster is solid, has no cracks, and is smooth and level, as paint will only emphasize any problems. Badly cracked or loose plaster should be removed. If there are any large holes, a piece of wire mesh, expanded metal, or heavy hardware cloth is used as a backing for the patching plaster. The edges of the hole should be dampened to give better adherence for the patching plaster. Small cracks should be enlarged to about 1/8 of an inch wide in a V-shaped manner. Again the edges are moistened to provide a good bond with the patching compound. All cracks, even if hairline, must be repaired as they will only enlarge with time. To achieve a smooth and level wall, the surface must be sanded with a fine sandpaper and, before the paint is applied, the fine dust must be brushed from the wall surface. Plaster is extremely porous, so a primer-sealer is required, which may be latex, alkyd, or oil-base.

Gypsum Wallboard

On gypsum board, all seams must be taped and nail or screw holes filled with spackling compound or joint cement; these filled areas should then be sanded. Care should be taken not to sand the paper areas too much as this causes a slight roughness that may still be visible after the final coat has dried, particularly if the final coat has any gloss. Gypsum board may also have a texture applied as seen in Chapter 3, page 75, and the luster selected will be governed by the type of texture.

Gypsum board must also be brushed clean of all fine dust particles before the primer is applied.

Metals

Metals must have all loose rust, **mill scale,** and loose paint removed before a primer is applied. There are many methods of accomplishing this removal. One of the most common and most effective is sandblasting, where fine silica particles are blow under pressure onto the surface of the metal. Small areas may be sanded by hand. The primer should be rust-inhibitive and specially formulated for that specific metal.

Masonry

Masonry usually has a porous surface and will not give a smooth top coat unless a block filler is used. The product analysis of the block filler shows a much larger percentage of calcium carbonate than titanium dioxide. One problem encountered with a masonry surface is *efflorescence*, which is a white powdery substance caused by an alkaline chemical reaction with water. An alkaline resistant primer is necessary if this condition is present. However, the efflorescence must be removed before the primer is applied.

WRITING PAINTING SPECIFICATIONS

Painting specifications are a way of legally covering both parties to the contract between the client and the painting contractor. There will be no misunderstanding of responsibility if the scope of the paint job is clearly spelled out, and most major paint companies include in their catalogues sample painting specifi-

Table 1-4
Coverage According to Method of Application

Method	Coverage per Hour
Brush	50–200 sq. ft.
Roller	100–300 sq. ft.
Spray	300–500 sq. ft.

cations covering terms of the contract. Some of these are more detailed than others. Table 1-4, Coverage According to Method of Application, and Table 1-5, Average Coat Requirements for Interior Surfaces, will aid the designer in calculating the approximate time required to complete the painting contract.

A time limit and a penalty clause should be written into the contract. This time requirement is most important, as painting is the first finishing step in a project and, if it is delayed, the final completion date is in jeopardy. The penalty clause provides for a deduction of a specific amount or percentage for every day the contract is over the time limit.

Information on surface preparation may be obtained from the individual paint companies. The problems created by incorrect surface treatment, priming, and finishing are never corrected by simply applying another coat of paint.

High performance paints should be selected if budget restrictions permit as high performance paints last several times longer than regular paints. This longer durability means business or commercial operations will not have to be shut down as frequently, thus the loss of business will more than offset the increase in cost. The words "high performance" should be included in the product description.

Table 1-5
Average Coat Requirements for Interior Surfaces

Surface	Vehicle	Number of Coats
Woodwork	Oil gloss paint	2–3 coats
	Semigloss paint	2–3 coats
Plaster	Alkyd flat	2–3 coats
Drywall	Alkyd flat	2–3 coats
	Vinyl latex	3 coats
Masonry	Vinyl latex	3 coats
Wood floor	Enamel	3 coats

Method of application should be specified: brush, roller, flat pad, or spray. The specifier must be sure that the method suits the material to be covered and the type of paint to be used. Also, primers or base coats must be compatible both with the surface to be covered and the final or top coat. When writing painting specifications, items to be excluded are just as important as items to be included. If other contractors are present at the site, their work and materials must be protected from damage. One area should be designated as a storage for all paint and equipment, and this area should have a temperature at or near 70°F, the ideal temperature for application of paints. All combustible material should be removed from the premises by the painting subcontractor.

The specifier should make certain that inspections are made prior to the application of each coat, as these inspections will more properly cover both client and contractor. If some revisions or corrections are to be made, they should also be put in writing and an inspection should be made before proceeding.

Cleanup is the responsibility of the painting contractor. This means that all windows and glass areas will be free of paint streaks or spatters. The area should be left ready for the succeeding contractor to begin work without any further cleaning.

Some states do not permit interior designers to sign the contract on behalf of their clients, while other states do allow this. The specifier will have to check state laws to see whether he/she or the client must be the contractual party.

How to Use the Manufacturer's Painting Specification Information

All paint companies have slightly different methods of laying out their descriptive literature, but a designer with the background material of this chapter will soon be able to find the information needed.

First, the material to be covered is listed, then the use of that material, and then the finish desired. Using wood as an example: The material is wood, but is it going to be used for exterior or interior work? If interior, is it to be used on walls, ceilings, or floors? Each different use will require a product suitable for that purpose. Floors will obviously need a more durable finish than walls or ceilings. Another category will be the final finish—flat, semigloss, or gloss? Will you need an alkyd, a latex, or, for floor use, a urethane? This is sometimes classified as the vehicle or generic type. The schedule then tells you which primer

or sealer is to be used in order to be compatible with the final coat. After the primer, the first coat is applied. This may also be used for the final coat or another product may be suggested. Drying time for the different methods of application may also be found in these catalogues. Two different times will be mentioned, one "dust-free," or "tack-free," meaning the length of time it takes before dust will not adhere to the freshly painted surface. In some cases, a quick drying paint will have to be specified, due to possible contaminants in the air. "Recoat" time may also be mentioned; this is important so that application of the following coat can be scheduled.

The calculated spreading rate per gallon will enable a specifier to calculate approximately how many gallons are needed for the job, thus enabling him/her to estimate material costs. Sometimes, in the more technical specifications, an analysis of the contents of the paint is included both by weight and by volume (see "How to Buy Paints," page 6). However, the most important percentage is the volume amount. This is the only way to compare one paint with another. It is the type and percentage of these ingredients that makes paints differ in durability, application, and coverage.

If paint is to be sprayed, there will be information on lowering the **viscosity** and, for other methods of application, the maximum reduction permitted without spoiling the paint job. Most catalogues also include a recommended thickness of film when dry which is expressed as so many mils **DFT**. This film may be checked with specially made gauges.

Table 1-6 is an example of information that may be found in three major paint catalogues. It is not a comparison chart as printed, but could be utilized as such if similar products were used.

PROBLEMS WITH PAINT AND VARNISH AND HOW TO SOLVE THEM

Temperature should ideally be around 70°F, but it can vary from 50°F up. Cold affects viscosity, causing slower evaporation of the solvents, which results in sags and runs. High temperature lowers viscosity, also causing runs and sags. High humidity may cause less evaporation of the solvent, giving lower gloss and allowing dirt and dust to settle and adhere to the film. Ven-

Table 1-6
Typical Paint Specifications

Material	Surface	Vehicle or Type	Luster or Finish	Primer	Final Coat	Type of Application	Drying Time		Thinner or Solvent	Coverage (sq. ft. per gal. dry mils)	% Nonvolatile by Volume	Company
							Dust Free Touch	Recoat				
Gypsum	Walls	Vinyl Acrylic		Quick-Drying Latex Sealer		Roller	10 mins	2–4 hrs	Water	350–450 sq. ft. 1.0–1.3 mils	28.9% ± 1.0%	PPG
		Acrylic	Flat		1–2 coats Speedhide® Acrylic Latex Interior Flat Wall Paint	Roller	30 mins	4 hrs	Water	400 sq. ft. 1.25 mils	31% ± 1.0%	PPG
Trim	Woodwork	Alkyd		Quick-Drying Enamel Undercoater		Brush	1–2 hours	24 hrs	Paint Thinner	450–500 sq. ft 1.5–1.7 mils	44.9% ± 1.0%	PPG
		Water-based Alkyd Resin	Eggshell		1–2 coats Quick-Dry Architectural Eggshell White	Brush	4–6 hours	24 hrs	Paint Thinner	425–450 sq. ft 1.9 mils	53.6% ± 1.0%	PPG
Plaster	Ceiling	Alkyd		Wall & Wood Primer		Roller	1–2 hours	16–24 hrs	Mineral Spirits	320 sq. ft. 2 mils	39.7% ± 2.0%	Sherwin-Williams
		Latex Vinyl Acrylic	Semigloss		1–2 coats Style Perfect Latex Semi-gloss Enamel	Roller	1/2 hour	4 hrs	Water	400 sq. ft. 1.4 mils	32% ± 2.0%	Sherwin-Williams

tilation must be provided when paints are being applied, but strong drafts will affect the uniformity of luster.

Today, most paint starts out with a base and the pigments are added according to charts provided to the store by the manufacturer. Sometimes it may be necessary to change the mixed paint in hue and this can be done by the judicious addition of certain pigments. Therefore, it is vital that the designer be aware of the changes made by these additions.

Bibliography

Banov, Abel. *Paintings and Coatings Handbook.* Farmington MI: Torstar Corporation, 1973.

"Coating Systems," *New Construction and Maintenance.* Cleveland OH: Glidden.

"Enamel Paints," *Consumer Reports*, October 1980, pp. 629–633.

"50,000 Years of Protection and Decoration," *History of Paint and Color.* Pittsburgh PA: Pittsburgh Plate Glass Company.

How to Choose Your Painting Tools. Cleveland OH: Sherwin-Williams, 1977.

Innes, Jocasta. *Paint Magic.* New York: Van Nostrand Reinhold, 1981.

"Introduction to Paint Technology," *Painting Systems for Specifiers and Applicators.* Cleveland OH: Sherwin-Williams, 1983.

"Paints and Coatings," *A Guide for Professional Performance.* S. San Francisco CA: Fuller O'Brien, 1975.

Percival, Bob. *How-to-Do-It Encyclopedia of Painting and Wallcovering.* Blue Ridge Summit PA: TAB Books Inc., 1982.

Product and Painting Guide. Pittsburgh PA: Pittsburgh Paints, 1981.

Rowe, A.R. "With Paint . . . It's the Dry Film That Counts." *Decorative Products World*, November 1981, pp. 58–59.

Time-Life Books. *Paint and Wallpaper.* New York: Time-Life Books, 1976.

Wheeler, Gershon. "Interior Painting, Wallpapering and Paneling." *A Beginners Approach.* Reston VA: Reston Publishing Company, 1974.

Glossary

Binder. That part of a paint which holds the pigment particles together, forms a film, and imparts certain properties to the paint. It is part of solids and is also known as vehicle solids.

Calcium carbonate. An extender pigment.

Chalk resistance. A paint with a binder that resists decomposition caused by weathering (which causes loose or powdery pigments on the surface).

Coalescence. The merging into a single mass.

DFT. Dry film thickness. The mil thickness when coating has dried.

Flagged bristles. Split ends.

Flatting. Lowering of the gloss.

Flexibility. Ability of paint film to withstand dimensional changes.

Gloss. Luster. The ability of a surface to reflect light. Measured by determining the percentage of light reflected from a surface at certain angles (see Table 1-1).

Gum. A solid resinous material that can be dissolved and that will form a film when the solution is spread on a surface and the solvent is allowed to evaporate. Usually a yellow, amber, or clear solid.

Gypsum wallboard. Thin slabs of plaster covered with a heavy-weight paper covering.

Hiding power. The ability of paint film to obscure the substrate to which it is applied. Measured by determining the minimum thickness at which film will completely obscure a black and white pattern.

Humidity. The amount of water vapor in the atmosphere.

Kiln–dried. Controlled drying in an oven to a specific moisture content.

Luster. Same as gloss.

Mill scale. An almost invisible surface scale of oxide formed when iron is heated.

Mils. Measurement of thickness of film. One one-thousandth of an inch. One mil equals 25.4 microns (micrometers).

Oxidation. Chemical combination of oxygen and the vehicle of a paint that leads to drying.

Reduction. Lowering the viscosity of a paint by the addition of solvent or thinner.

Resins. A solid or semisolid material that deposits a film and is the actual film-forming ingredient in paint. May be natural or synthetic. *See* Gum.

Solvent. A liquid that will dissolve something, commonly resins or gums or other binder constituents, and evaporates in drying. Commonly an organic liquid.

Substrate. The piece or object that is to be painted.

Titanium dioxide. A white pigment providing the greatest hiding power of all white pigments. Nontoxic and nonreactive.

Tooth. The slight texture of a surface that provides good adhesion for subsequent coats of paint.

Vehicle. All of a paint except the pigment. The liquid portion of a paint.

Viscosity. The resistance to flow in a liquid. The fluidity of a liquid, i.e., water has a low viscosity and molasses a very high viscosity.

0-25 flame spread. Lowest acceptable rating for commercial and public buildings.

2

FLOORS

CONTENTS

WOOD

Wood was used in ancient times for flooring. According to the Bible, Solomon's Temple had a floor of fir, whereas the Romans only used wood on the upper floors of their buildings, using stone on the main floor. These stone floors persisted throughout the Dark Ages. In the peasant homes, of course, dirt was spread with straw; however, heavy, wide oak planks predominated in domestic structures.

The first wood floors were called *puncheon floors,* which were split logs, flat side up, fitted edge to edge, and smoothed with an ax or an adz. When saws became available to cut the wood into planks, white pine plank flooring of great widths was used in the Colonial period in the United States and was pegged in place.

In 18th and early 19th century America, sand was frequently spread over the wood floor to absorb dirt and moisture. Later, these floors were stained and then covered by Oriental rugs in the more wealthy homes; in the more modest homes, they were either left bare or covered by homemade rugs. When renovating an old pine plank floor, the knots, which are much harder than the surrounding wood, have a tendency to protrude above the level of the worn floor and must be sanded to give a smoother floor surface. In some early floors that have not been renovated, it is actually possible to trip over these knots because they extend so far above the level of the floors.

In the early 19th century, **stenciling** was done directly on the floor in imitation of rugs, parquet floors, and marble and tile patterns. Painted floors and **floorcloths** came to be highly regarded until the carpet industry spelled the decline of floorcloths in the 1830's and 1840's. Incidentally, these floorcloths are now making a comeback with textile designers such as Meyer Romanoff.

From the early 1700's in France, **parquetry** and **marquetry** were used. One of the most famous examples of this period is the beautiful parquet floor at the Palace of Versailles.

In 1885, the invention of a machine capable of making a **tongue-and-groove** in the edge of the wood, plus the use of **kilns,** combined to produce a draftproof hardwood floor.

In the Victorian era, inlaid border patterns using contrasting light and dark wood were put together in a very intricate manner.

End-grain wood was even used to pave streets at the beginning of the 20th century.

In the early 1920's, unit block flooring was introduced, making parquet floors more reasonably priced because each piece did not have to be laid down individually.

Wood as a material for floors has definitely made a comeback in recent years, particularly in contemporary homes. This is due in part to the use of polyurethane and urethane varnishes, which give an almost maintenance-free floor. Previously, a wood floor had to be stripped of wax build-up and frequently resanded and refinished.

Wood is basically divided into two broad categories: the hard woods coming from the deciduous trees, which lose their leaves in the winter, and the soft woods, which come from the conifers or evergreens. Actually, there is an overlapping of hardness because some woods from the evergreens are harder than those from the broad-leafed trees.

The harder woods will, of course, be more durable and this durability, together with color and texture, must be considered in both flooring and furniture construction. Ease of finish should also be considered when the wood is to have an applied finish.

Weight is usually a good indicator of the relative strength of wood. Because wood is a natural material, it absorbs or eliminates moisture depending upon the humidity to which it is exposed. Most shrinkage or swelling occurs in the width of the wood; the amount depends on the manner of the cut. **Quarter sawn** woods are the least troublesome.

Warping is the tendency of wood to twist or bend when drying. This may be in the form of a **bow, crook, twist,** or **cup** and, as these are terms frequently referred to in construction, they are illustrated in Figure 2-1. The moisture problem can be reduced to a minimum by using kiln-dried lumber, where wood is stacked in an oven in such a manner that heated air can circulate around the whole plank in order to obtain a uniform moisture content. Seven to eight percent is acceptable in flooring and furniture making, and 12 to 19 percent is acceptable for construction grades.

Wood is composed of many cells that run vertically, thus giving wood its straight **grain.** At frequent intervals, **medullary rays** thread their way between and at right angles to the vertical cells. They are most noticeable in plain oak and beech.

We have all seen pictures or drawings of the circular rings of trees. Some of the giant sequoias of California and the ancient oaks of Great Britain have been dated by rings showing hundreds of years of growth. These rings show the seasonal growth and are comprised of spring wood—formed early in the growing season—and the summer wood or late wood. In some trees the different time of growth is very obvious, such as in ash or oak, while in others, such as birch and maple, the seasonal growth is more blended. When there is an obvious difference in growth time, there is also a difference in weight and hardness. The faster-growing trees, usually those in more moderate climates, are softer than the same trees grown in northern areas where the growing season is shorter. Next to the bark is the sapwood that contains the food cells and that is usually lighter in color. Heartwood contains the now-inactive cells and is slightly darker due to chemical substances that are part of the cell walls.

Figure is the pattern of the wood fibers, and the wood grain is determined by the arrangement of the cells and fibers. Some are straight and others are very patterned; this is enhanced by the method of cutting the boards.

There are two principal methods of cutting lumber. One is plain sawed for hardwoods, and flat grained for softwoods. The second is quarter sawed for hardwoods, or edge grained for softwoods. When referring to maple as used as a flooring material, the words "edge grained" are used, even though maple is hardwood. Oak is quarter sawn, but fir cut in the same manner is called "vertical grain." As interior designers will probably be dealing mainly with hardwoods, the terms "plain sawed" and "quarter sawed" will be used from now on, with the exceptions as mentioned above. Each method has its own advantages: plain sawed is the cheapest, easiest, and most economical use of wood, while quarter sawing gives less distortion of wood from shrinkage or warping.

Each method of cutting gives a different appearance to the wood. Plain sawing gives a cathedral effect, while quarter sawing gives more of a straight-

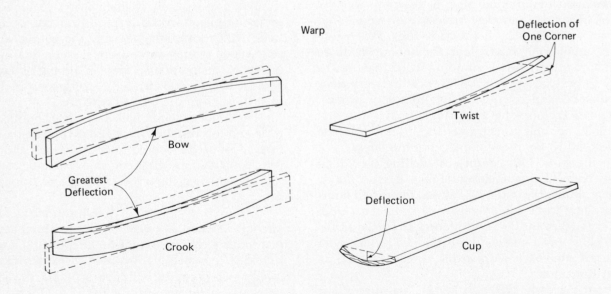

FIGURE 2-1. Warp

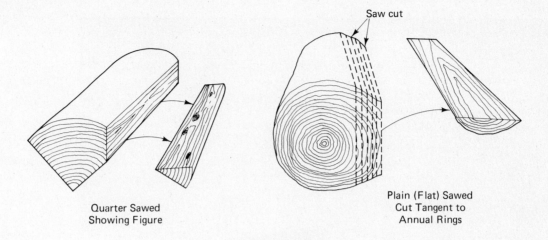

FIGURE 2-2. Quarter Sawed and Plain Sawed.

line appearance. As saw mills cutting logs into boards will produce 80 percent plain to 20 percent quartered lumber, quartered oak flooring is extremely hard to find and is expensive. Most of all production is mixed cuts.

Veneer is a very thin sheet of wood varying in thickness from 1/8 to 1/100 of an inch. Wood over 1/4 inch thick is no longer considered veneer. The manner in which the veneer is cut also gives different patterns. The three methods are rotary sliced, flat sliced, and quarter sliced. (These will be discussed in more detail in the wall paneling chapter.) **Laminated** wood is used for some floors and is a sandwich with an uneven number of sheets of veneer with the face having the better veneers. Water-resistant glue should be used for bonding the layers together, and the sandwich is placed in a hot press where pressure of 150 to 300 pounds per square inch (**psi**) is applied. Heat around 250° permanently sets the adhesive and bonds the layers together into a single strong panel.

The more expensive and rarer cuts of wood are used as the face veneer, thus holding down the cost and preserving the supply of these rarer woods.

TYPES OF WOOD FLOORING

Strip

Strip flooring comes in narrow widths, 2 1/4 inches or narrower, and is tongue-and-grooved on both sides

and ends. This type of flooring is most commonly made of oak, although some other woods may be used, such as teak and maple. The strip flooring may be laid parallel to the wall as in Figure 2-3, the cover, and Figure 3-7, or diagonally as in Figure 2-4. Gymnasium floors are always constructed of maple, but require a special type of installation that provides a slight give to the floor.

Harris-Tarkett manufactures a prefinished laminated strip flooring, Longstrip Plank™. The top layer is one species of several fine hardwoods each 4mm thick (1/6 of an inch, approximately). This top layer of hardwood is pressure glued to a core layer of crossbanded pine strips and then bonded to a pine veneer backing. Tarkett wood floors are designed to be installed with 1/8-inch foam underlayment as a floating system. Precise factory milling has eliminated "eased edges" to create a visually perfect floor and simplify floor maintenance. The tongue-and-groove boards come in three-strip boards, 8 feet long, with an almost impervious Swedish finish. These boards are packed with from 29.8 to 36.7 square feet per carton, depending on species.

Regular strip flooring is sold by the board foot and 5 percent waste allowance is added to the total ordered.

Random Plank

Random width plank is available in widths from 3 to 8 inches; most installations are composed of three different sizes. The widths selected should correspond to the dimensions of the room in order to keep

FIGURE 2-3.
*Red oak strip flooring is used in a contemporary vacation home. The railing surrounding the dining area is fir. The ceiling is also fir and the kitchen has a ceramic tile counter. (*Architect: *Tom R. Zabriskie;* photograph: *Richard Springgate)*

FIGURE 2-4.
*A strip floor is laid diagonally to contrast with the strong vertical and horizontal lines. (*Architect: *Mammon & Reynolds;* photograph: *Richard Springgate)*

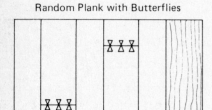

Random Plank with Butterflies

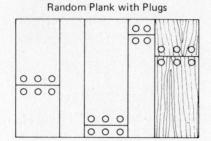

Random Plank with Plugs

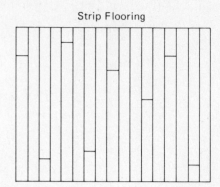

Strip Flooring

FIGURE 2-5. Types of Flooring.

the flooring in proper scale: the narrower ones for small rooms and wider ones for the larger rooms. Random plank comes with a **square** or **beveled edge** and may be **prefinished** at the factory or finished after installation.

Plank floors also have a tongue-and-groove side. The beveled edge prefinished tongue-and-groove installation does disguise any shrinkage, as the V-joint becomes a fraction wider, whereas with a square edge, the crack caused by shrinkage is more obvious. This is why it is important that all wood be stored in the climatic conditions that will prevail at the installation site. This will allow the wood to absorb or dissipate moisture and reach a stable moisture content.

In the past, some plank floors were installed using wooden pegs or plugs. A hole (or several holes in the case of a wide plank) was drilled about 1 1/2 to 2 inches from the end of the plank and a dowel was pounded into the floor joist and glued into place. Any excess dowel was cut and sanded flush with the floor. Many times, these plugs were constructed of a contrasting wood and became a decorative feature of plank flooring. In later years, screws were countersunk and short dowels of walnut, other contrasting woods, or even brass were glued in to cover the screws for decorative purposes only. Today, unfortunately, some prefinished floors may even have plugs made of plastic, which seems incongruous in a wood floor. Another decorative joining procedure was the butterfly or key, where a dovetail-shaped piece of wood was used at the end joint of two boards (see Figure 2-5).

Plank flooring is sold by the square foot and a 5 percent waste allowance is generally added to the total square footage.

Parquet

Parquet is individual pieces of wood, 3/8, 5/16, 1/2, or 3/4 of an inch thick, joined together to form a variety of patterns. These small pieces are held together by various methods: using a **metal spline,** gluing to a mesh of paper, or gluing to a form of cheesecloth. This holds the small pieces of wood in the pattern.

There are many patterns, as can be seen from Figure 2-6, and most manufacturers make a similar variety of patterns, but the names may vary. One company will name a pattern Jeffersonian, another Monticello or even Mt. Vernon, but they are basically variations of the same pattern. This particular design is made with a central block surrounded by **pickets** on all four sides. The center may be made of solid wood, a laminated block, or contain five or six strips going in the same direction. Or there may be a standard unit of four **sets** in the center (see Figure 2-7). For other examples of parquet, see Figures 2-8, 2-9, 3-37.

To minimize the expansion problems caused by moisture, the oak flooring industry has developed several types of parquets. One of the strip parquets has been described before; others are the acrylic-impregnated and the laminated floors.

Parquets such as PermaGrain® acrylic wood and Gammapar® have been treated with a liquid acrylic that has been forced under pressure into the porous structure of the wood. The wood is then subjected to irradiation, which causes the acrylic to impart to the wood an extremely abrasion-resistant finish. Dyes and fire retardants may be added to the acrylic, if required.

Hartco produces a prefinished, acrylic-impregnated parquet floor that is not radiated. The stain

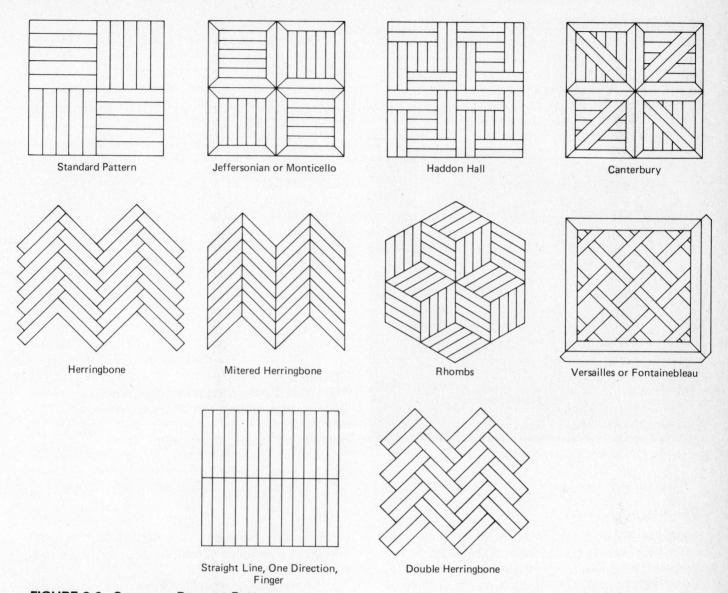

Standard Pattern   Jeffersonian or Monticello   Haddon Hall   Canterbury

Herringbone   Mitered Herringbone   Rhombs   Versailles or Fontainebleau

Straight Line, One Direction, Finger   Double Herringbone

FIGURE 2-6. Common Parquet Patterns.

penetrates throughout the wood so that worn areas need only be retouched with a topcoat. The floor never needs sanding, staining, or refinishing. With all these impregnated woods, it must be remembered that the color cannot be changed as it has penetrated the whole depth of the wood. This can be an asset or a liability, depending upon your requirements.

Hartco's new Pattern-Plus™ is designed to enable the creation of unlimited designs and floor patterns. Each piece is engineered with a tongue-and-groove to interlock with the other pieces. The individual units come in four lengths: 9, 18, 27, and 36 inches, all 3/8 of an inch thick and 4 1/2 inches wide. By mixing or matching lengths, original floor patterns may be created.

Hartco manufactures parquet squares with a 1/8 of an inch thick, 3 pound density polyethylene foam backing for residential use. For commercial installations, a 1/16 of an inch thick, 6 pound density foam is used. This extra density will stand up to the traffic in public areas.

The laminated block is a product that displays far less expansion and contraction with moisture changes and, therefore, can be successfully installed below

FIGURE 2-7.
A 3/4 inch Monticello pattern by Chicksaw faithfully reproduces the Thomas Jefferson design. (Photo courtesy of Chicksaw-Memphis Hardwood Flooring Company)

grade (see Figure 2-11) in basements, in humid climates, and even fit tight to vertical obstructions. The blocks can be glued directly to the concrete with several adhesive types. One of the concerns in the past has been the ability of a laminated block to be sanded and refinished. Because the face layer is oak, with proper maintenance, the initial service life can be expected to be 20 to 30 years. Any of the laminated products on the market today can be sanded and refinished, using proper techniques and equipment, at least twice, so the expected life of a laminated block floor is 60 to 90 years.

A new product from Harris-Tarkett is Dura Park™ which is a tongue-and-groove, square-edged block that may be arranged in a wide variety of patterns. Instead of the traditional sets in a square, Dura Park™ comes in a unit 4 9/16 by 18 7/8 inches and 5/16 of an inch thick which produces, according to manner of installation, the traditional set block, alternating parallel design, stairstep, or basketweave pattern. It is glued over dry concrete or wood subfloors.

Masonite also produces a Squar-Edge™ tongue-and-groove prefinished parquet floor in 12 3/4 inch squares.

Parquet floor comes packed in cartons with a specific number of square feet. When ordering parquet flooring, only whole cartons are shipped, thus the allowance for cutting may be taken care of with the balance of the carton.

Most woods for flooring are quarter sawed or plain sawed, but some species are cut across the growth rings (end-grained). Kentucky Wood Floors produces a mesquite floor that is cut in this manner. Mesquite is harder than most wood species and has a dark warm color of its own. The heart of a piece of mesquite has a small irregular crack that radiates across in two or three directions. This wind shake gives each block its own special signature. Mesquite rounds are set in a Latex and rock-hard wood putty grout.

Another end-grain pattern is formed by small cross-cut pieces that are attached together into blocks or strips with the end grain exposed. The thickness may

FIGURE 2-8.
A Haddon Hall patterned oak parquet flooring is the background for this contemporary dining room grouping. A shiny reflective base sets off the high-gloss painted wall. (Photograph courtesy of Milo Baughman Design; furniture by Thayer Coggin, Inc.)

vary from 1 to 4 inches, depending upon the manufacturer. Some use tetrachlorophenol to penetrate the blocks, while others use a penetrating oil finish. One and a half inches of end-grain block has insulating qualities equal to 23 inches of concrete. Some end-grain block floors are still in use after more than 40 years of heavy industrial use. These blocks absorb noise and vibration and have been installed in museums and libraries.

There are on the market special custom designed borders for use in the Victorian or older style homes. These borders are made of contrasting woods and vary in width from 4 inches up to 20 inches.

To achieve another custom look, parquet floors may be laid in specially designed patterns, usually using contrasting types of wood (see Figure 2-10).

Grade Levels

Figure 2-11 illustrates the difference between on, above, and below grade. Above grade is not a problem for installation of wood floors because no moisture is present. As mentioned earlier, moisture is the major cause of problems with wood. *On grade* means that the floor is in contact with the ground. The floor usually has

FIGURE 2-9.
A herringbone oak parquet floor adds an interesting background to the carpeted seating area. The custom designed ceiling is oak, incorporating a dropped luminary system. Note that in the conference room in the background, the areas of carpeting and parquet are reversed. (Architect: *Eduard Dreier, A.I.A.;* photograph: *Richard Springgate)*

FIGURE 2-10.
*A custom designed wood floor is laid diagonally
to the wall but is also parallel to the stairs. The
reflective surround of the floor is polished
marble. (*Designer: *Ruben De Saavedra;*
photograph: *Daniel Eifert)*

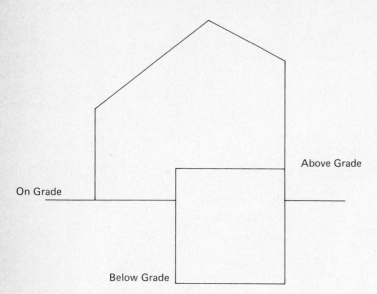

FIGURE 2-11. Grade Levels.

Installation Procedures

Slabs must be free of dust, grease, or oil stains and must be level. As has been stressed in the paint chapter and will be repeated throughout this textbook, **SURFACE PREPARATION IS EXTREMELY IMPORTANT.** The completed floor is only as good as the subfloor. Any high spots should be ground down and low spots filled in using the correct patching compound. One floor installer related a story about a client who complained of a loose wood floor installed on a slab. When the loose wood was removed, not only did the wood come up, but attached to it was the material used as a filler for the low spots. The person who leveled the floor had used an improper patching compound.

The following instructions are taken from the *Hardwood Flooring Installation Manual* published by the National Oak Flooring Manufacturers Association (NOFMA) Technical Service. There may be some slight variations in installation procedures, depending upon the area of the country.

a drainage gravel as a base, covered by a polyethylene film to prevent moisture from migrating to the surface. The concrete is then poured on top of this polyethylene sheet.

Below grade means a basement floor and the presence of moisture is an even greater problem. The polyethylene film should be lapped at the joints. Reinforcing rods are placed on top of the film and then the concrete is poured. All freshly poured concrete should be allowed to **cure** for 30 to 60 days. The rubber mat test will show if moisture is present. A rubber mat is placed on the cement surface and left for 24 hours and, when removed, if the concrete surface is dry, then there is no moisture present. This test should be done even if the slab has been in place over two years. The polyethylene film is of the utmost importance in insuring a subsurface that is properly moisture-free for installation of any floor.

Only laminated wood floors may be installed below grade, but the manufacturer's installation procedures must be followed exactly. Karpawood© and Asian Rosewood© imported by Bangkok Industries are 50 percent harder than red oak, almost inert, and therefore very useful for on or below grade installations.

The following is a very detailed description of the installation of wood floors. Many of these procedures will be followed when installing other types of flooring.

PLYWOOD ON SLAB METHOD. This system uses 3/4 inch or thicker exterior plywood as the subfloor nailing **base.** A 4 mil or heavier polyethylene film is laid out over the entire slab, with the edges overlapping 4 to 6 inches and extending under the base on all sides. It does not require imbedding in **mastic.** Plywood panels are laid out loosely over the entire floor. The first sheet of every other run is cut so end joints are staggered 4 feet. One-half inch of space is left at wall lines and 1/4 to 1/2 of an inch between panels (for expansion purposes). At door and other vertical obstructions where moulding will not be used to cover the void, the plywood is cut to fit, leaving 1/8 of an inch space. A minimum of nine nails are used per panel, starting at the center of the panel and working toward the edges to be sure of flattening out the plywood and holding it securely.

SCREEDS METHOD. This method uses flat, dry 2 by 4 inch **screeds** (sometimes called sleepers) of random lengths from 18 to 48 inches. They must be preservative-treated with a product other than creosote, which might **bleed** through and stain the finished floor. The slab is prepared by installing the vapor barrier in asphalt mastic and screeds are imbedded 12 to 16 inches on centers (**o.c.**) at right angles to the finished floor. The joints are staggered and screeds are lapped by at least 5 inches. A vapor barrier is applied for insurance over the screeds. The screeds method is suitable for strip or plank flooring up to 4 inch widths. The plywood on slab is used for wider planks. Three-quarter inch parquets and block are normally laid in asphalt mastic, but a good moisture barrier is very important.

INSTALLATION OF STRIP FLOORING WHEN LAID ON PLYWOOD-ON-SLAB, ON SCREEDS, AND PLYWOOD OR BOARD SUBFLOORS. A good grade 15 pound asphalt-saturated building paper is lapped 4 inches at the seams. This keeps dust out, retards moisture from below, and helps prevent squeaks in dry seasons.

For best appearance, the strip flooring is laid in the longest direction of the room or building. The walls are never used as a starting point because they are never truly square. The first strip is nailed 3/4 of an inch from the wall; this gap is for expansion and will be hidden by base moulding. Seven to eight loose rows of flooring are laid out end to end in a staggered pattern, with end joints at least 6 inches apart. A nailing machine drives a special barbed fastener through the tongue of the flooring at the proper angle but, due to the proximity of the wall, the power nailer is used only after several rows have been hand nailed. Three-quarter inch tongue-and-groove parquet and block are laid in mastic on wood subfloor or over a moisture barrier, as previously described. Figure 2-12 shows the various notch sizes that may be specified for spreading the mastic. Hardening time varies from 2 to 48 hours. The 3/4 inch parquet may be laid with edges parallel to the wall or at a 45° angle to the wall.

Wood parquet must always be installed in a pyramid or stair step sequence rather than in rows to avoid misaligned pattern. (see Figure 2-13).

Reducer strips may be used at the doorway if there is a difference in level between two areas, and are available to match the wood floor. Most wood floor mastics take about 24 hours to dry, so do not walk or place furniture in the room during that time period. Laminated planks must be rolled with a 150-pound roller before the adhesive sets.

An unfinished wood floor is sanded with the grain using progressively finer grits until the floor is smooth and has an almost shiny appearance. After vacuuming to eliminate any dust particles, finishing materials specifically manufactured for use on wood floors are applied. For open-grained wood such as oak, a filler and/or stain may be used after sanding to provide a more highly reflective surface.

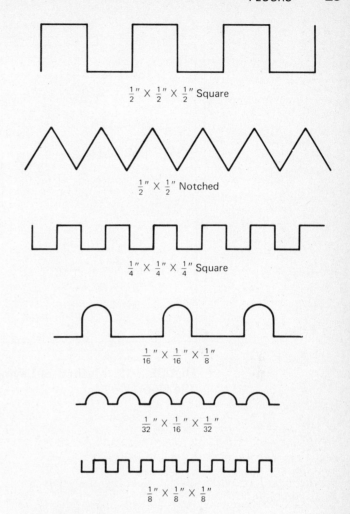

$\frac{1}{2}'' \times \frac{1}{2}'' \times \frac{1}{2}''$ Square

$\frac{1}{2}'' \times \frac{1}{2}''$ Notched

$\frac{1}{4}'' \times \frac{1}{4}'' \times \frac{1}{4}''$ Square

$\frac{1}{16}'' \times \frac{1}{16}'' \times \frac{1}{8}''$

$\frac{1}{32}'' \times \frac{1}{16}'' \times \frac{1}{32}''$

$\frac{1}{8}'' \times \frac{1}{8}'' \times \frac{1}{8}''$

FIGURE 2-12. Trowel Sizes.

Maintenance

It is the general housekeeping type of cleaning that prolongs the life of a wood floor. The main problem with maintenance of any floor is grit. This can be removed by dust mop, broom, or vacuuming. If the floor is the type that may be waxed, a thin coat of wax should be allowed to dry and harden. Then an electric bristle brush buffer is used. As old wax holds dirt and grease and a buildup of "scuffs," it should be removed periodically by means of a solvent type of wax remover specifically designed for wood floors. Food spills may be wiped up with a damp cloth.

Most factory-finished or prefinished wood floors have a wax finish that may be renewed with a paste wax. However, custom finishes such as polyurethane and Swedish should not be waxed. Manufacturers of

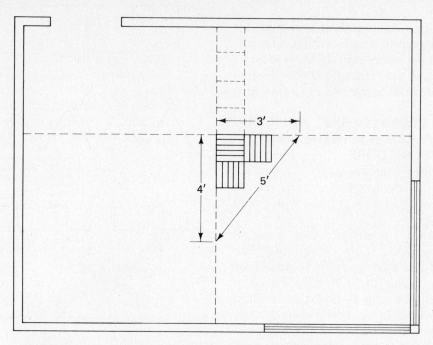

FIGURE 2-13. Method of Laying Out a Parquet or Tile Floor.

acrylic wood provide special cleaning materials for their products.

MARBLE

Marble was formed by layers of shells being subjected to tremendous heat and pressure, forming a **metamorphic** limestone composed predominantly of crystalline grains of calcite or dolomite or both, having interlocking or mosaic texture. Commercially, the term *marble* is used for crystalline rock composed predominantly of one or more of the following minerals: calcite, dolomite, or serpentine, and capable of taking a polish. There are literally hundreds of varieties of marble throughout the world, each with its own unique color and composition.

The largest proportion of all marbles are formed from the recrystallization of limestone. Most of these marbles are highly crystalline and usually white, although streaks or cloudings may be present. A second group is the onyx marbles. Essentially, they consist of calcium carbonate and are chemical deposits that have not resulted from metamorphism of preexisting limestone, but rather from processes of solution and precipitation. It is because of this dissolving of the calcium carbonate that successive layers may have different colors. Such banding gives beautiful decorative effects.

The third type of marble comprises the verd antiques. The name is applied to marbles of prevailing green color, consisting chiefly of serpentine, a hydrous magnesium silicate. Verd antiques are highly decorative stones, the green being interspersed at times with streaks or veins of red and white.

The colors of marble are as varied and numerous as the areas from which it is quarried. The famous Carrara marble is pure white. Pinks, reds, yellows, and browns are caused by the presence of iron oxides, whereas the blacks, greys, and blue-greys result from bituminous deposits. Silicate, chlorite, and mica provide the green colors.

Marble is the most ancient of all finished materials currently in use today and the Carthage Marble Corporation has provided the following interesting history of marble and its uses:

Some authorities believe that the onyx marble of Algeria was employed by the Egyptians as early as 475 B.C. It was also used to construct most of the buildings in the ancient North

African city of Carthage, from which the marble center at Carthage, Missouri, gets its name. This translucent marble, so delicately clouded with yellow and brown, seems to have been known to many of the early Mediterranean peoples and was used for the first buildings of Ancient Rome, yet the quarries were not rediscovered in modern times until 1849.

Historically, the men who preceded the early Hindus, Greeks, and Romans used marble as the most highly prized of all building materials. Biblical references indicate that marble was used in King Solomon's Temple at Jerusalem, and in the palace of Sushun more than one thousand years before Christ. Parian marble from the Aegean Sea was found in the ruins of Ancient Troy.

The marble industry came of age during the great architectural activity of the Roman Empire. As many as forty-two different quarries were known and developed by the ancient Romans, and all but two of these have been used in modern times. The oldest known Italian quarry is the Porta Santa quarry on Chias, which was worked as early as 660 B.C. Marble from this quarry was used in the Stadium of Palatine, the Julian Basilica, and the Basilica of St. Peter and St. Paul. It was, however, the Italian city of Carrara which gained prominence as the recognized center of art, architecture, and marble production—prominence which it maintains to this very day.

Near Carrara are quarries producing many of the world's most famous and most vividly colored marble, but it is the marble known as Carrara White which has been the beloved favorite of sculptors past and present.

The Parthenon in Athens was built of the celebrated Pentelic marble quarried at Mount Pentelicus in Attica. Phidias used this same marble for the frieze of the Parthenon and portions of this frieze known as the **Elgin Marbles** are intact today and greatly treasured by the British Museum.

The Taj Mahal, built in the early part of the 17th century, was known as the "gem of buildings," and is constructed entirely of white marble. Inside, the sunlight filters through marble screens as delicate as lace and the white marble walls are richly decorated with floral designs picked out in onyx, jasper, carnelian, and other semiprecious stones.

The early settlers of New England, especially Vermont, discovered marble that has been used extensively for over 150 years. The vast marble deposits in Missouri, however, were unknown until seven years after the Civil War. Other deposits of marble are found in Georgia and other Appalachian Mountain States, with some western states also having smaller deposits.[1]

Marble floors were used in the Baroque and Rococo periods in Europe. During the French Empire, black and white marble squares were used and remain a popular pattern for marble floors today. In the formal halls of Georgian homes, the marble floors were appropriate for the mahogany tables and chairs. In his Barcelona Pavilion, Mies Van der Rohe used great slabs of marble as free-standing partitions, and today marble is used for furniture, floors, and both interior and exterior walls. (See marble floors in Figures 2-10, 2-14, 3-8.)

Marble is a very strong material; however, there is 50 percent or more breakage and waste at or in a marble quarry which is the primary reason some marble costs more than others. These broken pieces are then used for byproducts such as **terrazzo** and marble dust.

Marble is a relatively heavy and expensive material for use on floors, due to the necessity of using the conventional, thick bed installation method. One method of cutting down weight and cost is to use a layer of fiberglass and/or epoxy resins as a backing for thin layers of marble. This method may also include a cellular aluminum honeycomb as used in an imported marble panel. Another method uses a 1/4 of an inch thick layer of marble backed by a 1 inch thick piece of Styrofoam. This latter method also provides a marble floor that is warmer to the touch than one made of thicker marble. A third method uses 3 mm of natural stone, then a .5mm of resin impregnated woven rovings of glass fiber which covers a 12.7 (or 25.4mm) of cellular aluminum honeycomb, backed with another layer of glass fiber.

Zeta Marble produced by Tecnomarmi and imported by Marble Technics is quarried from blocks of first quality marble and onyx and is the result of a special patented industrial process involving the resin bonding of different marbles. Zeta marble is available

[1]Carthage Marble Corp.

in 6 by 12 by 1/2 inch, or 20 by 20 inch sizes and is made up of strips of marble, which gives a solid but slightly striped effect, or of different types of marbles producing a definite striped effect.

There are also many new **agglomerate** marble tiles on the market. These agglomerates differ from terrazzo (see page 51) in that the percentage of marble and the size of the marble spalls are considerably greater. These tiles are composed of a vacuum-formed mixture consisting of 90 to 95 percent marble/5 to 10 percent resin, and are available as floor tile or marble wall veneers.

The following properties need to be considered for marble floors:

Density. Averages 0.1 pound per cubic inch. This figure may be used to calculate the weight of the marble.

Water absorption. Measured by total immersion of a 2 inch cube for 48 hours and varies from 0.1 to 0.2 percent, which is less than other natural stones. The maximum absorption as established by ASTM is 0.75 percent.

Abrasion resistance. Measured by a scuffing method that removes surface particles in a manner somewhat similar to the action of foot traffic. A value of 10 has been established as the minimum acceptable value for marble selected for general floor use.

A polished or glossy finish is not recommended for floors. Smooth satin or honed (a velvety, smooth surface with little or no gloss) or sand-rubbed (a flat nonreflective surface) should be specified (see Figures 2-10, 2-14, 3-8, 8-6, and 8-7).

When using marble or any other of the natural stones, it is necessary to calculate the weight of these materials and be sure the subfloor is strong enough to support the extra weight. This, of course, is where the 1/4 inch materials come into use, especially for remodeling, where the floor was probably not constructed to bear these heavy stones.

One of the newer materials to provide rigidity to the subfloor is the glass mesh mortar unit or Backer Board, with one of the brand names being Wonder Board.® This board, 7/16 of an inch thick, consists of five layers. The core is expanded shale, light weight concrete covered on both sides with a fiberglass mesh reinforcement. The outside layer is a skim coat of a high density portland cement surface. The subfloor suggested is a 1/2 of an inch minimum thickness plywood firmly fastened to floor joists with nails and construction adhesive. The floor joists should be 16 inches o.c. maximum. A layer of latex modified sand-

portland cement mortar is applied with a 1/4 by 1/4 by 1/4 inch notched trowel. The Wonder Board is placed on top and nailed in place every 6 to 8 inches, using 2 inch nails that penetrate through to the floor joists. The subfloor is now ready for the installation of materials requiring the thin-set method.

INSTALLATION METHODS. There are several associations that are responsible for codes and standards based on the consensus of their membership. The natural stones such as marble, travertine, and slate use the specifications and test methods contained in the American Society for Testing and Materials (ASTM), Section 4 Construction; volume 04.08 Soil and Rock; Building Stones. The ceramic tile industry uses the American National Standards Institute (ANSI) A108 for installation specifications. A copy of these specifications and test methods may be obtained from the respective organizations (see Appendix B).

As this is the first hard surface material covered in this textbook, installation methods will be detailed because, basically, the same methods are used for all natural stones, ceramic tile, quarry tile, and other types of flooring.

The only exception to the similarity of installation is that a marble setter **butts** tiles together, resulting in 1/16 of an inch width space which may be filled in with portland cement if desired or left unfilled. A tile setter, however, is accustomed to working with **cushion-edged** tile and so will leave a wider space between the tiles. It is necessary to state the spacing of the tiles and whether or not **grout** is to be used.

Thick-set or thick-bed *must* be used for setting materials of uneven thickness such as flagstone and other similar materials. It may also be used for hard-surfaced materials with uniform thickness. A layer of mortar is spread on the substrate to a depth of 3/4 to 1 1/4 inches and allowed to set for one hour. Then the tiles are placed on the mortar and tapped into place until the surface is level. The mortar used on floors is a mixture of portland cement and sand, roughly in proportions of 1 : 6.

Sometimes the tiles or stones are moistened on the bottom to aid in adhering qualities, or a thin layer of portland cement may be buttered or spread on the stone, which is then set in place.

Thin-set or thin-bed is only for materials of even thickness, such as pavers or tiles. This involves spreading a mastic or adhesive on the substrate with a trowel. An oil-based mastic should be avoided when installing marble as it stains the marble. These spreading rates are controlled by the use of a trowel with a

FIGURE 2-14.
A colorful marble tile is used on the floor in front of the windows of the bank teller stations. Above the marble floor is a marble shelf, which is repeated at the customer service area on the left. Columns are covered with sheet brass. Ceilings are acoustical panels. (Architects: Thomas, Petersen, Hammond, & Associates; interiors: The Richins Co.; photograph: Richard Springgate)

specified notch depth, which limits the amount of material to be spread (see Figure 2-12).

NORMAL MAINTENANCE. The following information is taken from the booklet "How to Keep Your Marble Lovely," which is available from the Marble Institute of America, Inc. (see Appendix A). Marble floors should be washed with clean luke-warm water, and twice a year a mild detergent can be used. The floor is rinsed thoroughly with clean water. Any residue could make the floor slippery. It should be remembered that all stones and many man-made, hard-surfaced materials are to some degree porous and should, therefore, be protected from oil and water-borne stains.

Most old stains require the use of a poultice which consists of white paper toweling or a white powdered household cleaner to form a paste. The poultice should be soaked in the proper solution depending on the type of stain and covered with a sheet of plastic that has been taped down around the edges to keep the moisture from evaporating while the stain is drawn out of the marble—from up to 48 hours, depending upon the type of stain.

To remove organic stains such as tea or coffee and leached colors from paper or textiles, the surface is washed with clean water and a poultice is applied soaked in either hydrogen peroxide (20 percent volume) or household ammonia (full commercial strength). Oil stains and mustard are soaked in Amyl Acetate or Acetone. (*Caution:* Amyl Acetate and Acetone are highly flammable and should only be used in a well-ventilated area and kept away from flame or sparks.) For rust stains, a poultice is soaked in commercial rust remover.

TRAVERTINE

Travertine is a porous limestone formed from the precipitation of mineral springs and has holes in it which resulted from escaping gas. When it is to be used on the floor, travertine should be filled with an epoxy resin. As travertine is creamy colored, this resin may be opaque, with a creamy color, or transparently clear. The opaque filler does not reflect the light as well as the surrounding polished travertine, whereas the clear epoxy gives a three-dimensional appearance to the holes and takes on the shine of the travertine (see Figures 2-15, 3-32, and 4-2).

MAINTENANCE. The maintenance of travertine is the same as for marble.

GRANITE

Granite is technically an igneous rock having crystals or grains of visible size. These grains are classified as fine, medium, or coarse.

Colors are white, gray, buff, beige, pink, red, blue, green, and black but, within these colors, the variegations run from light to dark. The color gray, for example, may be light, medium, or dark gray or vary between dark and purplish gray, or dark and greenish gray. It is important to see an actual sample of the type of granite to be used. The National Building Granite Quarries Association recommends submitting duplicate 12 by 12 inch samples to show the full range of color, texture, and finish, with the designer retaining one set and the other being returned to the granite supplier for his guidance.

In addition to color, the finish is important. The following definitions were set up by the NBGQA:

Polished. Mirror gloss, with sharp reflections.

Honed. Dull sheen, without reflections.

Fine rubbed. Smooth and free from scratches; no sheen.

Rubbed. Plane surface with occasional slight "trails" or scratches.

Thermal. Plane surface with flame finish applied by mechanically controlled means to insure uniformity. Surface coarseness varies, depending upon grain structure of the granite.

As with other stones, polished granite should not be used for floors because the mirror gloss and color will eventually be dulled by the abrasion of feet.

The same method of veneered construction used to make thinner and lighter weight marble squares is also used with granite, and for the same reasons.

When a feeling of permanence and stability is needed, granite is a good choice.

INSTALLATION. Granite is installed using the same methods as for marble, especially for the honed-face stones. When some of the more textured finishes are used, especially when the granite has not been cut to a specific size, a mortar joint is used.

MAINTENANCE. Granite floors, particularly those with rougher surfaces, require ordinary maintenance of dirt removal by means of a brush or vacuum cleaner. The more highly finished granite surfaces should be maintained in a similar manner to marble.

FIGURE 2-15.
The diagonally laid travertine floor and pool surround are a focal point of this condominium foyer. The filled travertine has been laid with the grain in the same direction to blend in with the diagonal installation. The ceiling is mirrored. (Architect: Ken Hanson; interior designers: Gayl Baddeley, A.S.I.D., and William Coltrin-Fleming, A.S.I.D.,; photograph: Richard Springgate)

Grout

Grout is the material used to fill the joints between tiles. The type of grout employed, if any, depends on which variety of tile is being used. Therefore, not only is the type of grout important, but also the spacing of the tile.

The Tile Council of America states that portland cement is the base of most grouts and is modified to provide specific qualities such as whiteness, uniformity, hardness, flexibility, and water retentivity. The commercial portland cement grout for floors is usually gray (colors are also available) and is designed for use with ceramic mosaics, quarry, and paver tile. Damp curing is required. *Damp curing* is the process of keeping the grout moist and covered for several days, resulting in a much stronger grout.

When a sand-portland cement grout is used, the proportion of cement to fine sand varies depending on the width of the joint; 1 : 1 for 1/8 inch joints, 1 : 2 for up to 1/2 inch widths, and 1 : 3 for joints over 1/2 inch wide.

Grouts with sand are not usually used with highly reflective tiles, as the roughness of the grout is not compatible with the high gloss. For glazed tiles, use portland cement grout or mastic grout. There are special grouts available that are chemical resistant, while some are fungus and mildew resistant, and others of a latex composition are used when any movement is anticipated.

FLAGSTONE

Flagstone was used on the floors during the Tudor period in England. *Flagstone* is defined as thin slabs of stone used for flagging or paving walks, driveways, patios, etc. It is generally fine-grained **sandstone, bluestone, quartzite,** or slate, but thin slabs of other stones may be used. One-inch-thick bluestone flagging in random multiple pattern compares very favorably in price to premium vinyl tiles.

The stone may be irregularly shaped as it was quarried, varying in size from 1 to 4 square feet, or the edges may be sawed to give a more formal appearance. Thickness may vary from 1/2 to 4 inches; therefore, the flagstone must be set in a thick mortar base in order to produce a level surface (see Figure 2-16).

The extra thickness of the flagstone must be taken into consideration when positioning the floor joists. One client had flagstone drawn and specified on her blueprints, but the carpenter misread the plans and presumed that it was to be a flagstone patterned floor and not the real thing. The client arrived at the house one day to discover that the entry way did not have the lowered floor necessary to accommodate the extra thickness of the stone. The contractor had to cut all the floor joists for the hall area, lower them 4 inches, and then put in additional bracing and supports in the basement—a very costly error.

Another point to remember with flagstone is that the surface is usually slightly uneven because it comes from naturally cleaved rock; therefore, flagstone is not suitable for use under tables and chairs as the legs will rock. An entrance hall of flagstone is very durable but needs to be protected from grease.

The grout used is a sand-portland cement type and fills all areas where the flagstones adjoin.

MAINTENANCE. There are sealing compounds on the market that make flagstone **impervious** to any staining and wear. These compounds are available in gloss and matte finishes and protect the treated surface against the deteriorating effects of weathering, salts, acids, alkalies, oil, and grease. The gloss finish does seem to give a rather unnatural shiny appearance to the stone but, where the impervious quality rather than the aesthetic quality is of prime importance, these sealers may be used. Vacuuming will remove dust and siliceous material from the surface and a damp mop will remove any other soil from the sealed surface.

SLATE

Slate was also used as a flooring material in the Tudor period in England (1500–1558) and, in 17th century France, slate was combined with bands of wood. Slate is a very fine-grained metamorphic rock cleaved from sedimentary rock shale. One of the characteristics of slate is that this cleavage allows the rock to be split easily into relatively thin slabs. The most common colors for slate range from gray to black, but green, brown, and red are also available. In areas of heavy traffic, the honed black slate does, however, have a tendency to show the natural scuffing of shoes and the scratches give the black slate a slightly grayish appearance. All stones will eventually show this scuffing and, therefore, highly polished stones should be avoided as a flooring material.

Different finishes are available in slate, as in other stones. The Structural Slate Company describes the following finishes:

FIGURE 2-16.
A metal faced door opens into a flagstone entry-way. The chest of drawers is topped with a carved mirror. Walls are covered by a silk wallcovering. (Architect: Eduard Dreier, A.I.A.; interior designers: Gayl Baddeley, A.S.I.D., and William Coltrin-Fleming, A.S.I.D.; photograph: Richard Springgate)

FIGURE 2-17.
Natural cleft slate has been used as a flooring in the kitchen of a condominium at a ski area. (Architect: *Max J. Smith;* photograph: *Richard Springgate)*

Natural cleft. The natural split or cleaved face. It is moderately rough with some textural variations. Thickness will have a plus or minus tolerance of 1/8 of an inch.

Sand-rubbed. This has a slight grain or stipple in an even **plane.** No natural cleft texture remains. Finish is equivalent to **60-grit** and is obtained by wet sand on a rubbing bed.

Honed. This finish is equivalent to approximately **120-grit** in smoothness. It is semipolished, without excessive sheen.

The standard thickness of sawed flooring slate is 1/2 inch. Also available are 3/4 and 1 inch thicknesses, and these are suitable for both interior and exterior use.

One-half inch slate weighs 7 1/2 pounds per square foot, 3/4 inch weighs 11 1/4 pounds, and 1 inch weighs 15 pounds. The absorption rate of slate is 0.23 percent. One-quarter inch slate is used for interior foyers in homes and commercial buildings using the thin-set method. This thickness is an excellent remodel item over wood or slab, and gives a rug level effect when it adjoins carpet. One-quarter inch slate weighs only 3 3/4 pounds per square foot.

The thicker slate is available in rectangles and squares in sizes from 6 by 6 inches to 24 by 24 inches in multiples of 3 inches, whereas the sizes for 1/4 inch slate are 6 by 6 inches to 12 by 12 inches also in multiples of 3 inches.

As can be seen from the above types, slate is available for both thin-set and thick-set applications. When thin-set mastic or adhesive is used, a 1/4 by 1/4 inch notched trowel held at a 45° angle is suggested.

There are, however, several points to remember with both types of installations. If grout is used with slate (the spacing varies from 1/4 to 1/2 inch), it is important that any excess be cleaned off because grout that has dried on the slate surface will probably never come off. If grout is not used, the slate tiles are butted against each other. Joint lines are staggered so no lines are more than 2 to 3 feet in a straight line.

Thick-bed installation is similar to flagstone. All joints should be 1/2 inch wide flush joints and should be **pointed** with 1 : 2 cement mix the same day the floor is laid to make joints and setting bed **monolithic.**

MAINTENANCE. A slate floor is easily maintained with mild soap and water. While waxing is not harmful, it detracts from the natural beauty of the stone, turns the floor to a darker shade, and may yellow the grout.

CERAMIC TILE

Due to the fact that ceramic tile was one of the most durable materials used by ancient civilizations, archaeologists have been able to ascertain that thin slabs of fired clay, decorated and glazed, originated in Egypt about 4700 B.C. Tile was, and frequently is, used in Spanish architecture to such a degree that a Spanish expression for poverty is "to have a house without tiles." The Spanish also use ceramic tile on the **risers** of stairs.

In England, many abbeys had tile mosaic floors and the European cathedrals of the 12th century also had tile floors. The very ancient tiles were used to make pictures on the walls, with the pattern covering many tiles. A good example is the bulls and dragons in the Ishtar gate from Babylon, now in the Pergamon Museum in Berlin. Later, each tile was highly decorated with very intricate patterns or four tiles were used to form a complete pattern. Eighteenth and 19th century tiles used a combination of these two types.

Tiles were named after the city where they first originated—Faience from Faenza in Italy, Majolica from Majorca, and Delft tiles from the town of Delft in Holland. Delft tiles, with their blue and white designs, are known worldwide.

Today, European use of ceramic tile for all purposes greatly exceeds usage in the United States, although in the West and Southwest, ceramic tile is being used more frequently and for more purposes than in other areas of the country (see cover photograph and Figures 2-18, 3-2, 3-11, 7-2, and 8-5).

Most glazed ceramic tiles for interior use are produced by the dust-press process. A mixture of damp, white-burning clays and other ceramic materials are forced into steel dies under heavy pressure. After pressing, the tile is inspected for smoothness, size, and imperfections. It may then be fired at a high temperature to form a **bisque,** a tile ready to be glazed. A glaze of ceramic materials and mineral pigments is sprayed on the bisque and a second firing at a lower temperature fuses the glaze to the bisque. Some glazed tiles are produced with a single firing. In this process the tile is pressed, allowed to cure, given a coat of glaze, and then fired in the kiln.

Tiles are also made by extrusion, a slush-mold process, or a ram-press process. In the extrusion process, the clay is mixed to the consis-

FIGURE 2-18.
In this restaurant, large scale paintings, glass doors, and movable room dividers are balanced by 24 inch square Italian ceramic floor tiles. (Italian ceramic tile by Marazzi, USA: designer: Teresa Pomodoro; photograph courtesy of Italian Tile Center)

tency of thick mud and forced through a die. The machine cuts the clay to proper lengths as it comes from the die. In the slush-mold process, a wet mixture of clay is poured into molds and allowed to set. The tiles are then removed from the molds, glazed, and fired in a kiln. In the ram-press process, tiles are formed between two steel dies. This method produces larger tiles of any shape or surface texture. The tiles are glazed and fired in the same manner as dust-pressed tiles.[2]

It is the temperature and the proportions of the ingredients that dictate the use—walls, floors, interior or exterior, and residential or commercial.

There are many types of finishes and patterns available in ceramic tile, ranging from a very shiny, highly reflective glaze to a dull matte finish. Tile may be solid colored or handpainted with designs, as seen in Figure 2-19.

The surface texture of the tile has a great deal to do with the reflectance qualities. For example, a perfectly smooth tile will have a much higher reflectance

Table 2-1
Porosity Variances

Type	Water Absorption Rate
Impervious	0.5% or less
Vitreous	More than 0.5% but less than 3%
Semivitreous	More than 3% but less than 7%
Nonvitreous	More than 7%

rate than a rough surface tile even though they may have identical glazes.

When ceramic or quarry tile is used on the floor, it is usually finished at the base with combination trim tiles having a **bullnose** at the top and a **cove** at the bottom in the same material as the floor tile (see Figure 2-20). If ceramic tile is to be continued onto the wall surface, a cove base is used.

CERAMIC MOSAIC TILE

Ceramic mosaic tile is usually formed by the dust-pressed method, 1/4 to 3/8 inch thick, with a facial area of less than 6 square inches. Pigments and, if required, abrasives are added to the porcelain or clay mixture, distributing the color throughout the tile. Ceramic mosaic tile is fired in kilns with temperatures reaching 2,150°F. It is impervious, stainproof, dent-proof, and frostproof. Because of a mosaic tile's small size, the individual tiles are mounted on a sheet to facilitate setting. Backmounted material may be perforated paper or a fibermesh. Face mounted tiles have paper with a water soluble adhesive applied to the face of the tile, which is removed prior to grouting (see Figure 2-21).

A paver tile has the same composition and physical properties as a mosaic tile, but is thicker and has a facial area of more than 6 square inches (see Figure 2-22).

Glazed tile is not recommended for floor use for two reasons. First, the surface can become extremely slippery when wet; second, some wearing and scratching can occur over a period of time, depending on type of use. Of course, if moisture and wear are not a problem, then glazed tile may be used.

FIGURE 2-19.
Italian ceramic tiles display colorful tulips in bloom. The 8 by 8 inch tiles are high-gloss and are appropriate for bathroom floors and walls. (Ceramic Tile by S.P.E.A. "Elite Series," available through Amaru Tile Selections, N.Y.)

[2]Don A. Watson, *Construction Materials and Processes.* (New York: McGraw Hill, 1972), p. 271. Reprinted, with minor changes, by permission of the publisher.

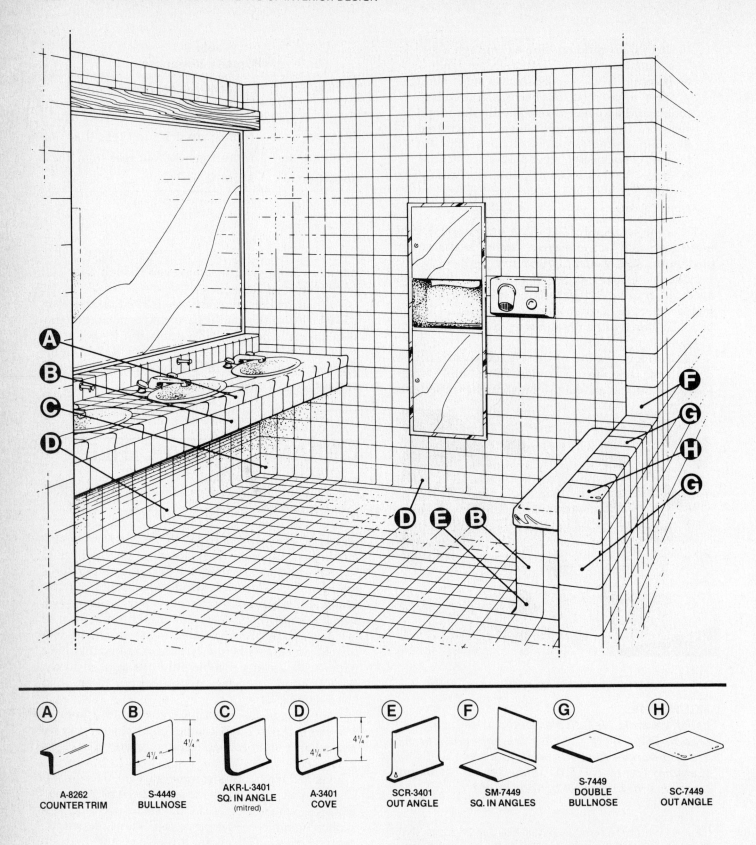

A
A-8262
COUNTER TRIM

B
S-4449
BULLNOSE

C
AKR-L-3401
SQ. IN ANGLE
(mitred)

D
A-3401
COVE

E
SCR-3401
OUT ANGLE

F
SM-7449
SQ. IN ANGLES

G
S-7449
DOUBLE
BULLNOSE

H
SC-7449
OUT ANGLE

FIGURE 2-20. Tile Trim. (Reprinted with permission of American Olean)

FIGURE 2-21.
*A clean contemporary plaid design is created using 2 by 2, 2 by 1, and 1 by 1 inch porcelain ceramic mosaic tile. The rugged, unglazed mosaics provide superior slip resistance and will not wear or fade. (*Tile: *American Olean Tile Company;* designer: *Robert Metzger)*

FIGURE 2-22.
The lobby of an office building has pavers on the floor and a reflective linear metal ceiling. The wall hanging becomes the focal point of the area. (Architects: *MHT Inc.;* interior design: *Conant Associates;* photograph: *Richard Springgate)*

The *Handbook for Ceramic Tile Installation* is published by the Tile Council of America, Inc., each year and contains Tables 2-2 and 2-3, which will help the designer to choose the correct tile for every type of use, and from that table be able to specify a Handbook Method Number, grout, and setting method. This handbook is also a guide in developing job specifications.

As can be seen from Tables 2-2 and 2-3, ceramic tile for floor use may be installed by both thick- and thin-set methods.

Specialty Tiles

Conductive tile is made from a special body composition by adding carbon black or by methods resulting in specific properties of electrical conductivity while retaining other normal physical properties of tile. These tiles are used in hospital operating rooms, certain laboratories, or wherever sparks from static electricity could cause an explosion, due to the presence of oxygen. Conductive tile should be installed using a conductive dry-set mortar with an epoxy grout.

Pregrouted tiles usually come in sheets of up to 2.14 square feet that have already been grouted with silicone rubber. Pregrouted tiles save on labor costs because the only grouting necessary is between the sheets, rather than between individual tiles.

Slip-resistant tiles contain abrasive particles that are part of the tile. Other methods of slip-resistance may be achieved by grooves or patterns on the face of the tile.

Some tiles are self-spacing because they are molded with **lugs.** Other means of spacing are achieved by using plastic spacers to insure alignment of tiles and an even grout area.

When ordering any tile, add 2 percent extra of each color and size for the owner's use. This will make replacements due to damage immediate and the color will match exactly.

QUARRY TILE

Quarry tile is strong, hard-body tile made from carefully graded shale and fine clays, with the color throughout the body. Depending upon the geographic area where the clays are mined, the colors will vary from the warm brown-reds to warm beiges. The face of quarry tile may be solid colored, variegated with lights and darks within the same tile, or *flashed* where the edges of the tile are a darker color than the center. The tiles are extruded in a half-inch-thick ribbon and then cut to size. The quality of the clays and temperatures at which they are fired (up to 2,000°F) provide a wide variety of finished products. Quarry tile is generally considered stain resistant but not stain proof.

The rugged, unglazed surface of quarry tile develops an attractive **patina** with wear. An abrasive grit surface is available where slip resistance is important. Almost all quarry tile is manufactured unglazed in order to retain the natural quality of the tile, but some quarry tile is available glazed (see Figure 2-23).

Quarry tile may be installed by either thick- or thin-set methods. The grout is either a sanded portland cement mix or an epoxy grout with a silica filler.

MAINTENANCE. Ceramic or quarry tile may be cleaned with a damp mop if the soil is light, or with water and a detergent if the soil is heavier. It must be remembered that tile and grout are two different materials, with grout being the more porous. Any soil that is likely to stain the grout should be removed as soon as possible.

It is the responsibility of the tile installer to remove all excess grout as part of the installation contract.

MEXICAN TILE

Clay, taken directly from the ground, is shaped by hand into forms. Therefore, Mexican tile differs from ceramic and quarry tile in that the proportion of ingredients in the clay are not measured. It is allowed to dry in the sun until it is firm enough to be transported to the kiln. As Mexican tile is a product of families working together, it is not uncommon to find a child's handprint or a dog or cat paw imprinted in the surface of the tile. Leaf prints may also be noticed where they drifted down when the tile was drying. These slight imperfections are part of the charm of using Mexican tile.

Due to the relatively uneven thickness of Mexican tile, it should be installed using the thick-set method (see Figure 2-24). If being used in a greenhouse or similar area where drainage is possible, Mexican tile may be laid in a bed of sand, which will accommodate any unevenness of the tile. All cracks or joints are then filled in with sand.

Table 2-2
Floors, Installation Performance Levels

FLOORS
INSTALLATION PERFORMANCE LEVELS
Performance-Level Requirement Guide

Use Guide to find Performance Level required. Then consult Selection Table at right and choose installation which meets or exceeds it. For example: Method F113, rated Heavy, can also be used in any area requiring lower Performance Level.

GENERAL AREA DESCRIPTIONS		RECOMMENDED PERFORMANCE-LEVEL RATING
Office Space Commercial Reception Areas	a) General	Light
Public Space in Restaurants and Stores, Corridors, Shopping Malls	a) General	Moderate
Kitchens	a) Residential b) Commercial c) Institutional	Residential or light Heavy Extra Heavy
Toilets, Bathrooms	a) Residential b) Commercial c) Institutional	Residential Light or Moderate Moderate or Heavy
Hospitals	a) General b) Kitchens c) Operating Rooms	Moderate Extra Heavy Heavy—use Method F122
Food Plants, Bottling Plants, Breweries, Dairies	a) General	Extra Heavy
Exterior Decks	a) Roof Decks b) Walkways and Decks on Grade	Extra Heavy—use Method F103 Heavy, Extra Heavy—use Method F101 or F102
Light Work Areas, Laboratories, Light Receiving and Shipping, etc.	a) General	Moderate or Heavy

Notes:
  Consideration must also be given to (1) wear properties of surface of tile selected, (2) fire resistance properties of installation and backing, (3) slip-resistance.
  Tile used in installation tests listed in Selection Table were unglazed unless otherwise noted. Unglazed Standard Grade tile will give satisfactory wear, or abrasion resistance, in installations listed. Decorative glazed tile or an especially soft body decorative unglazed tile should have the manufacturer's approval for intended use. Color, pattern, surface texture and glaze hardness must be considered in determining tile acceptability on a particular floor.
  For waterproof floors (to prevent seepage to substrate or story below), refer to Method F121 and also specify setting method desired.
Selection Table Notes:
  Tests to determine Performance Levels utilized representative products meeting recognized industry standards: Dry-Set mortar — TCA Formula 759; epoxy mortar and grout — TCA Formula AAR-II; and epoxy adhesive — TCA Formula C-150.
  a. Data in Selection Table based on tests conducted by Tile Council of America, except data for F144 and RF Methods which are based on test results from an independent laboratory through Ceramic Tile Institute.
  b. Floor covered after grouting with polyethylene sheeting. Water added to entire surface on second day and sheeting replaced.
  c. Rates "Heavy" if Dry-Set is wet cured for three days before grouting.
  d. Floor may show surface wear under constant steel wheel traffic.

Source: 1984 Handbook for Ceramic Tile Installation. Copyright © 1983 by Tile Council of America, Inc. Reprinted with permission.

Specification must include Handbook Method Number, grout, setting method and tile description as tabulated to achieve the intended performance level.

Handbook Method Number	Case	Page	Description	Grout	Comments On Use
F116		13	Organic adhesive on concrete Ceramic mosaic or glazed floor tile	Wet cured[b] 1 pc: 1 sand	Dry-Set or Latex-portland cement mortar preferred
F142		16	Organic adhesive on wood Ceramic mosaic or quarry tile	Latex-portland cement	Residential, low cost, bathroom, foyer
F143		16	Epoxy mortar on wood Ceramic mosaic tile	Wet cured[b] 1pc: 1 sand	High bond strength in residential use
TR911		29	Epoxy adhesive over existing resilient tile Ceramic mosaic or quarry tile	Latex-portland cement	Residential renovation
F141		16	Portland cement mortar on wood Ceramic mosaic tile	1 pc: 1 sand	Depressed wood subfloor in residence
F143		16	Epoxy mortar on wood Ceramic mosaic tile	ANSI A118.3 epoxy	Best for wood subfloors
F144[a]		17	Latex-Portland cement mortar on glass mesh mortar unit. Ceramic mosaic or quarry tile	Latex-portland cement	Light weight installation over wood subfloor
RF511[a]	6,11	24	Glass mesh mortar unit / matting	Commercial portland cement	Concrete subfloor
F112		12	Dry-Set mortar on cured mortar bed Ceramic mosaic tile	Wet cured[b] 1 pc: 1 sand	Economy for smooth surface
F113		12	Dry-Set mortar on concrete[c] Ceramic mosaic tile	Latex-portland cement	Economy
F113 F115		12 13	Dry-Set mortar on concrete[c] Ceramic mosaic tile	ANSI A118.3 epoxy	Mild chemical resistance
F122		14	Conductive Dry-Set mortar Conductive tile	ANSI A118.3 epoxy	Hospital operating rooms, other special
RF511[a] RF511	5 8,10	24 24	Glass mesh mortar unit / matting Portland cement mortar / matting	Commercial portland cement	Wood subfloor Concrete subfloor
F111 F112		12 12	Portland cement mortar Ceramic mosaic tile	1 pc: 1 sand	Smoothest floor surface
F112		12	Dry-Set mortar on cured mortar bed Quarry Tile	Wet cured[b] 1 pc: 2 sand	Economy for smooth surface
F113		12	Dry-Set mortar on concrete Ceramic mosaic tile	Wet cured[b] 1 pc: 1 sand	Best general thin-set method
F122		14	Conductive Dry-Set mortar Conductive tile	Wet cured[b] 1 pc: 1 sand	Hospital operating rooms, other special
RF511[a] RF511	7,9 12	24 24	Portland cement mortar / matting Portland cement mortar / matting	Commercial portland cement	Wood subfloor Concrete subfloor
F111 F112 F101		12 12 11	Portland cement mortar Quarry tile or Packing house tile	1 pc: 2 sand	Smooth, hard service best ceramic tile floor
F113 F102		12 11	Dry-Set mortar on concrete Quarry tile or packing house tile	Wet cured[b] 1 pc: 2 sand	Best general thin-set method
F113 F114 F115		12 13 13	Dry-Set mortar on concrete Quarry tile or Packing house tile	ANSI A118.3 epoxy	General, on concrete, for mild chemical resistance
F143		16	Epoxy mortar on wood Quarry tile or packing house tile	ANSI A118.3 epoxy	Hard service on wood subfloor, chemical resistance
F131 F132		14 15	Epoxy mortar on concrete Quarry tile or packing house tile	ANSI A118.3 epoxy	Chemical resistance
F134		15	Chemical resistant mortar on acid resistant membrane, packing house tile[d]	Furan or ANSI A118.3 epoxy	For continuous or severe chemical resistance

Source: 1984 Handbook for Ceramic Tile Installation. Copyright © 1983 by Tile Council of America, Inc. Reprinted with permission.

FIGURE 2-23.
In a room adjoining the outdoors, the 6 inch hexagonal quarry tile from American Olean adds beauty and practicality and sets off the classic-style furniture. (Interior designer: Ian Lipton; photograph courtesy American Olean)

FIGURE 2-24.
The rustic quality of Mexican tile in the lower lobby is a foil for the contemporary architecture, creating an eclectic look. Alternating clear and mirrored acrylic strips are suspended from the ceiling acting as interesting space dividers. (Architect: Ralph Edwards; photograph: Richard Springgate)

Mexican tile is extremely porous—the most porous of all tile—due to its natural qualities. This does present a problem during installation and grouting, as grout stains will show if not removed promptly. Clear varnish or liquid plastic generally have not proven satisfactory as a finish for Mexican tile.

The most durable and least porous finish is obtained by using a generous amount of boiled linseed oil. A second coat of linseed oil is used to even up the absorption of the tile. The porous parts are recoated until an even layer is obtained. Any excess oil is mopped up. (*Caution:* Oil rags are combustible.)

A clear paste Tre-wax is applied by scrubbing the tile with a fiber scrub brush, using approximately one pound per 125 square feet. Just before the wax dries it should be buffed. If an antique look is desired, brown paste Tre-wax is used, but it should be applied to only one tile at a time so the color is evenly spread. It should dry 20 to 30 minutes. The brown wax does not dry cloudy as does the clear, so it should be buffed just before it is dry. A sealing coat may then be applied.

MAINTENANCE. Keep the floor free of dust and dirt by sweeping or vacuuming and, when the wax shows signs of wear, apply another coat of wax and buff.

GLASS TILE

A glass tile manufactured in France and imported by the Briare Company, Inc. is composed of impervious, dense, and homogeneous glass. This glass mass is physically stable and inert; its porosity is nil and it is unaffected by chemical agents (alkalies, greases, hydrocarbons, industrial fumes, sea air, and all types of acid except hydroflouric). The pressing and vitrification at the second stage of firing gives it a distinctive appearance. These tiles are used for floors and also for walls in both interior and exterior commercial and residential applications. Glass tile is very suitable for moderate commercial uses such as in restaurants or offices. Heavy traffic may wear away the glaze, but the brilliant color of the tile will remain unchanged because the color is present through 100 percent of the mass.

The Domino Briare is available in a circle of approximately 11/16 and 3/16 of an inch thick. Of particular interest to interior designers, this product can be manufactured in any custom color to suit design requirements (minimum order 5,500 sq. ft.). The tiles come mounted on a 12 by 12 inch nylon mesh.

INSTALLATION. Either the latex-portland cement mortar or the epoxy-mortar methods of installation are recommended, due to the impervious nature of Briare. The grout within the joints should be semi-dry, and any excess is easily removed by rubbing the tile with a rough, clean cloth, such as burlap.

The Briare Design Service recommends a gray grout with light-colored glass tiles and a black or dark gray with dark-colored ones. Gray, being a neutral color, tends to fade into the background, allowing the beauty of the tile to come forward. A white grout is to be strictly avoided as it makes the outline of the grout stand out and visually "washes out" the tile.

MAINTENANCE. Simple cleaning with clean water and a sponge or mop should suffice. Any oily deposits should be removed by using soap and water and then rinsing with clean water. Polishing is never required.

GLASS BLOCK

Glass block is an 8-inch square of solid glass that is 3 inches thick. Vistabrick® provides excellent light transmission and good visibility with high impact strength. These blocks may be used as pavers and as covers for light fixtures recessed in floors. This material is used where special light effects are required.

MAINTENANCE. Same as for glass tile.

CONCRETE

Concrete is a mixture of water, portland cement, and an **aggregate** that may be sand, gravel, or rocks (1 1/2 inches in diameter or larger) or it may be a combination of sand and rocks. The final product will vary considerably, depending on the type and size of the aggregate used and the chemical and physical properties of the cement binder.

A concrete floor is low-cost as compared to other materials and is very durable. However, it is difficult to maintain unless the surface has been treated with a floor sealer specially manufactured to produce a dust-free floor. Color may be added when the concrete is mixed. A concrete floor looks less like an unfinished floor or subfloor if it is grooved into squares. Also, any cracking is more likely to occur in these grooves and be less visible. Concrete floors are being used in passive solar homes because the large mass absorbs the rays of the sun during the day and radiates the heat back at night.

MAINTENANCE.

Dry concrete will absorb alkaline salts, such as carbonates and trisodium phosphate. These absorbed salts will crystallize in the pores of the cement and increase in size as they pick up moisture. Subsequent harsh washings cause additional damage and complicate the problem of maintenance. Prewetting, therefore, should be standard procedure before using any cleaning solution on a concrete floor . . . Wetted concrete should be washed with a hot synthetic detergent, as soap will react with the lime and cause a scum . . . Well-sealed, dense concrete is easy to maintain and is less subject to injury from routine washing and scrubbing.[3]

TERRAZZO

Terrazzo was used as a flooring material during the Italian Renaissance. However, terrazzo, as we know it today, was not produced until after the development of portland cement in the 18th century. Terrazzo is a composite material, poured in place or precast, consisting of marble chips, **seeded** or unseeded with a binder that is cementitious, noncementitious (epoxy, polyester, or resin) or a combination of both. See Figure 4-10 for terrazzo tile.

The National Terrazzo and Mosaic Association explains that the chips are mixed with the **matrix** in a ratio of two parts aggregate to one part matrix before pouring. After the terrazzo topping is poured in place (in a monolithic installation), additional chips are sprinkled or seeded and troweled into the terrazzo topping to achieve the proper consistency.

Terrazzo that is poured into forms should be cured at least seven days and then ground on a water-coated surface, first with a coarse grit and then with successively finer grits.

[3]Adapted by permission of the American Library Association from Bernard Berkeley, *Floors: Selection and Maintenance* (LTP Publications no. 13), pp. 241–42. Copyright © 1968 by the American Library Association.

The NTMA gives the following sizes for aggregates:

Standard—1/16 to 3/8 inch chips.

Venetian—1/4 to 1 1/16 inch chips.

Palladian—3/8 inch thick **spalls** up to 5 inches in breadth.

The binder may be gray or white portland cement, or it may be colored to blend or contrast with the marble chips. Divider strips of brass, zinc, or plastic are attached to the subfloor and are used for several purposes—as expansion joints to take care of any minor movement, as dividers when different colors are poured in adjacent areas, and as a means of enhancing a design motif, logo, or trademark. Precast tiles of terrazzo inlaid in a resilient thermoset resin mortar come in approximately 12 by 12 inch squares with a 3/16 inch thickness (see Figure 4-10).

MAINTENANCE. The National Terrazzo and Mosaic Association specifically warns that soaps and scrubbing powders containing water-soluble inorganic salts or crystallizing salts should never be used in the maintenance of terrazzo. Alkaline solutions will sink into the pores and, as they dry, will expand and break the cells of the marble chips and matrix, causing **spalling.** (This is similar to the problem with cement floors.)

After the initial cleaning, the floor should be allowed to dry and then be sealed as soon as possible. This sealing is for the cement portion of the floor. The cleaning program for terrazzo is as follows: (1) daily sweeping, (2) regular damp-mopping to prevent dirt accumulation, (3) machine buffing to remove traffic marks and restore luster, (4) sealing as needed in high traffic areas, and (5) periodic machine scrubbing to remove heavy accumulation of dirt.

Stain removal for terrazzo is the same as for marble.

EXPOSED AGGREGATE

When an exposed aggregate floor is specified, the type of aggregate to be used is extremely important, as this is the material visible on the finished floor. River stone gives a smooth rounded texture but, today, the river stone effect may be achieved by tumbling the stones in a drum to remove the sharp edges.

While the concrete is still **plastic,** the selected aggregate is pressed or rolled into the surface. Removal of the cement paste, by means of water from a hose when the concrete is partially hardened, will expose the aggregate and display the decorative surface. For interior use, most of the aggregate should be approximately the same size and color, but other values within that hue may also be used, with a scattering of white and black stones.

One drawback to the use of exposed aggregate is that, like any other hard-surfaced material, exposed aggregate is not sound absorbent and is hard on the feet for prolonged standing.

A clear polyurethane finish specially formulated for masonry surfaces can be applied. This gives a finish that brings out the natural color of the stone, similar to the way a wet stone has more depth than a dry one. The coated exposed aggregate seldom seems to soil. A vacuum brush used for wood floors will pick up any loose dirt from between the stones.

BRICK

Brickmaking is an ancient art going back before recorded history to 9,000 or 10,000 years ago. All these early bricks consisted of clay and possibly straw mixed together with water to form a plastic mass that was put into molds and baked in the sun. The earliest recorded use of brick is in the Bible when the Egyptians made the Israelites work "in mortar and in brick" (Ex. 1:14). Burnt brick was used in the Tower of Babel and also in the wall surrounding the city of Babylon.

The Chinese also used brick in the 3rd century B.C. for building part of the Great Wall. The Romans used sun-dried bricks until about 14 A.D., at which time they started using bricks burnt in kilns. The Romans took this knowledge of brickmaking to Europe and Britain but, after they left in 410 A.D., the art died out and was not restored until the 11th and 13th centuries.

The first brick buildings in the United States were built in Virginia around Jamestown by British settlers and on Manhattan Island by the Dutch. The bricks used in Virginia were probably made locally as there are records of brick being exported in 1621.

Of course, the Aztecs of Mexico and Central America also used **adobe** bricks for building purposes. The Pyramid of the Sun in Teotihuacan, Mexico, which was constructed in the 15th century, still stands today.

Until about the mid-1850's, brick was molded by hand; from then on it was made using mechanical means. Bricks are made by mixing clays and shales

with water and are formed while plastic into rectangular shapes with either solid or hollow cores.

During the process of heating the bricks, the clay loses its moisture content and becomes rigid but it is not chemically changed. It is during the higher temperatures used in burning the brick that it undergoes a molecular change. When the temperature is raised further the grains fuse together, closing all pores, and the brick becomes vitrified or impervious.

The color of the brick depends on two factors: curing time and the temperature of the kiln. The red color comes from the oxidizing of iron to form iron oxide. The lighter colors (the salmon colors) are the result of underburning. If a higher, longer heat is applied, the brick will be harder. The harder bricks have a lower absorption rate and higher compression rate than the softer ones.

Because brick is heavier than most hard-surfaced flooring, care should be taken to see that the subfloor is strong enough to support the extra weight. See Figure 2-25 for a brick floor.

There are two methods of installing brick as a flooring material. One is mortarless, with the brick being set in a cushion of sand; the second is mortar set, with the brick set in a l/2 inch bed of mortar with mortared joints. In the mortarless installation, two layers of 15 pound felt are laid on the subfloor. Then a 1/2 inch cushion of sand and portland cement is spread on the felt and the bricks are laid as close together as possible and tapped into place. The use of the herringbone pattern or running bond is suggested because of the interlocking nature of these patterns. (See the herringbone pattern in Figure 2-6 and the running bond in Figures 2-25 and 3-3.) Fine sand is brushed across the top of the bricks to fill in any possible cracks.

With the mortar installation, the plywood subfloor is spread with a polyethylene film, then 1/2 inch of mortar is put down. The bricks are jointed with mortar and laid in the mortar bed. The excess mortar is cleaned off and the joints are leveled by using a rough rag. The density of the mortar joints is increased if they are **tooled,** leaving the mortar level with the surface of the brick.

The same ingredients that make brick may be used to make brick pavers. The difference between brick and brick pavers is the thickness, with the pavers being only 3/4 inch thick. All other properties are the same. These pavers may be installed by the same methods, but an adhesive may also be used as with thin-set ceramic tile, except that the grout, if used, should contain sand to be compatible with the brick texture.

FIGURE 2-25.
The lobby of this office building has a brick floor laid in a running bond without a mortar joint. The ceiling is Hunter Douglas' Box 4 Renovation ceiling system, engineered expressly for renovation work. The carrier system was attached to the existing grid ceiling and panels were snapped into place. It eliminated costly downtime and any need to modify light or ventilation systems. (Courtesy of Hunter Douglas, Inc., Architectural Building Products Division)

One of the newer products on the market is an acrylic impregnated brick made by PermaGrain Products, Inc. This PermaBrick® acrylic brick flooring is made in a similar manner as the PermaGrain wood flooring. It is a special technique for transforming the natural earthen material into an indestructible and, in the case of the F-Series, impervious brick paver. The F-Series is 2 1/4 by 7 1/2 inches and the S-Series is 3 5/8 inches; both are 5/16 inch thick. Both series have three colors. The S-Series has a mottled stone appearance and is **semivitreous.**

INSTALLATION. The PermaBrick Bonding Agent/Grout adheres the brick to the substrate and is also the grout. Six colors are available. The two methods of installation are single-step and two-step. In general, large jobs should be installed using the two-step method.

Single-step method: The Bonding Agent is applied with a 1/2 by 1/2 by 1/2 inch square notched trowel, and the Bonding Agent/Grout is spread in straight furrows. Each tile is pressed firmly into place so a squeeze-up of material occurs. Excess Bonding Agent/Grout is cut off and wiped off from the brick with a dampened sponge.

Two-step method: This is similar to the thin-set method, using a 1/4 by 1/4 by 1/4 inch square notched trowel. Bricks should set at least 4 hours (overnight is better). The surface of PermaBrick is dampened with a sponge and grouted with Bonding Agent/Grout.

MAINTENANCE. Brick may be vacuumed, swept, damp mopped, or spray buffed.

LINOLEUM

Linoleum was first invented more than a hundred years ago and was the only resilient flooring material available on the market for many years. Modern technology has now produced vinyl sheet flooring and, therefore, linoleum is no longer being manufactured in this country. However, many people still persist in calling sheet vinyls "linoleum" out of habit and, although the components of the two products are very different, the end results do appear similar.

ASPHALT TILE

Like linoleum, asphalt tile is another flooring material that is gradually being phased out due to advanced technology. Actually, at the moment there is very little asphaltic material in this tile. Asphalt tile is very inexpensive but does not have resistance to stains and can be softened by mineral oils or animal fats. The individual tiles are brittle and have poor recovery from indentation. Any of the solvents will permanently damage the surface. Nine inch by nine inch squares are available in the darker shades in a marbleized pattern.

INSTALLATION OF RESILIENT TILE. Asphalt, vinyl asbestos, vinyl, cork, and other resilient tiles are all installed using the thin-set method. The most important step in this installation procedure is to be sure the subfloor is smooth and level. Due to the thin nature of these tiles, any discrepancies in the subfloor will be visible on the surface of the tile. One friend was extremely disturbed to find that her newly installed floor had developed a wavy and bumpy appearance after only several weeks because the wood subfloor had not been sanded.

The subfloor is troweled with the suggested adhesive and, as with the installation of parquet floors, the walls should not be used as a starting point (see Figure 2-13).

MAINTENANCE. All resilient tile floors should be washed using only a damp mop as an excess of water is likely to cause raised or uneven tiles due to moisture penetrating through the joints to the subfloor. Asphalt tile may have a factory coating for protection during shipping and installation and, if this is present, it should be removed before further treatment. There are many liquid waxes on the market that may be used for residential use, but the solvent types of paste waxes should never be used on asphalt tile. For commercial installations, Hillyard Chemical Company makes cleaners and waxes that may or may not require buffing. This company specializes in floor treatments and supplies finishing and maintenance information for every type of flooring discussed in this book. Many janitorial supply companies also produce suitable maintenance cleaners and waxes for commercial installations.

Vinyl composition and vinyl tile floors are all maintained in the same manner as asphalt tile.

VINYL ASBESTOS (VINYL COMPOSITION)

Vinyl asbestos is the most commonly used floor tile for less expensive installations. Vinyl asbestos consists of blended compositions of asbestos fibers, vinyls, resins, plasticizers, coloring pigments, and fillers formed into thin sheets under heat and pressure. The thin sheets, without backing, are then cut into tiles (see Figure 2-26).

In recent years the word "asbestos" has connoted an image of adverse health effects. Some studies have shown asbestos fibers to be injurious to the health in their loose state, but the tiles themselves are safe provided they are not sanded or the original surface disturbed.

The words "vinyl composition" and "reinforced vinyl" are now used to avoid the word "asbestos." The tile contents may be checked to see if asbestos is present. Most vinyl composition tiles, in fact, are no longer manufactured with asbestos.

The thickness, or **gauge,** as it is sometimes called, is 1/16, 3/32, and 1/8 inch. For commercial and better residential installations, the 1/8 inch gauge is the best choice. The advantages of vinyl composition tiles are that it (1) is inexpensive, (2) is easy to install and maintain, (3) may be installed on any grade, (4) resists acids and alkalies, and (5) withstands strong cleaning compounds. The disadvantages are that it (1) has low impact resistance, (2) has poor noise absorption, and (3) is semiporous as compared to solid vinyls and solid rubber.

MAINTENANCE. See Asphalt Tile.

VINYL TILE

Vinyl tiles are homogeneous or, in other words, solid vinyl with the color throughout the tile. They are available in the traditional marble and travertine designs and also in brick, slate, and stone patterns. Solid color vinyl tiles are used as feature strips or for borders. Borders should be of approximately the same width at all walls. Vinyl tiles are constructed of polyvinyl chloride with mineral fillers, pigments, plasticizers, and stabilizers.

Several companies manufacture a vinyl floor with real wood veneer literally sealed between solid vinyl. The top layer is made of a transparent 0.20 of an inch thick, pure vinyl, which permits the natural color and texture of the wood grain to be visible, yet protected.

Vinyl wall base effectively trims off a resilient floor installation and also helps hide minor wall and floor irregularities. Its distinctive profile consists of a reclining curvature at the top and a descending thintoe line which conforms snugly with wall and floor. Some vinyl coves can be hand-formed to make the corners, while others come with both inside and outside corners preformed. The cove wall base comes either in 20 foot rolls or 48 inch strips in 2 1/4 inch or 4 inch heights. (see Figure 2-27).

INSTALLATION. Tiles are installed with a specified adhesive in a pyramid fashion (see Figure 2-13).

MAINTENANCE. The new tile floor should not be washed, just damp mopped for a week to allow the adhesive to set. Spots of adhesive can be removed with a clean white cloth dampened with paste wax or lighter fluid. Periodic sweeping with a soft broom or vacuum will prevent buildup of dust and dirt. Spills should be cleaned immediately. Damp mopping with a mild detergent is sufficient for slightly soiled floors, or scrubbing with a brush or machine for heavy soil. Soap-based cleaners should not be used because they can leave a dulling film. The floor should then be rinsed with clean water. The floor should never be flooded, and excess dirty water should be removed with a mop or vacuum. Azrock states that no-wax floors can be damaged by intense heat, lighted cigarettes, and rubber- or foam-backed mats or rugs. If stubborn stains persist, try rubbing the spot with alcohol or lighter fluid.

RUBBER

Rubber tiles are made of butadiene styrene rubber and synthetics and are available in 9 and 12 inch squares, with a thickness of either 3/32, 1/8, or 3/16 inch. The tiles are usually marble or travertine patterned, laid at right angles to each other. They may be laid below grade and are extremely sound absorbing.

Sheet rubber comes in 36 3/4 inch untrimmed widths, also in the marbleized patterns. A solid color sheet rubber is becoming increasingly popular where excessive dirt or excessive moisture are likely to be tracked inside. These sheets have raised discs or studs with beveled edges, causing the dirt to drop down below the wear surface, which lowers the abrasion on the wear surface. The same thing happens with water; it, too, flows below the wear surface, which prevents the hazard of a slippery surface. This type of sheet may also be cut into 17 13/16 inch squares and then heat sealed. The same material is available for stair treads and provides a safe covering for stairs. While the original purpose of this tile was stated above, many installations are purely for aesthetic rather than utilitarian reasons. (see Figure 2-28).

FIGURE 2-26.
Vinyl composition floor tile from Azrock creates the formal feeling of black and white marble tile without the weight and expense of marble. (Courtesy of Azrock Floor Products)

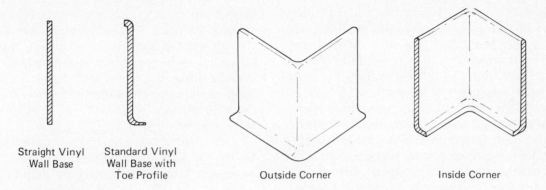

Straight Vinyl
Wall Base

Standard Vinyl
Wall Base with
Toe Profile

Outside Corner

Inside Corner

FIGURE 2-27. Vinyl Cove Base.

FIGURE 2-28. Close Up View of a Raised Disc Rubber Flooring.

MAINTENANCE. The RCA Rubber Company, an Ohio Corporation of Akron, Ohio, suggests the following maintenance for their floors. For new installations, clean the floor thoroughly with a good grade of mild detergent cleaner. Remove detergent from the floor and rinse with a solution of 10 percent Clorox® in warm water. When the floor is dry, use a high speed buffer. New floors will require more frequent buffing until a high sheen is acquired. For further maintenance, dry dust or mop floors (no mops treated with mineral oil or other petroleum products). Periodically mop the floors using a 5 percent solution of Clorox® in water.

SHEET VINYL

Sheet vinyl comes in 6, 9, or 12 foot widths and is manufactured by two methods, inlaid or rotogravure. Most inlaid sheet vinyls are made of thousands of tiny vinyl granules built up layer by layer then fused together with heat and pressure. The result is a soft, hefty flooring with a noticeable depth of color and a crafted look. Inlaid vinyls are thick and soft. Some have extra layers of foam cushioning to provide comfort underfoot and muffle footsteps and other noises. Color and pattern go all the way through the vinyl layer.

Rotovinyls, also called *rotogravure vinyls*, are made by a rotogravure process that combines photography and printing. Almost any image that can be photographed can be reproduced on a rotovinyl floor. The printed layer is protected by a topping (called the *wear layer*) of vinyl resin either alone or in combination with urethane. The vinyl resin composition produces a satin-gloss surface, whereas urethane creates high-sheen results. A mechanical buffer with a lamb's wool pad will bring back the satin-gloss of the vinyl resin composition wear layers. When comparing data on vinyl sheet flooring, you will note that the wear layer of vinyl resin composition is usually thicker than the wear layer made of urethane or any combination of urethane and other products. This difference is due to the fact that urethane cannot be applied in more than a 2 mil thickness. Wear layers in domestic sheet vinyls may vary from .010 to .025 inch, while commercial wear layers may be as high as .050 inch.

All rotovinyls are made with an inner core of foamed or expanded vinyl, which means they are cushioned to some extent. But, at the lower end of the price scale, cushioning may be quite thin.

Most sheet vinyls come with a no-wax finish which stays shiny most of the time without the necessity of waxing the floor. It must be remembered, however, that this finish may wear off where the surface is subjected to heavy traffic and in other wear areas, such as under the tables and chairs. Some manufacturers sell a compound that will renew the shine, but the worn surface on some types of material may still show through this shine.

All sheet vinyls are flexible enough to be coved up the **toe space** to form their own base. This eliminates any seams where moisture might collect.

INSTALLATION. All good sheet vinyl installations have chemically welded seams, which fuse the surface of the sheets into a seamless, one-piece floor. Sheet vinyls should also be rolled with a 100 pound roller to eliminate air pockets and form a good bond between the backing and the adhesive.

Furniture should be equipped with the proper loadbearing devices; otherwise, indentations will mar the vinyl surface. Most manufacturers recommend limiting the static loan to 75 psi (see Figure 2-30).

Particular attention should be paid to these protective loadbearing devices when a highly cushioned vinyl has been installed. Heavy refrigerators and kitchen or office equipment must not be dragged across the floor as this will damage and tear the very cushioned surfaces. These items should be "walked" across the floor on a piece of plywood or particle board.

MAINTENANCE. Maintenance is the same as for vinyl tiles, bearing in mind that no-wax does not mean no maintenance.

CORK

Due to its extremely porous and fragile qualities, cork is not used alone as a flooring material but is combined with resins to provide greater durability and easier maintenance. Plain cork with no additives is extremely resilient and has good sound absorbency. When cork is combined with vinyl some of the resiliency and noise reduction is lost, but the added durability and ease of maintenance more than compensate for these losses.

Designer Cork™, a vinyl clad floor from PermaGrain Products, Inc., is a 1/8 inch thick, 12 by 12 inch tile, or 6 by 36 inch Accent Plank composed of three layers. The bottom is a bonded vinyl moisture barrier, the middle a natural cork layer with the cork edges sealed against moisture. The top layer is a 20

FIGURE 2-29.
*An informal seating area has a Congoleum
Valuflor "Addison" pattern sheet vinyl floor.
(Photograph courtesy of Congoleum Corporation,
Resilient Flooring Division)*

mil transparent vinyl-bonded wear surface. Designer Cork is available in eight color pattern treatments. Due to the excellent insulating qualities of cork, it cannot be used over radiant heating systems.

INSTALLATION. PermaGrain Products, Inc., suggests using Armotex AS-422,™ manufactured by Armstrong, as an underlayment for all their products. Armotex disperses excessive substrate moisture away from direct contact with the flooring panel itself. This is especially beneficial in high moisture locales and below grade installations. A 48-hour waiting period is suggested before the PermaGrain products are installed. The adhesive is applied using a 1/16 by 1/16 by 1/16 inch square-notched trowel. The final procedure after installation is rolling with a 100 to 150 pound roller. PermaGrain suggests that plywood is much superior to particle board for the underlayment.

MAINTENANCE. Designer Cork may be damp mopped or spray buffed by machine. Designer Cork should never be waxed, but, if desired, a good quality nonyellowing vinyl dressing may be used. The floor may be protected from indentations, as seen in Figure 2-30.

FORMED-IN-PLACE OR POURED FLOORS

Formed-in-place floors come in cans and are applied at the site in a seamless floor installation. The basis of these "canned floors" may be urethane, epoxy, polyester, or vinyl, but they are all applied in a similar manner. First, as with all other floor installations, the surface must be clean, dry, and level. Second, a base coat of one of the above materials is applied to the substrate according to directions. Third, colored plastic chips are sprinkled or sprayed on the base and several coats of the base material are applied for the wear layer.

This flooring seems to be popular in veterinary offices where a nonskid and easily cleaned surface is desirable. It can also be coved up a base like sheet vinyl, eliminating cracks between floor and base. Of course, this type of flooring may be used in any area where cleanliness is of paramount importance.

MAINTENANCE. Maintenance is the same as sheet vinyl.

TYPE OF LOAD	KENTILE FLOORS INC. RECOMMENDS	KENTILE FLOORS INC. DOES NOT RECOMMEND	TYPE
Heavy Furniture more or less permanently located, should have composition furniture cups under the legs to prevent them from cutting the floor.	 RIGHT — Wide Bearing Surfaces Save Floors	 WRONG — Small Bearing Surfaces Dent Floors	Composition Furniture Cups 
Frequently Moved Furniture requires casters. Desk chairs are a good example. Casters should be 2" in diameter with soft rubber treads at least 3/4" wide and with easy swiveling ball bearing action. For heavier items that must be moved frequently, consult the caster manufacturers as to the suitable size of equipment that should be used.	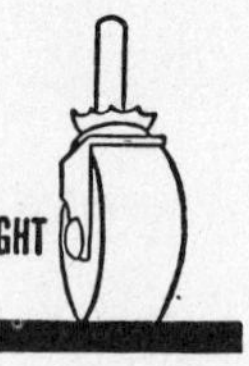 RIGHT — Rubber Rollers Save Floors	 WRONG — Hard Rollers Mark Floors	Rubber Wheel Casters 
Light Furniture should be equipped with glides having a smooth, flat base with rounded edges and flexible pin to maintain flat contact with the floor. They should be from 1¼" to 1½" dia., depending upon weight of load they must carry. For furniture with slanted legs apply glides parallel to floor rather than to slanted ends of legs.	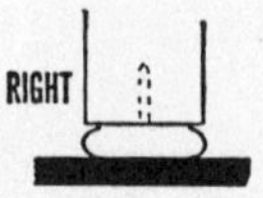 RIGHT — Use Flat Bearing Surfaces	 WRONG — Remove Small Metal Domes	Flat Glides with Flexible Shank 

FIGURE 2-30. Static Load for Furniture.

VINYL-COATED FABRIC FLOORS

It is now possible to have a fabric made into a vinyl floor, enabling designers to custom design their own floors. Fabric is permanently bonded between heavy layers of long life, clear polyvinyl chloride (PVC). It may be applied on or above grade, over plywood, wood, or concrete floors. The surface has a slightly embossed finish.

A sample of the fabric is sent to the manufacturer to determine if it is suitable for coating. The minimum order is 32 square feet or 4 by 8 feet. Sheet sizes are 4 by 4 feet and 4 by 8 feet. Tiles may be cut in 9 or 12 inch squares.

INSTALLATION. Installation is identical to any other vinyl product.

MAINTENANCE. Maintenance is the same as for vinyl tiles.

PLASTIC LAMINATE

Where **access flooring** is essential, Wilsonart® Perma-Kleen™ may be specified. This access floor tile is used in data processing centers and electronic clean rooms because of its excellent static dissipation and electrical resistance. Perma-Kleen is bonded to oil-free steel, aluminum, wood, or particle board access floor components, using moisture-resistant adhesive following the manufacturer's instructions.

MAINTENANCE. Same as for vinyl tiles.

Bibliography

Ackerman, Phyllis. *Wallpaper, Its History, Design and Use.* New York: Frederick A. Stokes Company, 1923.

Berendsen, Anne. *Tiles. A General History.* New York: Viking Press, 1967.

Berkeley, Bernard. *Floors: Selection and Maintenance.* Chicago IL: Library Technology Program, American Library Association, 1968.

Burch, Monte. *Tile, Indoors and Out.* Passaic NJ: Creative Homeowners Press, division of Federal Marketing Corporation, 1981.

Dezettel, Louis M. *Masons & Builders Library* (Vols. I & II). Indianapolis IN: Theodore Audel, division of Howard W. Sams & Co. Inc.

Ellis, Robert Y. *The Complete Book of Floor Coverings.* New York: Charles Scribner & Sons, 1980.

Entwisle, E.A. *The Book of Wallpaper, A History and an Appreciation.* Trowbridge, England: Redwood Press Ltd., 1970.

Feirer, John L. *Woodworking for Industry.* Peoria IL: Charles A. Bennett, 1979.

Hand, Jackson. *Walls, Floors and Ceilings.* New York: Book Division, Times Mirror Magazines, Inc., 1976.

Kicklighter, Clois E. *Modern Masonry.* South Holland IL: Goodheart-Willow Co., 1977.

Landsmann, Leanne. *Painting and Wallpapering.* New York: Grosset & Dunlap, 1975.

Meilach, Dona Z. *Tile Decorating with Gemma.* New York: Crown Publishers, 1978.

Practical Encyclopedia of Good Decorating and Home Improvement. New York: Greystone Press, 1971.

Salter, Walter L. *Floors and Floor Maintenance.* New York: Halstead Press, 1974.

Sunset Books. *Remodeling with Tile.* Menlo Park CA: Lane Publishing Co., 1978.

Time-Life Books. *Floors and Stairways.* Home Repair & Improvement. Alexandria VA: Time-Life Books, 1978.

Watson, Don A. *Construction Materials & Processes.* New York: McGraw-Hill, 1972.

Glossary

Access Flooring. Raised flooring providing access to the area beneath.

Adobe. Unburnt, sun-dried brick.

Agglomerate. Marble chips and spalls of various size, bonded together with a resin.

Aggregate. The solid material in concrete, mortar, or grout.

Base. A board or moulding at the base of a wall that comes in contact with the floor; protects the wall from damage (see Figure 5-1).

Beveled. In wood flooring, the top edge is cut at a 45° angle.

Bisque. Once-fired clay.

Bleed. Upward penetration of the creosote through the wood surface.

Bluestone. A hard sandstone of characteristic blue, gray, and buff colors, quarried in New York and Pennsylvania.

Bow. Longitudinal curvature of lumber (see Figure 2-1).

Bullnose. A convex rounded edge on tile (see Figure 2-20).

Butts. Close together, leaving no space.

Cove. A concave rounded edge on tile (see Figure 2-20).

Crook. The warp of a board edge from the straight line drawn between the two ends (see Figure 2-1).

Cup. Deviation of the face of a board from a plane (see Figure 2-1).

Cure. Maintaining the humidity and temperature of freshly poured concrete for a period of time to keep water present so it hydrates or hardens properly.

Cushion-edge. Tiles with a slightly rounded edge.

Eased. Slightly rounded.

Elgin Marbles. (Pronounced with a hard g.) Lord Elgin, the British Ambassador to Turkey from 1799 to 1802, persuaded the Turkish Government in Athens to allow him to remove the frieze of the Parthenon to the British Museum in London to prevent further damage.

Floorcloths. Printed canvas used in early 1800's.

Gauge. Thickness of tile.

Grain. Arrangement of the fibers of the wood.

Grout. Material used to fill in the spaces between the tiles.

Impervious. Less than 0.5 percent absorption rate.

Kiln. An oven for controlled drying of lumber or firing of tile.

Laminated. Bonding of two or more layers of material.

Lugs. A projection attached to the edges of a ceramic tile to provide equal spacing of the tiles.

Marquetry. Inlaid material in reference to wood flooring that has been fitted in various patterns and glued to a common background.

Mastic. An adhesive compound.

Matrix. The mortar part of the mix.

Medullary rays. Ribbons of tissue extending from the pitch to the bark of a tree, particularly noticeable in oak.

Metal spline. Thin metal wire holding the strips of parquet together.

Metamorphic. Changes occurring in appearance and structure of rock caused by heat and/or pressure.

Monolithic. Grout and mortar base become one mass.

o.c.. Abbreviation for on center; example: measurement from the center of one stud to the center of an adjacent stud.

120-grit. A medium fine grade of sandpaper.

Parquetry. Inlaid wood flooring, usually set in simple geometric patterns.

Patina. Soft sheen achieved by continuous use.

Pickets. Wood strips pointed at both ends, used in parquet floors in patterns such as Monticello.

Pointed. Act of filling the joints with mortar.

Plane. Flat and level surface.

Plastic. Still pliable and soft, not hardened.

Psi. Pounds per square inch.

Prefinished. Factory finished when referring to wood floors.

Quarter sawn. Wood sliced in quarters lengthwise which shows the grain of the wood to best advantage (see Figure 2-2).

Quartzite. A compact granular rock, composed of quartzite crystals usually so firmly cemented as to make the mass homogeneous. Color range is wide.

Reducer strip. A tapered piece of wood used at the joining of two dissimilar materials to compensate for difference of thickness.

Riser. The vertical part of a stair.

Sandstone. Sedimentary rock composed of sand-sized grains naturally cemented from mineral materials.

Screeds. 2 x 4's between 18 and 48 inches in length, laid flat side down and randomly placed to support subfloor.

Seeded. Sprinkling of marble chips on top of a base.

Semivitreous. 3 percent but not more than 7 percent moisture absorption.

Sets. Groups of parquet set at right angles to each other, usually four in a set.

60-grit. A medium sandpaper.

Spall. A fragment or chip, in this case, of marble.

Spalling. Flaking of floor due to expansion of components.

Square. Edges cut at right angles to each other.

Stenciling. Method of decorating or printing a design by painting through a cut-out pattern.

Terrazzo. Marble chips, of similar size, combined with a binder that holds the marble chips together. This binder may be cementitious or noncementitious (epoxy resin).

Toe space. Area at base of furniture or cabinets that is inset to accommodate the toes.

Tongue-and-groove. A wood joint providing a positive alignment (see Figure 6-2).

Tooled. A mortar joint that has been finished by a shaped tool while the mortar is plastic.

Twist. A spiral distortion of lumber (see Figure 2-1).

Veneer. A very thin sheet of wood varying in thickness from 1/8 to 1/1000 of an inch.

Vitreous. 0.5 percent but less than 3 percent moisture absorption.

Walls

CONTENTS

In floors, the weight of the flooring material was spread over a large area; however, when the same materials are used on walls, they create a heavy dead load. Thus, walls, whether constructed or veneered with granite, stone, brick, or concrete block, must have a foundation prepared to withstand this additional weight. **Compressive strength** is also important for wall installation materials.

There are two types of walls: load-bearing and nonbearing. The interior designer needs to know the difference. *Loadbearing walls* are those that support an imposed load in addition to their own weight; a *nonbearing wall* is just for utilitarian or aesthetic purposes.

The architect deals with both, but the interior designer probably deals more with nonbearing walls. A load-bearing wall should never be removed or altered without consulting an architect or engineer.

GRANITE

Granite is used wherever a feeling of stability and permanence is desired. This is probably why one sees a preponderance of granite in banks and similar institutions. The properties of granite are the same as

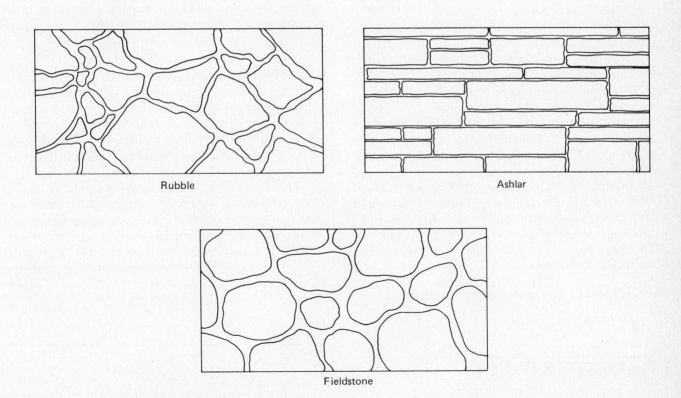

Rubble

Ashlar

Fieldstone

FIGURE 3-1. Types of Stonework.

were mentioned in the previous chapter. The only difference is that granite walls may be polished or honed, as abrasion is not a problem with walls. However, Figure 3-2 shows a rubble granite wall where the stone has been left in its original rough-hewn state.

INSTALLATION. Anchors, **cramps,** dowels, and other anchoring devices should be type 304 stainless steel or suitable **nonferrous** metal. A portland cement sand mortar is used and, where applicable, a sealant is used for pointing the joints.

MAINTENANCE. If required, the granite wall may be washed with a weak detergent solution and rinsed with clear water. To restore the shine, buff it with a lamb's wool pad.

MARBLE

Marble has the same elegant and formal properties whether used for walls or for floors (see Figures 8-6 and 8-7). Marble is also used as a fireplace surround in Figure 3-27, and as protective strips on the corner of a wall (see Figure 3-8).

According to the Marble Institute of America, interior marble wall facing may be installed by either mechanical fastening devices utilizing nonstaining anchors, angles, dowels, pins, cramps, and plaster spots or in a mortar setting bed to secure smaller units to interior vertical surfaces. The overall dimensions of the marble determine the setting method. Resilient cushions are used to maintain joint widths which are then pointed with white cement or other approved material (see Figures 8-6 and 8-7).

In addition to the traditional sizes, new thin marble veneers that are backed with lighter weight materials have less weight per square foot and, depending on job conditions, may be set in either a conventional full mortar bed or by any of the several newer thin-bed systems.

MAINTENANCE. The same as for marble floors, see page 34.

TRAVERTINE

When travertine is used in wall applications, it is not necessary to fill the voids. Unfilled travertine gives an interesting texture to the wall surface but, for a perfectly smooth installation, filling is required. Like flooring, wall applications of travertine may be filled with a clear, translucent epoxy or an opaque epoxy matching the color of the travertine. Filled travertine does tend to have less sheen on the filled area than on the solid area. The surface of the travertine may be left in its rough state, providing texture, or it may be cut and sanded or ground smooth.

INSTALLATION. Installation methods for travertine are the same as for marble.

STONE

This type of wall is usually a veneer and may be constructed of any type of stone. **Rubble** is uncut stone or stone that has not been cut into a rectangular shape. **Ashlar** is stone that is precut to provide enough uniformity to allow some regularity in assembly. The rubble masonry is less formal and also not as strong as the other types of bonds due to the irregularly shaped bonds. Rubble also requires the use of more mortar. Uniform mortar joints are a mark of good craftsmanship. **Fieldstone** or **cobble** has a more rounded feeling than does ashlar or rubble.

MAINTENANCE. Stonework should be cleaned with a stiff brush and clean water. If stains are difficult to remove, soapy water may be used followed by a clean-water rinse. Stonework should be cleaned by sponging during construction, which facilitates final cleaning. The acids used to clean brick should never be used on stone walls.

Regular maintenance consists of brushing or vacuuming to remove dust. It is important to remember that, generally, igneous types are impervious, but sedimentary and metamorphic stones are more susceptible to stains. Stone walls should not be installed where grease or any substance that may stain the stone is present.

BRICK

The surface of the brick may be smooth, rough, or grooved. Bricks with these surface textures create interesting wall designs with interesting shadows. Bricks

FIGURE 3-2.
The massive two-story wall is made of rough cut granite rubble carefully laid with a minimum of visible mortar. The redwood walls repeat the diagonal lines of the glass skylight which are again repeated in the ceiling. The ceramic tile used on the floor of the lobby is very suitable for the proximity of the ski slopes. (Architect: Eduard Dreier, A.I.A.; photograph: Richard Springgate)

are obtainable in whites, yellows, grays, reds, and browns and may be ordered in special sizes or shapes.

The standard brick size is 3 7/8 inches wide by 8 1/4 inches long and 2 1/2 inches high. Those laid so as to expose the long side in a horizontal position are called **stretchers,** while vertically they are called *soldiers*. When the end of the bricks show horizontally, they are called **headers,** but vertically they are called *rowlocks* (see Figure 3-3). The *bond* is the arrangement of brick in rows or courses. A *common bond* is defined as bricks placed end to end in a stretcher course with vertical joints of one course centered on the bricks in the next course. Every sixth or seventh course is made up of headers to tie the face brick to the backing. A bond without headers is called a *running bond*. See Figure 3-3 for types of brick bonds.

The joints in a wall installation are extremely important as they create shadows and special design effects. The joints of a brick wall are normally 1/2 of an inch thick. The mortar for these joints consists of a mixture of portland cement, hydrated lime, and sand. The joints in brickwork may serve different purposes—some are for shadows or decorative effects and some on exterior walls aid in providing a waterproof seal (see Figure 3-6). If a V-shaped or **beaded** joint is made with a trowel, the mortar is compressed and the joint tends to be more watertight.

Masonry walls may be hollow masonry, where both sides of the wall are visible, or they may be veneered. When both sides are visible, the **header course** ties the two sides together. A veneered wall is attached to the backing by means of metal ties (see Figure 3-5).

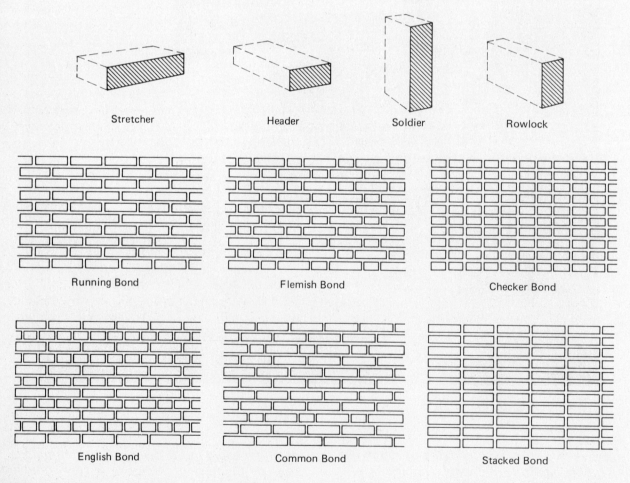

FIGURE 3-3. Stretchers, Headers, and Brick Bonds.

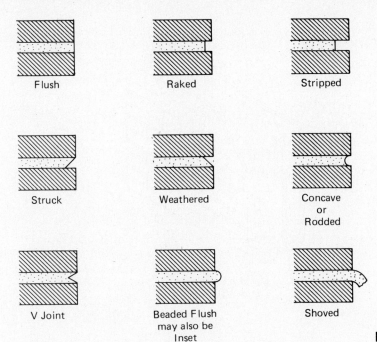

Flush

Raked

Stripped

Struck

Weathered

Concave
or
Rodded

V Joint

Beaded Flush
may also be
Inset

Shoved

FIGURE 3-4. Mortar Joints for Brick Walls.

INSTALLATION. Brick and concrete block are both installed by masons. Bricks are placed in a bed of mortar and mortar is laid on the top surface of the previous wythe, or row, so as to cover all edges. The brickbonds may be any of the types shown in Figure 3-3. The face of the joint is finished as shown in Figure 3-4.

MAINTENANCE. The major problem with finishing brick walls is the **mortar stain,** which occurs even if the mason is skilled and careful. To remove mortar stain, the walls are cleaned of surplus mortar and dirt then scrubbed with a solution of trisodium phosphate, household detergent, and water, then rinsed with water under pressure. If stains are not removed with the above treatment, then a solution of muriatic acid and water is used. The acid should be poured into the water to avoid a dangerous reaction. Just the bricks themselves should be scrubbed. The solution should not be allowed to dry but should be rinsed immediately with clean water. For cleaning light colored bricks, a more diluted solution of muriatic acid and water should be used to prevent burning.

Regular maintenance for bricks includes brushing and vacuuming to remove dust that may have adhered to the rough surface. Masonry walls that may come in contact with grease, such as in kitchens, should either be impervious or sealed to prevent penetration of the grease.

CONCRETE

Currently, many architects of contemporary buildings, particularly in the commercial, industrial, and educational fields, are leaving the poured concrete walls exposed on the interior. The forms that are used for these walls may be patterned or smooth, and this texture is reflected on the interior surface. The ties that hold the forms together do leave holes which, if properly placed, may provide a grid design (see Figure 3-6).

From the interior designer's point of view, a poured concrete wall is a *fait accompli*. The surface may be left with the outline of the forms showing, or it may be treated by the following methods to give a different surface appearance: bush hammering, acid etching, and sandblasting. Bush hammering is done with a power tool that provides an exposed aggregate face by removing the sand-cement matrix and exposes the

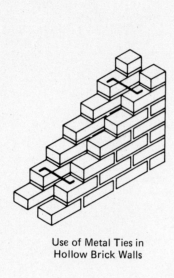

Use of Metal Ties in
Hollow Brick Walls

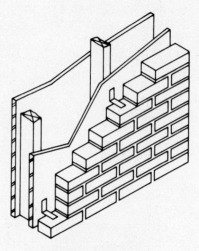

Use of Metal Ties in a
Brick Veneer Wall

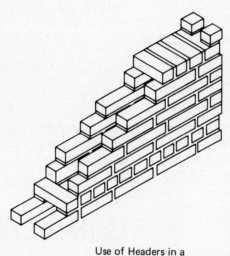

Use of Headers in a
Hollow Brick Wall
Visible from Both Sides

FIGURE 3-5. Metal Ties.

aggregate. Sandblasting provides a textured surface. Bush hammering produces the heaviest texture, while the texture from sandblasting depends on the amount and coarseness of sand used. Acid etching just removes the surface.

The main problem facing the designer is using materials and accessories that will be compatible with cast concrete. Obviously, they need to imply weight and a substantial feeling, rather than any delicacy or formality.

CONCRETE BLOCK

Concrete block is a hollow concrete masonry unit composed of portland cement and suitable aggregates. Walls of this type are found in homes, but are more frequently used in commercial and educational interiors. There are several problems with concrete block. First, it has extremely poor insulating qualities if used on an exterior wall. Second, if used on an

FIGURE 3-6.
Cast concrete wall on the left is in extreme contrast to the adjacent gold leaf area inside a symphony hall. The ceiling is a prefinished V-joint, tongue-and-grooved on all four sides, flooring material. Custom built walls have been curved to follow the contour of the brass railing. The background shows a large scale brick wall with a stripped mortar joint. (Architects: Fowler, Ferguson, Kingston, & Ruben; photograph: Richard Springgate)

outside wall and moisture is present, efflorescence will form. Third, it has a fairly rough surface which is difficult to paint, although this may be accomplished by using a specially formulated paint and a long-nap roller.

A block wall made of concrete block with a ground surface is shown on the cover of this book. The grinding process smooths the surface and exposes the aggregate. This particular wall is used as a passive solar collector and was installed using an adhesive rather than conventional mortar.

INSTALLATION. The mason erects a concrete block wall in a similar manner to a brick one except that, while a brick wall is only viewed from one side, a concrete block is often visible from both sides; therefore, the joints need to be finished on both sides of the block. Concrete block may be erected in either a running bond pattern or stacked (see Figure 3-3).

MAINTENANCE. Concrete block is not cleaned with acid to remove mortar smears or droppings, as with brick. Excess mortar should be allowed to dry and then be chipped off. Rubbing the wall with a small piece of concrete block will remove practically all of the mortar. For painting see Chapter 1.

GLASS BLOCK

In the 1920's and 1930's the use of glass block seemed to be limited to the side of the front door and bathrooms, but is now one of the revived materials for use in the 1980's. This is due to modern technology and the innovativeness of today's architects and designers. The use of glass block is only for nonload-bearing installations. This, however, should not be a limiting factor in the utilization of glass block.

Glass, one of man's most useful products, is also one of the oldest (about 4000 B.C.). In ancient times, formed pieces of colored glass were considered as valuable as precious stones. *Glass block* by definition is composed of two halves of pressed glass fused together. The hollow in the center is partially **evacuated,** which provides a dead air space with good insulating qualities.

The construction of the block is such that designs may be imprinted on both the inside and outside of the glass surfaces. These designs distribute and control the direction of the light rays. This is the most important reason for using glass block. Other reasons

are the insulating properties, ease of maintenance, and elimination of dust and dirt (see Figures 3-7, 7-8, and 7-9).

Standard glass block is 3 7/8 inches thick with the thinline being 3 1/8 inches thick. Glass block is obtainable in 6, 8, and 12 inch squares, and some styles come in a 4 by 8 inch rectangular block. The thinline block has the additional advantage of 20 percent less weight.

Pittsburgh Corning Corporation, the only domestic manufacturer of glass block, produces a variety of glass block that may be used for both exterior and interior purposes. One of the newest exterior glass blocks is solar-reflective, having a highly reflective, thermally bonded, oxide surface coating that reduces both solar heat gain and transmitted light. These reflective blocks are available with a gray reflective finish on one or both faces. A bronze appearance is achieved with a bronze edge coating and a reflective finish on one face.

The most transparent of glass blocks have smooth and clear exterior and interior surfaces. This type of block may be used for passive solar collection.

The outer faces of the ARGUS® glass block are light-diffusing units that disperse the light uniformly inside the structure, while the pattern pressed into the block's inner surfaces gives attractive light reflection without glare. They provide moderate light transmission and brightness, total privacy, and good solar heat control.

Specialty blocks such as VISTABRICK® are solid glass and provide maximum protection from vandalism and forcible entry. Also available in the standard glass block is an "LX" fibrous glass insert which controls light transmission glare, brightness, and solar heat gain. It also increases thermal resistance.

Glass block may also be of curved panel construction. It is suggested that the curved areas be separated from the flat areas by intermediate expansion joints and supports. The radius minimums are shown in Table 3-1.

INSTALLATION. The mortar-bearing surfaces of glass block have a rough coating that acts as a bond between the block and the mortar. An optimum mortar mix is one part portland cement, one part lime, and three parts sand. Panel reinforcing strips are used in horizontal joints every 16 to 24 inches of height, depending on which block is used. Expansion strips are used adjacent to **jambs** and **heads.** Joints are **struck** while plastic and excess mortar is removed immediately. Mortar should be removed from the face of the block with a damp cloth before final set occurs.

FIGURE 3-7.

The dining area is partially shielded from the living room by a glass block divider surrounding the grand piano. The glass block was erected using a clear silicone, with the gritty edge surface of the block removed to increase transparency. The strip floor is a continuation of the one shown on the cover. On the far walls are insulating acoustic panels covered with fabric. The house was constructed by the same method used in commercial buildings. Therefore, the ceiling is the underside of the metal deck used for the poured concrete floor of the second level. The dining room table is polished granite; the bronze sculpture is by Frank Riggs. (Architects: Joseph Linton and Wayne Bingham; photograph: Richard Springgate)

Table 3-1
Radius Minimums for Curved Panel Construction

Block Size	Outside Radius in Inches	Number of Blocks in 90° Arc	Joint Thickness in Inches	
			Inside	Outside
6 × 6	52 1/2	13	1/8	5/8
4 × 8	36	13	1/8	5/8
8 × 8	69	13	1/8	5/8
12 × 12	102 1/2	13	1/8	5/8

Courtesy of Pittsburgh Corning Corporation.

MAINTENANCE. Ease of maintenance is one of the attractive features of glass block. Mortar or dirt on the face of glass block may be removed by the use of water, but not with abrasives (steel wool, wire brush, or acid).

PLASTER

The Egyptians and ancient Greeks used plaster walls which were then painted with murals. The frescoes of early times were painted on wet plaster, which absorbed the pigment and dried as an integral part of the plaster. The frescoes of Michelangelo's Sistine Chapel still retain their original brilliant color even after 400 years. Plaster was also used for very intricate moldings and decorations. Today, plaster covered walls are only used in commercial installations and the more expensive custom-built homes.

Lath is the foundation of a plaster wall. In the Pyramids in Egypt the lath was made of intertwined reeds. The construction of the half-timbered homes of the English Tudor period are often referred to as daub and wattle, the daub being the plaster and the wattle the lath, this time a woven framework of saplings and reeds. When any restoration work is done on houses built prior to the 1930's, the lath will probably be found to be thin wood strips nailed to the studs about 3/8 inch apart.

Modern day lath is either gypsum board, metal, or masonry block. The gypsum lath consists of a core of gypsum plaster between two layers of specially formulated, absorbent paper. The gypsum lath is 3/8 or 1/2 inch thick, 16 inches wide by 48 inches long, and is applied horizontally with the joints staggered between courses. Other sizes are also available. Special types of gypsum lath may have holes drilled in them for extra adhesion or have a sheet of aluminum foil on one side for insulating purposes.

Metal lath is used not only for flat areas but also for curved surfaces and forms. Metal lath is a mesh that is nailed to the studs. The **scratch coat** is troweled on and some plaster is squeezed through the mesh to form the mechanical bond, whereas the bond with gypsum board is formed by means of **suction. Beads** or formed pieces of metal are placed at exterior corners and around **casings** to provide a hard edge that will not be damaged by traffic.

Plaster used to be troweled on the lath in three different coats: The first coat bonded to the lath; the second was the brown coat; and the third, the finish coat, was very smooth. The first two coats were left with a texture to provide tooth. A three-coat plaster job is still done sometimes, but two coats or even one may be used to complete the finished surface.

As mentioned in the chapter on paint, due to its extreme porosity, plaster must be sealed before proceeding with other finishes.

GYPSUM WALLBOARD

Gypsum wallboard has the same construction as the gypsum board lath, but sheets are normally 4 feet wide and 8 feet long, but may be obtained in lengths of up to 16 feet. The edges along the length are always tapered, but some types are tapered on all four edges. This allows for a filled or taped joint. This wallboard is also obtainable with a foil back which serves as a vapor barrier on exterior walls. Another method of vapor barrier preparation is using a polyethylene sheet stapled to the studs before erecting the gypsum wallboard.

In new construction, a 1/2 inch thickness is recommended for single layer application; for laminated two-ply applications, two 3/8 inch thick sheets are used. Table 3-2 lists the maximum member spacing for the various thicknesses of gypsum board.

The horizontal method of application is best adapted to rooms in which full-length sheets can be used, as it minimizes the number of vertical joints. Today, screws are usually used rather than nails, as they can be installed by mechanical means and will not pull loose. They are placed 6 to 8 inches o.c. with the heads slightly below the surface. The ceilings are done first and then the walls. A very good **dry wall** installation may also have an adhesive applied to the

Table 3-2
Non-load Bearing Walls Maximum Frame Spacing (1)

Base and Finish Assembly	Frame Spacing	
	Inches	mm
1/2″ IMPERIAL Gypsum Base		
one layer, 1-coat system	16	406
one layer, 2-coat system	16 or 24 (2)	406 or 610 (2)
two layers, 1 & 2 coat system	24	610
5/8″ IMPERIAL Gypsum Base		
one layer, 1-coat system	16 or 24 (2)	406 or 610 (2)
one layer, 2 coat system	24 (2)	610 (2)
two layers, 1 & 2 coat system	24	610

(1) For perpendicular or parallel application-perpendicular preferred for maximum strength, parallel application not recommended for ceilings. For fire-rated construction, see test report. (2) 24″ spacing requires joint treatment with DURABOND compound and PERF-A-TAPE Reinforcing Tape.

Reproduced with permission of U.S. Gypsum Company.

studs before installing the panels, in which case screws may be further apart.

A thorough inspection of the studs should be made before application of the gypsum wallboard to ensure that all warped studs are replaced. If this is not done, the final appearance of the wallboard will be rippled. Of course, this problem is not present when metal studs are used as in commercial construction.

After all the sheets have been installed, outside corners are protected by a metal corner or bead. Joint cement, spackling compound—or, as it is called in the trade, "mud"—is applied to all joints with a 5 inch wide spackling knife. Then, the perforated tape is placed so as to cover the joint and is pressed into the mud. Another layer of compound is applied, **feathering** the outer edges. After drying, the compound is sanded and a second or even a third coat is applied, the feathering extending beyond the previous coat. All screw holes are filled with joint cement and sanded smooth. Care must be taken to sand only the area that has been coated with joint cement, because sanding the paper layer will result in a roughness that will be visible, particularly when a painted semigloss or gloss finish is to be applied. In fact, the Gypsum Association suggests that a thin skim coat of joint compound be applied over the entire surface to provide a uniform surface for these paints. The dry-wall installer should be informed of the final finish so that attention can be paid to special finishing.

ALL seams or joints must be taped regardless of length because, if they are not taped, cracks will soon appear. The outside beads have joint cement feathered to meet the edge.

The surface of the wallboard may be left smooth, ready for painting or a wallcovering, or it may have some type of texture applied. The latter is done for several reasons. Aesthetically, a texture may be more desirable to eliminate glare and is also more likely to hide any surface discrepancies caused by warping studs and/or finishing of joints. The lightest texture available is called an *orange peel,* with the surface appearing just as the name suggests. Another finish is a skip-troweled surface where, after the texture has been sprayed on, a metal trowel is used to flatten some areas. The heaviest texture is a heavily stippled or troweled appearance similar to rough finished plaster. A texture is preferred whenever there is a **raking light** on the wall surface so that surface discrepancies are not quite so visible.

Gypsum wallboard may also be installed on a curved wall by qualified dry-wall installers. Only **simple** curves may be used. **Compound** curves cannot be fabricated (see Figure 3-8).

When water may be present, such as in bathrooms and kitchens, some building codes require the use of a water-resistant gypsum board. If a pliant wallcovering is to be used, all wallboard must be sealed or sized, as the paper of the gypsum board and the

FIGURE 3-8.
This interior design studio has gypsum wallboard curved to cover both walls and ceiling. Marble of two colors has been inset into the carpeted showroom. Marble strips are also used as a protection for the corners of the wall, serving both a utilitarian and decorative purpose. (Architect: *Cabel Childress;* interior designer: *Mary Ann Kipp, Corporate Interiors;* photograph: *Timothy Hursley/The Arkansas Office*)

backing of the wallcovering would become bonded together and the wallcovering would be impossible to remove.

Another type of wallboard is prefinished vinyl plastic in a variety of simulated finishes, including wood grains and other textures. It can be applied directly by adhesive to the studs or as a finish layer over a pre-existing wall. The edges may be square or beveled. Wood or metal trim must be applied at both floor and ceiling to create a finished edge.

WALLPAPER/ WALLCOVERING

The Chinese mounted painted rice paper on their walls as early as 200 B.C. Although mention of painted papers has been historically documented as early as 1507 in France, the oldest fragment of European wallpaper, from the year 1509, was found in Christ's College, Cambridge. This paper has a rather large scale pattern adapted from contemporary damask. Seventeenth century papers, whether painted or block printed, did not have a continuous pattern repeat and were printed on sheets rather than on a roll, as is the modern practice. The repetitive matching of today's papers is credited to Jean Papillon of France in the later 17th century. In the 18th century, England and France produced handprinted papers that were both expensive and heavily taxed.

Leather was one of the original materials to be hung as a covering for walls. The earliest decorated and painted leathers were introduced to Europe in the 11th century by Arabs from Morocco and were popular in 17th century Holland.

Flocked papers were used as early as 1620 in France. The design was printed with some kind of glue and then heavily sprinkled with finely chopped bits of silk and wool, creating a good imitation of damask or velvet. Flocked papers have been popular in recent decades, but are now falling from favor.

Scenic papers were used in the 18th century and many of them were handpainted Chinese papers. Wallpapers used in this country were imported during the second quarter of the 18th century, but domestic manufacturing did not really start until around 1800. Even then the quality was not equal to the fine imported papers.

After the Industrial Revolution, wallpaper became available to people of more moderate means and, thus, the use of wallpaper became more widespread. In the later 19th and early 20th centuries, William Morris provided the stimulating interest in wallpapers and their designs. In the first half of the 20th century, papers imitating textures and having the appearance of wood, marble, tiles, relief plasterwork, paneling, and moire silk were in demand.

In the late 1930's and 1940's, wallpaper was in style, only to be replaced by painted walls in the 1960's and 1970's.

Today, designers are more discriminating with the use of wallpapers or, as they will be known from now on, "wallcoverings." This change of name is due to the fact that, while paper was the original material for wallcoverings, today these wallcoverings may be all paper, paper backed by cotton fabric, vinyl face with paper or cotton backing, or fabric with a paper backing (see Figure 4-2). Foils or mylars have either paper or a nonwoven backing to ensure a smooth reflective surface.

The face of the paper wallcoverings is usually treated with a protective vinyl finish and provides a washable surface. "Washable" means wiping the surface with a damp cloth. Solid vinyl wallcoverings backed by woven cotton are more durable and are scrubbable.

Patterns

There are many collections available which have been researched by the manufacturer. By using these collections, the designer will be able to create the desired atmosphere.

Many of the Early American designs were inspired by the valuable brocades and tapestries that adorned the homes of the wealthy. Katzenbach & Warren has done extensive research into New England homesteads and their early papers. Since many were created before the machine age, they were often either painted entirely by hand or stenciled or printed by means of a wood block. The designs include small allover floral patterns, floral vine patterns, and flowing arabesques. Stencils with pineapples, the symbol of hospitality, and small stylized designs were also used. Katzenbach & Warren's Williamsburg Wallpaper Reproductions are copies from existing documents in the Williamsburg collection (see Figure 3-9).

Albert van Luit and Co., in their Winterthur Museum Collection, have meandering **chinoiserie** and the beautiful adaptation of an eight-panel scenic is the perfect background for English-style furniture. The scenic murals are hung above the chair rail (see Figure 3-10).

FIGURE 3-9.
This small step-and-repeat geometric is interpreted from the background motif of an antique textile in the Colonial Williamsburg collection. The document is a wool brocade made in England about 1770. The complementary WILLIAMSBURG™ border paper is interpreted from another textile from the same period. The leaf and dot stripe is based on one of the elements in a fabric swatch contained in a Dutch merchant's sample book that dates from 1790–1820. (Photograph courtesy of Katzenbach & Warren, Inc.)

For a French ambience, wallcoverings with delicate scrolls or lacy patterns are suitable for a formal background, while **toile-de-Jouy** and checks are appropriate for the French Country look. Wallcoverings for a formal English feeling range from symmetrical damasks to copies of English chintzes and embroideries.

Geometrics include both subtle and bold stripes and checks, as well as polka dots and circles. The colors used will dictate where these geometrics can be used (see Figure 3-11).

Trompe l'oeil patterns are three-dimensional designs on paper. Examples of realistic designs are a cupboard with an open door displaying some books, a view from a window, or a niche with a shelf top containing a piece of sculpture. These trompe l'oeil patterns are sold in a set.

Murals are large scale, nonrepeat, handscreened patterns done on a series of panels. They may be scenic, floral, architectural, or graphic in nature. Murals are sold in sets varying usually from two to six or more panels per set. Each panel is normally 28 inches in width and is printed on strips 10 to 12 feet in length. The height of the designs varies greatly, but most fall somewhere between 4 and 8 feet, although some graphics go from ceiling to floor (see Figure 3-10).

The pattern repeat is the distance between one point to the next repeated same point. This may vary from no repeat or match (as in a texture) to repeats as large as 48 inches. Therefore, for an exceptionally large repeat, additional paper should be ordered.

When a patterned wallcovering is hung, the left side of a strip will match or continue the design with the right side of the previous strip. If this match is directly across on a horizontal line, then it would be called a straight match. If the second strip has to be lowered in order to continue the design, this is called a drop match. A drop match does not necessarily mean that more wallcovering must be ordered, but must be taken into consideration when cutting the strips.[1]

[1] Schumacher, *A Guide to Wallcoverings. (New York: Author, n.d.)*

FIGURE 3-10.
This eight panel mural from Albert Van Luit is called "Cathay Chinois" and is very typical of the imported handpainted wallpapers used in the Georgian era. (Photograph courtesy of Albert Van Luit)

FIGURE 3-11.
A plaid wallcovering is used for both the ceiling and the soffit in this custom designed kitchen by Rubén De Saavedra, A.S.I.D. The kitchen has two sinks and ceramic tile both on the floor and the backsplash. The island has a solid wood counter; plastic laminate is used for the remaining tops. The large doors on the right are built-in refrigerators. (Photograph: *Daniel Eifert)*

Types

Textures include embossed papers, which hide any substrate unevenness, solid color fabrics, and grass-cloths. Embossed papers have a texture rolled into them during the manufacturing process. Care should be taken not to flatten the texture of embossed papers when hanging them.

Anaglypta® is an embossed product imported from England. This wallcovering provides the textured appearance of sculptured plaster, hammered copper, or even hand-tooled Moroccan leather. These highly textured wallcoverings are applied to the wall as any other product and, once painted, the surface becomes hard and durable. The advantage of these wallcoverings is that not only are they used on newly constructed walls in residential and commercial interiors, but they may also be applied after minimal surface preparation. In older dwellings and Victorian restoration projects, they provide the added advantage of actually stabilizing walls while covering moderate cracks and blemishes.

Fabrics should be tightly woven, although burlap is frequently used as a texture. The walls are pasted with a nonstaining paste and the fabric, with the selvage removed, is brushed onto the paste (see Figure 2-16).

Grasscloth is made of loosely woven vegetable fibers backed with paper. These fibers may be knotted at the ends and these knots are a decorative feature of the texture. Because these are vegetable fibers, width and color will vary, thus providing a highly textured surface. Due to the natural materials, it is impossible to obtain a straight-across match and, therefore, the seams will be obvious (see Figure 3-12). Woven silk is frequently included in grasscloth collections, and this finer texture gives a more refined atmosphere to a room (see Figure 2-16).

Flocked papers, as has been mentioned before, are one of the oldest papers on record. They are currently manufactured by more modern methods but still resemble pile fabrics. One problem with flocked papers is that, through abrasion or constant contact with the face of the paper, the flocking may be removed and a worn area will appear. A seam roller should never be used to press down the seams, as this also flattens the flocking.

Foils and mylars provide a highly mirrored effect with a pattern printed on the reflective surface. It is due to this high shine that the use of a lining paper is suggested to provide a smoother substrate. Foils conduct electricity if allowed to come in contact with exposed wires. In moist areas, some of the older foils had a tendency to show rust spots. This is why most

FIGURE 3-12.
*This informal seating is backed with a grasscloth-covered wall. Notice that the seams show.
(Photograph courtesy Milo Baughman Design;
furniture: Thayer-Coggin, Inc.)*

"metallic" wallcoverings are presently constructed of mylar. To achieve the best effect from foils, there should be an abundance of light in the room in order to reflect off the foil surface.

Kraft papers are usually hand-printed on good quality kraft paper, which is similar to the type used for wrapping packages. Unless specially treated these kraft papers absorb grease and oil stains, so care should be taken in placement of these types of wallcoverings.

For a cork faced paper, razor-thin slices of cork are applied by hand to tinted or lacquered ground papers. The base color shows through the natural texture of the cork and may blend or contrast with the cork itself. The sliced cork may also be cut into definite shapes for a repetitive pattern or it may be printed with a design. Cork also comes in 12 inch square tiles varying in thickness from 1/8 to 5/8 of an inch. These solid cork tiles are of varying texture and provide good heat and sound insulation.

Leather is cut into designs or blocks much as Spanish tiles because the limited size of the hide prohibits large pieces from being used. The color of the surface varies within one hide and from one hide to another; therefore, a shaded effect is to be expected.

Coordinated or companion fabrics are used to create an unbroken appearance where wallcovering and draperies adjoin. When using coordinated paper and fabric, the wallcovering should be hung first and then the draperies can be adjusted to line up with the pattern repeat of the wallcovering. The tendency is to call these companion fabrics "matching fabrics," but this is incorrect. It is extremely important to realize that paper or vinyl will absorb dyes in a different manner than will a fabric, and many problems will be resolved by the strict avoidance of the word "matching."

Lining paper is an inexpensive, blank paper which is recommended for use under foils and other fine quality papers. It absorbs excess moisture and makes a smoother finished wall surface. A heavier canvas liner is available for "bad walls."

Printing of Wallcoverings

Roller printing is used for the less expensive wallcoverings. The inks are transferred from a metal roller with raised design blocks to a large printing roller and then to the paper as it is fed through the press.

There are several means by which a wallcovering can be handprinted. First of all, it may be silk screened. A separate screen must be made up for each color used and the screens must be meticulously positioned so that the patterns match at the edges. In silk screening, the wallcovering must be allowed to dry between application of the different colors.

Block printing produces a similar effect to silk screening only, instead of the paint being squeezed through the open pores in the silk screen, the paint or color is rolled on a block where the negative or unwanted areas have been cut away. Block printing also requires positive positioning when printing.

Because silk screening and block printing are hand processes, a machine-like quality is not possible or perhaps even desirable. The pattern does not always meet at the seams as positively as does the roller-printed one. Matching should be exact in the 3 to 5 foot area from the floor, where it is most noticeable.

FIGURE 3-13. Custom Silk Screening.
(Photograph courtesy of Manuscreens, a Division of J. Josephson, Inc.)

Adhesives

There are several materials available to attach a wall-covering to the wall. The old stand-by is the wheat base paste and this is used for many wallcoverings. However, certain wallcoverings such as wetlook vinyls, handprints, naturals, and foils require a special adhesive. The manufacturer will always specify which type of adhesive is to be used. If fabric or grasscloth is to be hung, a nonstaining cellulose paste should be used. Regular vinyls are hung using a vinyl adhesive that is not the same as the special adhesive mentioned above.

Prepasted papers come with a factory-applied dehydrated cellulose or wheat paste. To activate this paste, cut strips are soaked in water for a designated number of seconds and then applied the same as regular wallpaper. The prepasted papers are usually less expensive and are mainly for use by the homeowner in a do-it-yourself project.

Strippable or peelable wallcoverings can be removed by simply prying up one corner and pulling off the whole strip. *Strippable* means that the base material used for the wallcovering is sufficiently strong to break away from the adhesive without shredding. *Peelable* means that the top layer of material will peel away from the substrate, leaving a suitable surface for repapering.

Most machine printed wallcoverings are **pretrimmed** at the factory, but the majority of handprints and hand-made textures are untrimmed.

Packaging

A single roll of an American wallcovering contains approximately 36 square feet of material regardless of the width, while a single roll of a European wallcovering contains 28 square feet. To make allowance for waste and matching patterns, it is advisable to calculate 30 usable square feet for a domestic wallcovering and 24 usable square feet for an imported one. This allowance is sufficient for a room with an average number of doors and windows but, for a room with window walls, more precise calculations should be made.

All wallcovering is priced by the single roll, but it is usually packaged in two or three roll bolts.

A double roll bolt is a continuous bolt containing the equivalent of two single rolls. The cost is twice the single roll price. The same applies to a triple roll bolt. By packaging wallcovering in bolts rather than in single rolls, the paperhanger has more continuous lineal yardage with which to work and, therefore, less waste.

When ordering handprints from a retail store, there are a few things one must know. There is a cutting charge if the wallcovering order requires a cut bolt. As the shading and even the positioning of the pattern on the roll may vary between dye lots or runs, SUFFICIENT BOLTS SHOULD ALWAYS BE ORDERED when the order is placed. The particular dye lot, which is stamped on the back of the roll, may not be still available if it is necessary to order more in the future. Opened or partially used bolts are not returnable and unopened bolts may be subject to a restocking charge.

Commercial Wallcoverings

Commercial wallcoverings are the exception to the single roll containing 36 square feet. Commercial wallcoverings are usually 52 to 54 inches wide and are packaged in 30-yard or more bolts. These wider coverings require a highly skilled professional paperhanger and a helper. The final appearance of the walls depends on the ability of the paperhanger.

Commercial wallcoverings are classified according to Federal minimum performance standards:

Type I: Light duty with a total weight of 7 to 12 ounces per square yard. The backing is scrim, usually of poly/cotton.

Type II: Medium duty with 13 to 21 ounces per square yard. Poly/cotton or **osnaburg** backing is usual.

Type III: Heavy duty with 22 ounces or more per square yard. Cotton broken twill is the backing.

The three types are further classified into Class 1: not mildew resistant and Class 2: mildew resistant.

Mildew is a fungus that flourishes in a moist, dark environment. If mildew is present or even suspected, the walls should be washed with a mixture of equal parts of household bleach and water. The correct paste or adhesive will also help prevent mildew from forming under the newly hung wallcovering. If proper precautions are not taken, any mildew that forms will permanently discolor the wallcovering.

Vinyl suede is fabricated from 100 percent vinyl, laminated to 100 percent woven cotton backing and is fully washable. These vinyl suedes come in 53 to 54 inches wide 30-yard bolts with a flame spread of 20.

With plain textures, grasscloths, and suedes, it is advisable to reverse the direction of every other strip. This will make a better finished appearance particularly if one side of the covering happens to be shaded a little more than the other.

If wood paneling is not permitted under the existing fire or building codes, a product called Flexwood® may be specified. Flexwood is made of carefully selected wood veneers permanently laminated to a fiber backing. It can be applied to straight or curved walls and wrapped around columns or pillars. It is available in 70 domestic and imported woods, with the veneers so carefully matched that joints are practically invisible after installation. Every sheet of Flexwood is factory matched and numbered in sequence to insure panoramic matching of the wall.

The recommended finish is a good alkyd varnish, which has a fast drying time and a low gloss. This material has a Class 1 flame spread rating of 15 when applied with the recommended adhesive.

All textile wallcoverings have good acoustic qualities and also good energy-saving insulation qualities. Textiles may be backed by paper and the fiber content may be 100 percent jute, or a combination of synthetics and wool, and jute and/or linen and cotton. These textiles usually have a flame spread rating of 25 or less and come in 28 inch wide double rolls 10 yards long or 36 inch wide double rolls 8 yards long. Some companies manufacture 100 percent wool faced, paper backed fabrics in 55-yard bolts. These textiles are hung on a prepasted wall using a ready-mixed heavy duty adhesive.

Sisal is another wallcovering which has high sound absorption and is also static-free. Rolls are 48 inches wide and 100 feet long. Sisal has an extremely prickly texture, as opposed to the other textiles, but this roughness can be an asset as in the following case: A school found that when students lined up outside the cafeteria, there was a tendency for the wall to get very dirty and be defaced by graffiti. Installation of sisal prevented both of these problems and also reduced the noise level.

One of the special surface treatments for wallcoverings is Tedlar®. This is a tough, transparent fluoride plastic sheet that is very flexible, chemically inert, and extremely resistant to stains, yellowing, corrosive chemicals, solvents, light, and oxygen. All the commercial wallcovering manufacturers have wallcovering products which are, or may be, surfaced with Tedlar.

Some companies offer special-order printing, with minimums of 50 rolls or more. These may be designs already in their line or special custom designs. Because these are handprints, they are expensive, but may solve a particular design problem.

INSTALLATION. Before hanging any wallcovering, the walls must be sized. Sizing is a liquid applied to the wall surface which serves several purposes. First, it seals the surface against alkali, also known as hot spots; second, it reduces absorption of the paste or adhesive to be used; and third, it provides tooth for the wallcovering. The sizing must be compatible with the paste or adhesive to be used.

Wallcoverings are installed in either of the following manners:

1. Table trimmed with a straight edge. This means cutting the selvage from both edges so that the panels can be butted. This procedure reduces the amount of surface adhesive residue and facilitates clean up.

2. Panels are overlapped on the wall and seams are made by double cutting through both sheets. Care must be taken NOT to cut into the substrate surface. Various hooked-knife-type cutting tools are available for this procedure. After the cut is made, the face strip may be removed and the adhesive cleaned off. L. E. Carpenter has the following extremely useful suggestions in their "A Practical Guide to Specification, Selection, Use and Care of Vicrtex Vinyl Wallcovering" booklet: "Remove excess paste from a seam before making the next seam. Vertical joints should occur at least 2 inches from inside and outside corners." They have also provided much of the information in this section.

Paste or adhesive is applied by means of a wide brush to the back of the wallcovering. Particular attention should be paid to the edges because this is where any curling will occur. The wallcovering is folded or **booked,** without creasing, in order to be carried from the pasting table to the wall, where it is carefully unfolded and hung in place. The first strip is always hung parallel to the **plumb line,** which has been previously marked. A seam roller is used on most wallcoverings, except as noted before. As has been mentioned already, for some wallcoverings, the paste must be applied to the wall rather than to the backing. THE MANUFACTURER'S INSTRUCTIONS FOR INSTALLATION METHODS SHOULD ALWAYS BE FOLLOWED. Inspect each roll for defects before cutting the first strip.

MAINTENANCE. All stains or damage should be corrected immediately. Paper faced wallcoverings should be tested to ascertain if the inks are permanent before cleaning fluids are applied. Vinyls may be scrubbed with a soft brush and water if they have been designated scrubbable. Foils are washed with warm water and wiped with a soft cloth to avoid any scratching. Hard water does have a tendency to leave a film on the reflective surfaces of foil.

Grasscloths, suedes, fabrics, sisal, and carpeting may be vacuumed to remove the dust. Again, always follow the manufacturer's instructions for maintenance.

It is suggested that vinyl covered walls be washed at least once or twice a year. Grease and oils, in particular, should not be allowed to accumulate. When removing stains from vinyl, cleaners should be used in the following order:

Step 1. Warm water.

Step 2. Warm water plus a mild soap, such as Ivory Snow®, or one of the commercially available vinyl cleaning products such as Vicrkleen™.

Step 3. Isopropyl Alcohol.

Step 4. Naphtha (recommended only after bulk of stain is removed with water or isopropyl alcohol).

TAMBOURS

Tambours may be either genuine wood veneer, metallic face laminate, or cork, laminated to a tempered hardboard core with brown fabric backing approximately 3/16 inch thick overall. Slats are cut 1/2 to 3/4

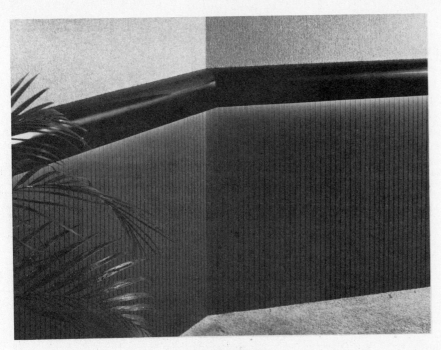

FIGURE 3-14.
Primeline® from Wilsonart® is used as a dado below a lighted chair rail. Primeline is a comprehensive new design line of tambour and grooved architectural surfacing. (Photograph courtesy of Ralph Wilson Plastics Co.)

inch o.c. with the angle of the groove varying between 28° and 60°. Standard dimensions are 24 inches wide by 96 inches slat length. A 120 inch length is available from some companies. Solid hardwood slats are also available in oak and maple (see Figure 3-14).

Flexible mirror may be clear, bronzed, or colored. This mirror is also bonded to a cloth back in square, rectangular, or diagonal pattern cuts and gives a multifaceted or broken reflection. Both the tambour and flexible mirror may be used vertically or horizontally on straight or curved walls.

INSTALLATION. The method of installation depends on the surface to which the tambour is to be attached. A special adhesive is usually required, but the manufacturers' instructions should always be followed.

WOOD

Wood is a renewable resource and a good natural insulator due to the millions of tiny air cells within its structure. For equal thickness, it is 4 times as efficient an insulator as cinder block, 6 times as efficient as brick, 15 times as efficient as stone, 400 times as efficient as steel, and 1,770 times as efficient as aluminum. The production of the final product is also energy efficient. One ton of wood requires 1,510 Kilowatt hours to manufacture, whereas one ton of rolled steel requires 12,000 Kilowatt hours, and one ton of aluminum requires 67,200 Kilowatt hours.

Wood for walls comes in two different forms: solid wood strips and plywoods.

Solid wood may be used on the walls of residences, but it is not usually used for commercial applications unless treated, due to the fire and building code restrictions. For residential use, redwood, cedar, and knotty pine are the most commonly used woods, but walnut, pecan, and many others may also be used (see Table 3-3).

There are several grades of redwood from which to choose. The Clear All Heart is unexcelled in **dimensional stability,** finish retention properties, and its well-known natural resistance to insects and decay. Clear All Heart gives a solid red color, whereas

Table 3-3
Comparative Table of Wood Species

SPECIES	BOTANICAL NAME	PRINCIPAL USES	APPEARANCE COLOR	FIGURE	GRAIN	RELATIVE COST Lumber	RELATIVE COST Plywood
ASH, White	Fraxinus, American	Trim, Frames & Cabinets	Creamy White to Light Brown	High	Open	100	175
BASSWOOD	Tilia, American	Decorative Molds Carving turnery	Creamy White	No figure	Closed	85	—
BEECH	Fagus grandifolia	Semi-exposed Cabinet Parts	Light to Pinkish	Medium	Closed	80	Not Gen. Available
BIRCH, Yellow, "Natural"	Betula alleghaniensis	Trim, Frames Panelling & Cabinets	White to Dark Red	Medium	Closed	100	100
BIRCH, Yellow, "Select Red" (Heartwood)	Betula alleghaniensis	Trim, Frames Panelling & Cabinets	Dark Red	Medium	Closed	150	150
BIRCH, Yellow, "Select White" (Sapwood)	Betula alleghaniensis	Trim, Frames Panelling & Cabinets	Creamy White	Medium	Closed	130	120
BUTTERNUT	Juglans cinerea	Trim, Frames Panelling & Cabinets	Pale Brown	High	Open	300	500
CEDAR, Western Red	Thuja plicata	Trim, Panelling Exterior & Interior	Reddish to Pinkish Brown nearly White Sapwood	Medium	Closed	100	100
CHERRY, Black	Prunus serotina	Trim, Frames Trim	Reddish Brown	High	Closed	160	200
CHESTNUT, Wormy	Castanea dentata	Panelling and Panelling & Cabinets	Greyish Brown	High	Open with Worm Holes	150	NA
FIR, Douglas Flat Grain	Pseudolsuga menziesii	Trim, Frames Panelling	Reddish Tan	High	Closed	100	80
FIR, Douglas Vertical Grain	Pseudolsuga menziesii	Trim, Frames Panelling	Reddish Tan	Low	Closed	100	NA
MAHOGANY, African Plain Sawn	Khaya ivornsis	Trim, Frames Panelling & Cabinets	Reddish Brown	Medium	Open	250	250
MAHOGANY, African Quarter Sawn	Khaya ivornsis	Trim, Frames Panelling & Cabinets	Reddish Brown	Low	Open	350	350
MAHOGANY, Tropical American, "Honduras"	Sweitenia macrophylla	Trim, Frames Panelling cabinets & Bar tops	Rich Golden Brown	Medium	Open	200	300
MAPLE, Hard "Natural"	Acer saccharum	Trim, Frames Panelling & Cabinets	White to Reddish Brown	Medium	Closed	75	150
MAPLE, Hard, "Select White" (Sapwood)	Acer saccharum	Trim, Frames Panelling & Cabinets	White	Medium	Closed	90	150
MAPLE, Soft "Natural"	Acer saccharum	Trim, semi-exposed Cabinet parts	White to Reddish Brown	Low	Closed	75	Not Gen. Available
OAK, Red Plain Sawn	Quercus ruba	Trim, Frames Panelling & Cabinets	Reddish Tan to Brown	High	Open	90	130
OAK, Red Rift Sawn	Quercus ruba	Trim, Frames Panelling & Cabinets	Reddish Tan to Brown	Low	Open	200	250
OAK, Red Quarter Sawn	Quercus ruba	Trim, Frames Panelling & Cabinets	Reddish Tan to Brown	Low	Open	200	250
OAK, White Plain Sawn	Quercus alba	Trim, Frames Panelling & Cabinets	Greyish Tan	High	Open	100	165
OAK, White Rift Sawn	Quercus alba	Trim, Frames Panelling & Cabinets	Greyish Tan	Low	Open	200	250
OAK, White Quarter Sawn	Quercus alba	Trim, Frames Panelling & Cabinets	Greyish Tan	Low figure accented with flakes	Open	200	250
PECAN	Carya species	Trim, Panelling & Cabinets	Reddish Brown with Dark Brown stripes	Medium	Open	100	200
PINE, Eastern or Northern White	Pinus strobus	Trim, Frames Panelling & Cabinets	Creamy White to Pink	Medium	Closed	100	NA
PINE, Idaho	Pinus monticola	Trim, Frames Panelling & Cabinets	Creamy White	Low	Closed	100	Not Gen. Available
PINE, Ponderosa	Pinus ponderosa	Trim, Frames Panelling & Cabinets	Light to Medium Pink	Medium	Closed	100	125
PINE, Sugar	Pinus lambertiana	Trim, Frames Panelling & Cabinets	Creamy White	Low	Closed	110	Not Gen. Available
PINE, Southern Yellow	Pinus echinata	Trim, Frames Panelling & Flooring Cabinets	Pale Yellow	High	Closed	65	Not Gen. Available
POPLAR, Yellow	Lirodendron Tulipifern	Trim, Frames Panelling & Cabinets	Pale Yellow to Brown with Green Cast	Medium	Closed	85	NA
REDWOOD, Flat Grain (Heartwood)	Sequoia Sempervirens	Trim, Frames Panelling	Deep Red	High	Closed	110	NA
REDWOOD, Vertical Grain (Heartwood)	Sequoia Sempervirens	Trim, Frames Panelling	Deep Red	Low	Closed	120	NA
ROSEWOOD, Brazilian	Dalbergia nigra	Solid Trim Incidental to Veneered Panelling	Intermingled Reds Browns, and Blacks	High	Open	NGA	780
SPRUCE, Sitka	Tideland spruce Picea sitchensis	Trim, Frames	Light Yellowish Tan	High	Closed	100	NA
TEAK	Techtona grandis	Trim, Frames Panelling & Cabinets	Tawny Yellow to Dark Brown	High	Open	400	400
WALNUT, Black	Juglans nigra	Trim, Frames Panelling & Cabinets	Chocolate Brown	High	Open	300	300
WALNUT, Nogal	Juglans nigra neotropica	Trim, Frames Panelling & Cabinets	Chocolate Brown	High	Open	200	NA

NOTE: Regional distribution differences may affect availability and cost relationship

(A) Rated from 1 to 4 as follows
1 In warehouse stock in good quantities and fair assortment of thicknesses and lengths

Reprinted by permission of the Architectural Woodwork Institute.

Table 3-3
Comparative Table of Wood Species (Continued)

PRACTICAL SIZE LIMITATIONS Thick	Width	Length	AVAILABILITY OF MATCHING PLYWOOD (A)	HARDNESS	DIMENSIONAL STABILITY (B)	FINISHING Paint	Transparent	REMARKS
1½"	7½"	12'	3	Hard	10/64	Not normally used	Excellent	Excellent where strength is required bold grain
1½"	7½"	10'	4	Soft	10/64	Excellent	Excellent	Best for mouldings no grain.
1½"	7½"	12'	4	Hard	14/64	Excellent	Good	North American Beech not generally used as show wood.
1½"	7½"	12'	1	Hard	12/64	Excellent	Good	One of the most common used
1½"	5½"	11'	2	Hard	12/64	Not normally used	Excellent	Rich Colour.
1½"	5"	11'	2	Hard	12/64	Not normally used	Excellent	Uniform Appearance.
1½"	5½"	8'	3	Medium	8/64	Not normally used	Excellent	Beautiful and Rich.
3¼"	11"	16'	1 & 3	Soft	10/64	Not normally used	Good	Decay resistant, rough texture favorite.
1½"	5½"	7'	2	Hard	9/64	Not normally used	Excellent	Rich Colour.
¾"	7½"	10'	4	Medium	9/64	Not normally used	Excellent	Very limited supply.
3¼"	11"	16'	1	Medium	10/64	Fair	Fair	Good supply.
1½"	11"	16'	4	Medium	6/64	Good	Good	Very limited supply.
2½"	11"	15'	3	Medium	7/64	Good	Excellent	Fine hardwood.
2½"	7½"	15'	3	Medium	5/64	Not normally used	Excellent	Limited supply.
2½"	11"	15'	3	Medium	6/64	Not normally used	Excellent	One of the world's finest cabinet woods.
3½"	9½"	12'	3	Very Hard	12/64	Excellent	Good	Plentiful supply, excellent properties.
2½"	9½"	12'	3	Very Hard	12/64	Not normally used	Excellent	Uniform appearance.
3¼"	9½"	12'	4	Medium	9/64	Excellent	Not normally used	Good utility hardwood.
1½"	7¼"	12'	1	Hard	11/64	Not normally used	Excellent	Excellent architectural wood, low cost widely used.
1-5/16"	5½"	10'	3	Hard	7/64	Not normally used	Excellent	Excellent architectural wood, limited supply.
1-5/16"	5½"	8'	1	Hard	7/64	Not normally used	Excellent	Excellent architectural wood, limited supply.
1½"	5½"	10'	2	Hard	11/64	Not normally used	Excellent	Wide Range of grain patterns and colour.
¾"	4½"	10'	3	Hard	7/64	Not normally used	Excellent	Limited availability.
¾"	4½"	10'	3	Hard	8/64	Not normally used	Excellent	Pronounced flake, very limited use and supply.
1½"	5½"	12'	3	Hard	11/64	Not normally used	Good	Subject to regional availability, attractive.
1½"	9½"	14'	3	Soft	7/64	Good	Good	True white pine, wide range of applications for general usage.
1½"	9½"	14'	4	Soft	8/64	Good	Good	True white pine, wide range of applications for general usage.
1½"	9½"	16'	3	Soft	8/64	Good	Good	Most widely used pine, wide range of applications for general usage.
3¼"	11"	16'	4	Soft	7/64	Good	Good	True white pine, wide range of applications for general usage.
1½"	7½"	16'	4	Medium	10/64	Fair	Good	An economical hard pine.
2½"	7½"	12'	3	Medium	9/64	Excellent	Good	Ideal interior hardwood excellent paintability.
2½"	11"	16'	1 & 3	Soft	6/64	Good	Good	Superior exterior wood high natural decay resistance
2½"	11"	16'	3	Soft	3/64	Excellent	Excellent	Superior exterior wood high natural decay resistance.
—	—	—	3	Very Hard	7/64	Not normally used	Excellent	Exotice figure, high cost.
3¼"	9½"	16'	4	Soft	10/64	Fair	Fair	Limited general available.
1½"	7½"	10'	2	Hard	6/64	Not normally used	Excellent	Outstanding wood for most applications, high cost.
1½"	4½"	6'	1	Hard	10/64	Paint not normally used	Excellent	Fine domestic hardwood extremely limited widths and lengths more readily available in veneer
¾"	9½"	9'	4	Medium	12/64	Not normally used	Good	Good substitute for juglans nigra where better widths and lengths required

2 In warehouse stock in fair quantity but not in thicknesses other than ¼" and ¾"; or sizes other than 4'-0" x 8'-0".
3 Produced on a special order only.
4 Not generally available

(B) These figures represent possible width change in a 12" board when moisture content is reduced from 10% to 5%. Figures are for plain sawn unless indicated otherwise in species column.

FIGURE 3-15.
The vertical grain of redwood produces these fairly even vertical stripes. The flat grain produces a more uneven patterned appearance. (Photograph courtesy of the California Redwood Association)

Clear redwood is also top quality but does contain some cream-colored sapwood and may also contain small knots and surface **checks.** This cream-colored sapwood may be attractive to some, but to others its random appearance is bothersome; therefore, the client needs to know the difference between the Clear All Heart and Clear.

Construction Heart is an economical all-purpose grade for decking and outdoor uses. The last two, Construction Common and Merchantable, are construction grades with knots and sapwood combined.

Redwood is available in vertical grain, equivalent to quarter sawed, and flat grain, cut at a tangent to the annual growth rings, exposing a face surface that appears highly figured or marbled.

For a stately atmosphere, Clear All Heart vertical-grained redwood enhances the effect. The smooth-faced redwood is referred to as *surfaced;* resawn has one surface roughened by resawing during manufacture, which generates an extra dimension of shadow,

contributing to a softened informal atmosphere. Boards range from 1/2 to 2 inches in thickness and 3 to 12 inches in width (see Figures 3-2, 3-17, and 3-18).

There are two types of cedar: aromatic cedar, which is used for mothproof closets, and regular cedar, which is used for both interior and exterior walls. Another soft wood frequently used for residential interiors is knotty pine where knots are part of the desired effect, unlike the top grade redwood.

Boards may be anywhere from 4 to 12 inches wide with tongue-and-groove for an interlocking joint, or **shiplap** for an overlapping joint. The tongue-and-groove may have the edges beveled for a V-joint or may be rounded or even elaborately molded for a more decorative effect. Shiplap boards come with their top edges beveled to form a V-joint, or with straight edges to form a narrow slot at the seams.

Square-edged boards are used in contemporary settings and may be board and batten, board on board, reverse board and batten, or contemporary vertical.

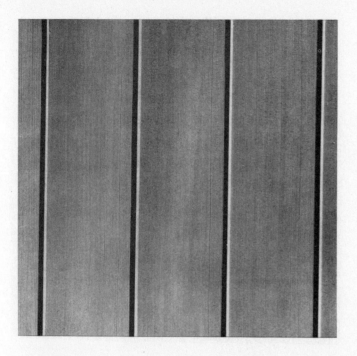
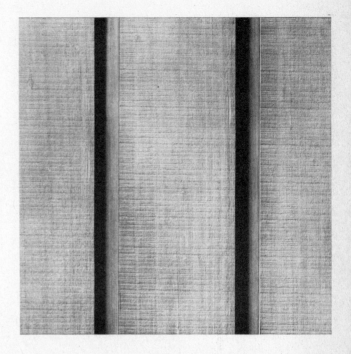

FIGURE 3-16.
On the left is surfaced vertical grain redwood with a V-joint. On the right, saw-textured shiplap redwood gives a rough horizontally lined surface. (Courtesy of the California Redwood Association)

FIGURE 3-17.
Clear All Heart redwood is installed in a diagonal chevron pattern on the wall. The V-joint causes shadows, thus emphasizing the joints. (Photograph courtesy of the California Redwood Association)

FIGURE 3-18.
This bedroom utilizes horizontal Clear redwood on the wall to the right and diagonal Clear redwood on the left wall. The built-in drawers are surfaced Clear All Heart redwood. Notice the light streaks caused by the sapwood. (Design: Marshall Roath; photograph: Allan Rosenberg, courtesy of California Redwood Association)

Board and batten consists of wide boards spaced about one inch apart, and a narrow 1 by 2 inch strip of batten is nailed on top to cover the one-inch gap. Board on board is similar to board and batten, except that both pieces of wood are the same width. Reverse board and batten has the narrow strip under the joint or gap. In contemporary vertical installations, the battens are placed on edge between the wider boards (see Figure 3-19).

For acoustical control, boards are often placed on edge and spaced 2 to 3 inches apart on an acoustical substrate.

The National Oak Flooring Manufacturer's Association suggests using oak flooring on the walls and ceiling. It is now possible to obtain a Class "A" 0-25 flame-spread rating (often required in commercial structures) by job-site application of an intumescent coating. The NOFMA supplies literature showing that using Albert DS Clear by American Vameg meets this standard. A beveled oak strip flooring gives a three-dimensional effect when installed on a wall.

Several companies manufacture paneling that comes prepackaged in boxes containing approximately 64 square feet. The longest pieces are 8 feet and the shortest 2 feet, with the edges beveled and tongue-and-grooved sides and ends. This type of paneling, although more expensive than regular strips, eliminates waste in a conventional 8-foot-high room.

INSTALLATION. Siding, plank, or strips may be installed horizontally, vertically, or diagonally. Each type of installation will give a completely different feeling to the room. Horizontal planking will appear to lengthen a room and draw the ceiling down, while vertical adds height to a room and is more formal. Diagonal installations appear a little more active and should be used with discretion or as a focal point of a room. Diagonal or herringbone patterns look best on walls with few doors or windows. Different application methods require different substrates.

If installed horizontally or diagonally over bare studs or gypsum board, no further preparation of the surface is needed. The strips are attached in the tongue area as with hardwood flooring, except that with wall applications, the nails penetrate each stud.

Vertical installations require the addition of nailing surfaces. The two types of nailing surfaces are blocking and furring. *Blocking* is the filling-in horizontally between the studs with a 2 by 4 inch piece of wood, in order to make a nailing surface. This blocking also acts as a fire stop. *Furring* is thin strips of wood nailed across the studs (see Figure 3-20).

When wood is to be used on an outside wall, a vapor barrier such as a polyethylene film is required. Also, wood should be stored for several days in the area in which it is to be installed so it may reach the correct moisture content. Some manufacturers suggest several applications of a water-repellent preservative to all sides, edges and especially the more porous ends. This is particularly important where high humidity persists.

One of the most innovative wall paneling systems is one imported from Germany called Profilewood®. The innovation is the clip system which is used to join and attach the panels to the studs. The Profilewood itself is not nailed to the studs, but rather is

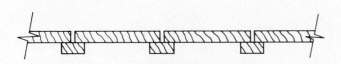

Board and Batten

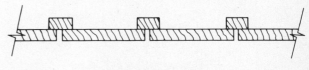

Reverse Board and Batten

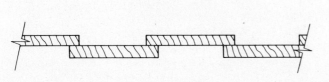

Board on Board

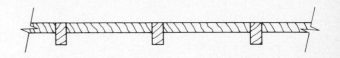

Contemporary Vertical Batten and Board

FIGURE 3-19. Boards and Battens.

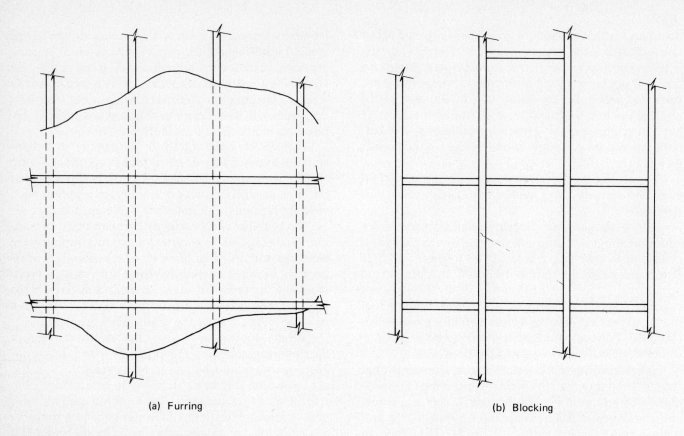

(a) Furring

(b) Blocking

FIGURE 3-20. Furring and Blocking.

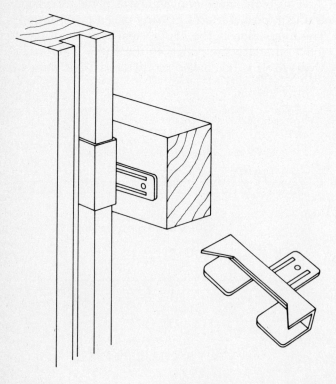

Profilewood

FIGURE 3-21. Profilewood® Metal Clip System Showing Installation Method.

held in place by the galvanized clips that are nailed to the studs, allowing for the natural shrinking and swelling of the wood. Profilewood is available in California Redwood, Western Red Cedar, Western Hemlock, Douglas Fir, and Sitka Spruce.

There are several suggested finishes for wood walls: wax, which adds soft luster to the wood; or a sealer and a matte varnish, where cleaning is necessary. The paneling may also be stained, but it is important to remember that if solid wood is used, the natural beauty of the wood should be allowed to show.

Plywood paneling

Plywood is produced from thin sheets of wood veneer, called *plies*, which are laminated together under heat and pressure with special adhesives. This produces a bond between plies that is as strong or stronger than the wood itself.

Plywood always has an odd number of layers which are assembled with their grains perpendicular to each other. Plywood may also have a lumber core or a particle board core. The lumber core is the most expensive plywood, but it is easily machined and has the most stable construction (see Figure 3-22).

The face veneer has the best quality veneer, and the back may be the same or of lesser quality, depending on its uses. Thus, a panel classified as N-A has an N grade on the face and an A grade on the back (see Table 3-4).

The manner in which the veneer is cut and the part of the tree from which it comes give the different patterns—rotary, flat sliced, or quarter sliced. *Rotary cut* is used for all construction plywood. The log is placed in a large lathe and, as the wood rotates against the sharp knife, the veneer peels off the log, in much the same manner as wrapping paper is pulled from a roll. The chief advantage to this method is that it produces wide, long sheets of veneer. Birch is one of the hardwoods cut by the rotary method, due to its uniformity of grain.

Flat slicing is the method of cutting veneer from wood the same way a potato is sliced. The veneer usually has a striped effect at the edges, with a larger, rather wide grain toward the center. Walnut is usually cut by this method.

Quarter slicing is the most costly method of veneer cutting. Quarter slicing is done for most fine imported

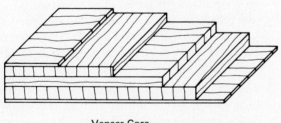

Veneer Core

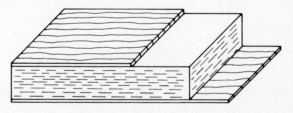

Particleboard Core

Lumber Core

FIGURE 3-22. Types of Plywood.

**Table 3-4
Veneer Grades of Plywood**

	N	Special order "natural finish" veneer. Select all heartwood or all sapwood. Free of open defects. Allows some repairs.
	A	Smooth and paintable. Neatly made repairs permissible. Also used for natural finish in less demanding applications.
	B	Solid surface veneer. Circular repair plugs and tight knots permitted.
Plugged	C	Improved C veneer with splits limited to 1/8 inch in width and knotholes and borer holes limited to 1/4 inch by 1/2 inch.
	C	Knotholes to 1 inch. Occasional knotholes 1/2 inch larger permitted providing total width of all knots and knotholes within a specified section does not exceed certain limits. Limited splits permitted in Exterior type plywood.
	D	Permits knots and knotholes to 2 1/2 inch in width and 1/2 inch larger under certain specified limits. Limited splits permitted.

Source: Hardwood Plywood Manufacturers Association. Reprinted by permission.

woods where a definite striped effect is desirable. Mahogany is a good example.

Other decorative veneer patterns may be obtained by using the crotch, burl, or stump of the tree. The crotch pattern is always reversed so that the pointed part, or V, is up. Burl comes from an area of damage of the tree, where the tree has healed itself and grown over the injury. It is a very swirly pattern. Olive burl is frequently used in contemporary furniture.

Because rotary cutting provides large sheets, matching of pattern is not necessary. However, matching of veneers in flat and quarter slicing is very important. Slip-matched veneers are laid next to each other as the veneer comes from the cutter, giving a repetitive pattern, but also nonmatching joints. Slip-matched veneers result in maximum color conformity

and are most commonly used with quartered and rift-sliced veneers. In book-leaf matched veneers, every other piece of veneer is turned over, thus giving a more united feeling to the veneer. The meeting edges produce a matching joint and effect maximum continuity of grain. Book-matching is used with either plain or quarter sliced veneer. End matching, sometimes known as butt matching, is used when the panel height desired exceeds the veneer length, and is achieved by progressively book-matching lengthwise as well as horizontally, thus producing a uniform grain progression in both directions. A four-way center and butt match is used on table tops or wall paneling to give extremely interesting patterns.

The following information is supplied by the Architectural Woodwork Institute, a not-for-profit organization representing the architectural woodwork manufacturers of the United States and Canada.

There are three methods of assembling the veneers within the panel face:

1. *Running Match.* Each face is made from as many veneer pieces as necessary. That portion left over from the last piece is used as the start of the next panel face. Maximum yield from the **flitch** is achieved by this method and is most commonly used in producing "premanufactured flitch" matched panel sets.

2. *Balance Match.* Each face is made from an odd or even number of equal-width veneer pieces. If the panel run is large, the number of veneer pieces per equal-width panel may eventually increase or decrease, as the individual veneer pieces vary in width within the total flitch. The face-matching method may be used in sequence-matched sets and is commonly used in blueprint-matched panels.

3. *Center Match.* Each face is made with an even number of equal width veneer pieces, which results in the same grain and figure occurring on each side of the vertical center line of the panel (see Figure 3-25).

Methods of matching panels

1. *Pre-manufactured Sets.* These are pre-manufactured and numbered sequence panel sets, usually 48 by 96 inches or 48 by 120 inches. They may be the product of a flitch or part thereof, with the number of panels usually varying from 6 to 12. If more than one set is required, no matching between the sets can be expected. Similarly, doors occurring within the panel run cannot be matched. These panels are best utilized in their near-full width, with neces-

TYPES OF VENEER CUTS:

The manner in which veneers are cut is an important factor in producing the various visual effects obtained. Two woods of the same species, but with their veneers cut differently, will have entirely different visual character even though their color values are similar.

In plywood manufacture there are five principal methods of cutting veneer. The veneer slicer and veneer lathe are the primary equipment employed.

The five methods are:

Rotary

The log is mounted centrally in the lathe and turned against a razor sharp blade, like unwinding a roll of paper. Since this cut follows the log's annular growth rings a bold grain figure is produced. Rotary cut veneer is exceptionally wide and matching at veneer joints is relatively difficult. Almost all softwood plywood is cut this way. Lengths in all hardwoods are limited to 10'.

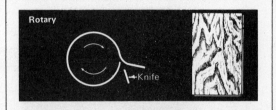

Plain slicing (or flat slicing)

The half log, or flitch, is mounted with the heart side flat against the guide plate of the slicer and the slicing is done parallel to a line through the center of the log. This produces a figure similar to that of plain sawn lumber.

Quarter slicing

The quarter log, or flitch, is mounted on the guide plate so that the growth rings of the log strike the knife at approximately right angles, producing a series of stripes, straight in some woods, varied in others.

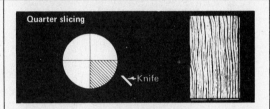

Half-round slicing

A variation of rotary cutting in which segments, or flitches, of the log are mounted off center in the lathe. This results in a cut slightly across the annular growth rings and visually shows modified characteristics of both rotary and plain sliced veneers. This method of cutting is often used on Red Oak.

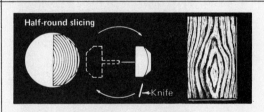

Rift-cut

Rift-cut veneer is produced in the various species of Oak. Oak has medullary ray cells which radiate from the center of the log like the spokes of a wheel. The rift, or comb grain effect, is obtained by slicing slightly across these medullary rays. This accentuates the vertical grain and minimizes the flake.

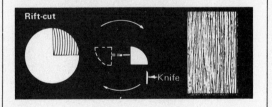

FIGURE 3-23. Veneer Types.
(Reprinted with permission of the Architectural Woodwork Institute)

TYPES OF MATCHING BETWEEN INDIVIDUAL VENEER PIECES

1. Book matching: This method is achieved by turning over every other veneer piece just as are the leaves of a book. The meeting edges thus produce a matching joint and effects maximum continuity of grain. This can be used with either plain or quarter sliced veneer.

2. Slip matching: With this method the veneer rotation is maintained but the pieces are joined side by side repeating the grain figure but with non-matching joints. This results in maximum color uniformity and is most commonly used with quartered and rift sliced veneers.

3. Random matching: This method results in a deliberate mismatch of veneers by random selection of the pieces from one or more flitches producing a casual or "board-like" effect.

4. End matching: This method is used when the panel height desired exceeds the veneer length and is achieved by progressively book matching lengthwise as well as horizontally, thus achieving a uniform grain progression in both directions.

The following illustrate the matching methods just described.

FIGURE 3-24. Book, Slip, Random, End Matching. *(Reproduced by permission of the Architectural Woodwork Institute)*

sary adjustments being made at wall ends or corners.

2. *Sequence-matched Panel Sets.* These sets are usually manufactured for a specific installation to a uniform panel width and height. If more than one flitch is required to produce the necessary number of panels, similar flitches will be used. This type of panel matching is best used when panel layout is uninterrupted and when the design permits the use of near-equal width panels. Doors occurring within the panel are not sequence-matched.

3. *Blueprint-matched Panel and Components.* This method of panel matching achieves maximum grain continuity, since all panels, doors, and other veneered components are made to the exact sizes required and in exact veneer sequence. If possible, flitches should be selected that will yield sufficient veneer to complete a prescribed area or room and, if more than one is required, flitch transition should be accomplished at the least noticeable predetermined location. This panel matching method is the most expensive, but it does express veneering in its most impressive manner (see Figure 3-26).

Rooms treated with paneling always produce a feeling of permanency. Architectural paneling is as different from ready-made paneling as a custom-made Rolls Royce is from an inexpensive production car. The ready-made paneling will be discussed later.

There are two grades of architectural paneling as defined by AWI:

Premium Grade: This is the highest grade available in both materials and workmanship, and is intended for the finest work. It is naturally the most expensive grade. It might be used throughout the entire building for monumental-type work, but most often is used in selected spaces within a building or for selected items.

Custom Grade: This is the normal grade in both material and workmanship, and is intended for high-quality regular work.

For a traditional type of paneling, stile and rail paneling is used. This consists of a panel that may be flat, raised, or have a beveled edge, together with the vertical side strips which are called **stiles,** and the horizontal strips which are called *rails.* The rails, stiles, and **mullions** may themselves be shaped into an **ovolo** or **ogee** moulding, or, to give a more intricate design, a separate moulding may be added. For raised panels under 10 inches in width, solid lumber may be used in custom grade, but for premium grade or wider panels, plywood is used with an attached edge of solid lumber which is then beveled (see Figure 3-29).

Since the detail and design options in this type of paneling are virtually unlimited, the AWI suggests that certain minimum information must be provided to properly estimate and detail this type of paneling:

1. Scale elevations of walls determining panel layout.

2. Determination by detail or instructions as to whether the panel mould is to be an applied moulding or whether it is to be a profiled portion of the stiles and rails. (Such profiles must be capable of being **coped.**)

3. Similar determination as to whether the panels are to be flat or raised.

Panels are assembled by means of mortise and tenon, or dowel joints. At the joining of the panel and the stiles and rails, a small space is left to allow for the natural expansion and contraction of the panel. This type of construction may sometimes be known as "floating panel construction." Panels that are glued have no allowance for this expansion and contraction, and may split if movement is excessive.

There are several methods of installing panels for acoustic control. The panels may be floated or raised, or batten mouldings of wood, metal, or plastic may also be used (see Figure 3-30).

FINISHING. The Architectural Woodwork Institute has specific standards for factory finishing of woodwork and their books entitled *Architectural Woodwork Quality Standards Guide Specifications and Quality Certification Program* and *Factory Finishing of Architectural Woodwork* should be consulted.

PREFINISHED PLYWOOD

Prefinished plywood paneling varies from 1/4 to 1/2 inch thick, and standard panel size is 4 by 8 feet, but is also available in 7 and 10 foot heights. The face of the plywood is grooved in random widths to simulate wood strips. This also hides the joining where each panel is butted up to the next, as outside edges are beveled at the same angle as the grooves.

The finish on this type of paneling is clear acrylic over a stained surface.

Some plywood paneling has a woodgrain reproduction on lauan plywood or on a paper overlay applied to lauan plywood and then protected with an oven-baked topcoat.

METHODS OF ASSEMBLING THE VENEERS WITHIN THE PANEL FACE

1. Running match: Each face is made from as many veneer pieces as necessary. That portion left over from the last piece is then used as the start of the next panel face. Maximum yield from the flitch is achieved by this method, and is most commonly used in producing "warehouse flitch" matched panel sets.

2. Balance match: Each face is made from an odd or even number of equal width veneer pieces. If the panel run is large the number of veneer pieces per equal width panel may eventually increase or decrease as the individual veneer pieces vary in width within the total flitch. This face matching method may be used in sequence matched sets and is commonly used in blueprint matched panels.

3. Center match: Each face is made with an even number of equal width veneer pieces which results in the same grain and figure occurring on each side of the vertical center line of the panel. The following illustrate the matching methods just described.

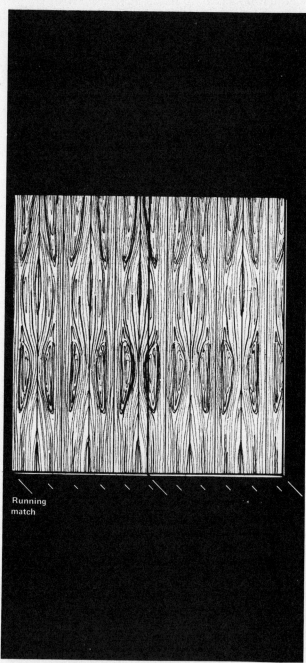

Running match

FIGURE 3-25. Assembly of Veneers Within the Panel Face.
(Reproduced by permission of the Architectural Woodwork Institute)

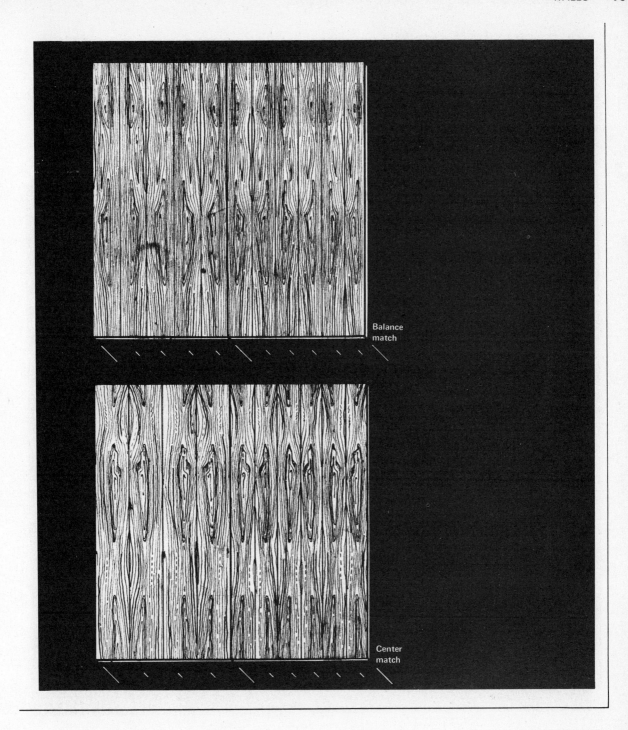

Balance
match

Center
match

METHODS OF MATCHING PANELS:

1. Warehouse matched sets: These are pre-manufactured and numbered sequence panel sets usually 48″ x 96″ or 48″ x 120″. They may be the product of a flitch or part thereof with the number of panels usually varying from 6 to 12 panels. If more than 1 set is required, no matching between the sets can be expected. Similarily doors occurring within the panel run cannot be matched. Best utilization of these panels is achieved by using them in their near full width with necessary adjustments being made at wall ends or corner.

2. Sequence matched panel sets: These sets are usually manufactured for a specific installation to a uniform panel width and height. If more than one flitch is required to produce the required number of panels similar flitches will be used. This type of panel matching is best used when panel layout is uninterrupted and when the design permits the use of near equal width panels. Doors occurring within the panel run are not sequence matched.

3. Blueprint matched panels and components: This method of panel matching achieves maximum grain continuity since all

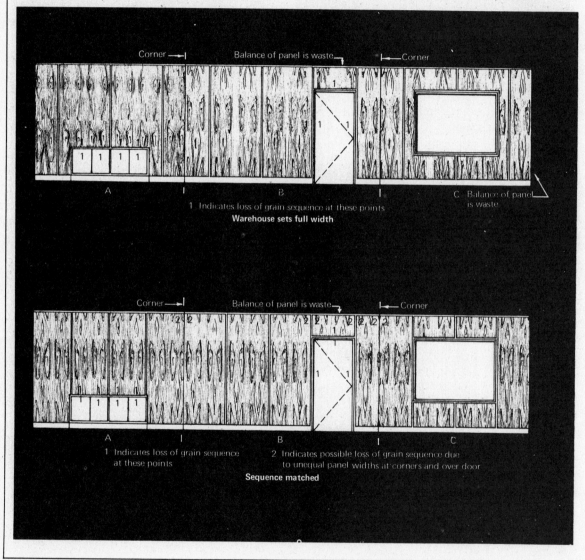

FIGURE 3-26. Matching Panels.
(Reproduced by permission of the Architectural Woodwork Institute)

panels, doors and other veneered components are made to the exact sizes required and in exact veneer sequence. If possible, flitches should be selected that will yield sufficient veneer to complete a prescribed area or room and if more than one is required, flitch transition should be accomplished at the least noticeable, pre-determined location. This panel matching method is the more expensive but does express veneering in its most impressive manner.

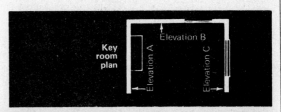

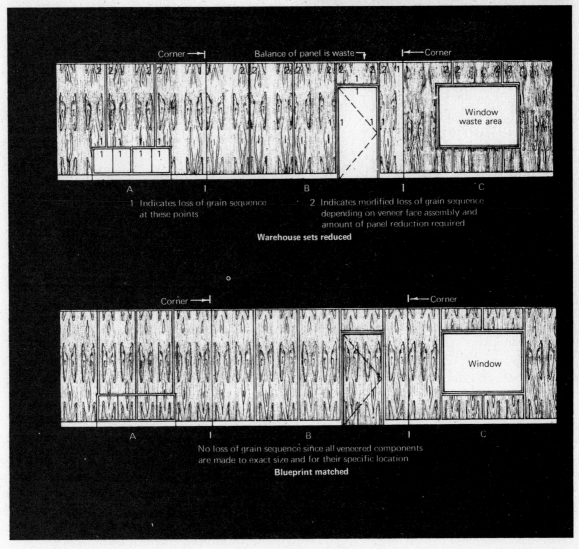

1 Indicates loss of grain sequence at these points
2 Indicates modified loss of grain sequence depending on veneer face assembly and amount of panel reduction required

Warehouse sets reduced

No loss of grain sequence since all veneered components are made to exact size and for their specific location

Blueprint matched

Stile+rail paneling
floating ' '

FIGURE 3-27.
The reception area of a law office reflects their prestigious practice with beautifully detailed woodwork and mouldings. Note the marble surround on the fireplace. (Architects: DeLaMare-Woodruff; interior designer: Raymond Jones; photograph: Richard Springgate)

FIGURE 3-28.
*Close-up detail of entrance arch shown in Figure 3-27. (*Architects: *DeLaMare-Woodruff;* interior designer: *Raymond Jones;* photograph: *Richard Springgate)*

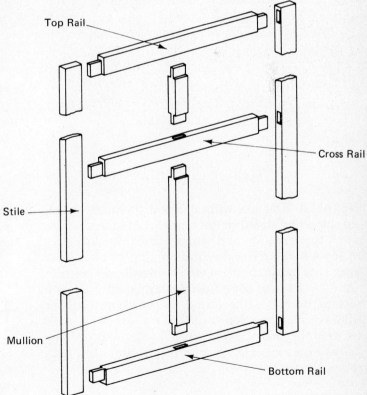

Top Rail

Cross Rail

Stile

Mullion

Bottom Rail

Typical Frame Parts

FIGURE 3-29. Frame Parts.

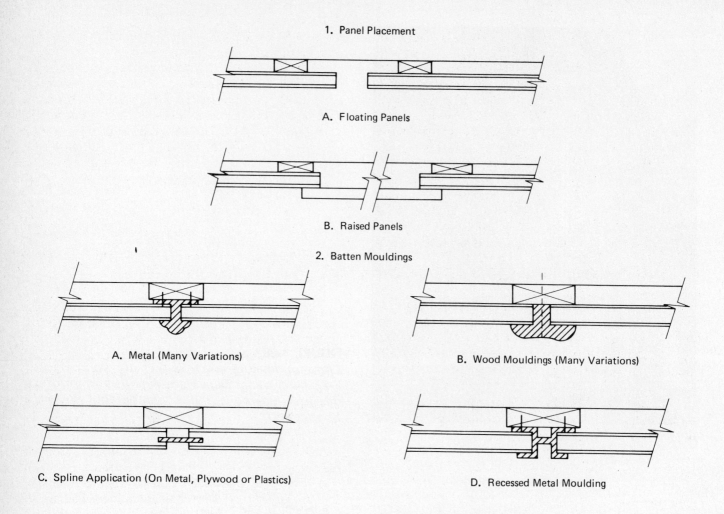

1. Panel Placement

A. Floating Panels

B. Raised Panels

2. Batten Mouldings

A. Metal (Many Variations)

B. Wood Mouldings (Many Variations)

C. Spline Application (On Metal, Plywood or Plastics)

D. Recessed Metal Moulding

FIGURE 3-30. Panel Installation for Acoustic Control.
(Courtesy of the Hardwood Plywood Manufacturers Association)

INSTALLATION. As with all wood products, paneling should be stored in the room for 24 hours to condition for humidity and temperature. Paneling may be applied directly to the stud framing, but it is safer from a fire hazard point of view to install over gypsum board. A 1/4 inch sound-deadening board used as a backing decreases the sound transmission. Nails or adhesive may be used to install the panels. If nails are used they may be color-coated when exposed fasteners are acceptable, or countersunk and filled with colored putty.

MAINTENANCE. Prefinished plywood panels require frequent dusting in order to prevent a build-up of soil which dulls the finish. Each manufacturer supplies instructions for maintenance of their particular product and these should be adhered to.

HARDBOARD

Sheets or planks of hardboard are manufactured of compressed wood fibers by means of heat and pressure. Hardboard sheets or planks consist of a textured hardboard base that is textured during the pressing process, usually in a wood grain pattern. A dark base coat is then placed on top. This layer gives the dark color to the V-joints. On top is the lighter precision coat that does not cover the V-joints. This precision coat is grained and coated with a melamine top coat that is baked on and that is resistant to most household chemicals and such staining agents as cosmetics and crayons. (Tape should not be applied to the panel surface because it may damage the surface.)

Marlite® brand plank is 1/4 inch thick, nominal 16 inch-wide module in 8-foot lengths, featuring a patented tongue-and-groove joinery system. Ten-foot lengths are available in some patterns. Marlite brand Monoplank® is a 1/4 inch thick nominal 6-inch wide module available in 8-foot lengths. It features a ship-lap joinery system.

Paneling is also available in 4 by 8 foot sheets and may utilize harmonizing mouldings between panels or it may be butted. Pigmented vertical grooves simulate joints of lumber planks and edges are also pigmented to match face grooves and to conceal butt joints. Hardboard panels are not to be used below grade, over masonry walls, in bathrooms, or in any area of high humidity.

When hardboard is covered with a photoreproduction of wood, it does not have the depth or richness of real wood, and is probably best used for inexpensive installations where price and durability are more important than the appearance of real wood. Because this paneling is not wood-veneered but rather a reproduction, the same manufacturing methods may be used for solid colors or patterns. Fast food restaurants and many businesses requiring the same feature of durability and easy cleaning use Marlite plank and Monoplank® and very unusual effects may be achieved. The plank and Monoplank may be used vertically, horizontally, and diagonally, provided the walls have had furring strips installed. They may also be installed over any sound, solid substrate.

Some hardboard is available in a stamped grille-type pattern or with holes (commonly known as Peg-Board®). The grille types are framed with wood and used for dividers. The perforated board is useful when hanging or storing items. Special hooks and supports are available for this purpose and are easily installed and removed for adjustment.

INSTALLATION. Thicknesses of hardboard vary from 1/8 and 3/16 inch to 1/4 inch. The 1/8 and 3/16 of an inch thicknesses must be installed over a solid backing, such as gypsum board. Panels are glued or nailed to the substrate.

MAINTENANCE. A lint-free cloth should be used. To remove surface accumulation such as dust and grease, a soft cloth dampened with furniture polish containing no waxes or silicones may be used. More stubborn accumulations may require wiping with a soft cloth dampened in a solution of lukewarm water and a mild detergent. The hardboard must be wiped dry with a clean dry cloth immediately following this procedure. (An inconspicuous area or scrap paneling should be used for experimental cleaning.)

PLASTIC LAMINATE

Plastic laminates are made from layers of kraft paper which have been impregnated with phenolic resins. The pattern layer is placed on top and covered by a translucent overlay of melamine. When all these layers are bonded with heat, 300°F, and pressure, 800 to 1,200 psi, the top translucent layer becomes transparent and forms the wear layer. The pattern layer may be solid color, metal, or a photoreproduction of wood or fabric (see Figure 3-31).

The vertical surface may either be .050 inch general purpose or .030 inch vertical surface. The .030 inch vertical surface type is not recommended on surfaces exceeding 24 inches in width. Plastic laminates for walls are quite often installed on the job site (see Figure 3-32).

Balancing or backing laminates are used to give structural balance and dimensional stability. They are placed on the reverse side of the substrate to inhibit moisture absorption through the back surface.

Where antistatic properties are required, a standard grade antistatic laminate is available.

METTLE MICA® laminate is anodized aluminum that is .025 of an inch thick and weighs 6 ounces per square foot. It comes with a 3.5 mil clear protective mask. This metal laminate is very suitable for walls and display cabinets, store fixtures, etc., and light duty horizontal surfaces. As with other high-pressure plastic laminates, a backing of equal thickness should be used to achieve a balanced construction. Plastic laminate is especially suitable for a wall treatment in a high humidity environment. Formica is the only manufacturer of the large 4 by 16 foot sheets that are very suitable for architectural paneling.

Several manufacturers of plastic laminate produce a laminate that does not have the usual dark edge associated with a square edge installation.

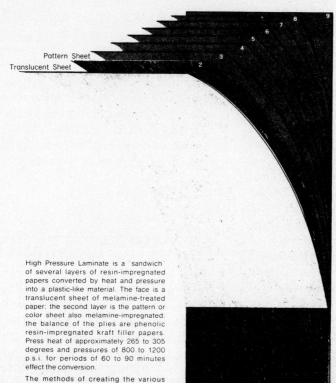

Pattern Sheet
Translucent Sheet

High Pressure Laminate is a "sandwich" of several layers of resin-impregnated papers converted by heat and pressure into a plastic-like material. The face is a translucent sheet of melamine-treated paper; the second layer is the pattern or color sheet also melamine-impregnated; the balance of the plies are phenolic resin-impregnated kraft filler papers. Press heat of approximately 265 to 305 degrees and pressures of 800 to 1200 p.s.i. for periods of 60 to 90 minutes effect the conversion.

The methods of creating the various available surface finishes vary. They are usually achieved by buffing, or polishing after pressing, or by the use of highly polished or minutely etched stainless steel or aluminum cauls (depending on the exact finish desired) that are placed in contact with the laminate face during the pressing sequence. No attempt will be made here to list the various surface finishes available, since most are unique to specific manufacturers, are subject to change and are well documented in their respective brochures.

High pressure laminates intended for general architectural usage are made in several types and thicknesses and for various purposes. These are:

.050" *General Purpose Type.* This is the type most universally used. It is suitable for either horizontal or vertical surfaces, and affords the maximum selection of colors, patterns and finishes. Since this thickness has the greater number of phenolic-impregnated plies, it is the most dimensionally stable and has the greatest impact resistance.

.030" *Vertical Surface Type.* As the name implies, this type is suitable for vertical surfaces only, such as wall panels and cabinet surfaces, and where maximum durability is not a prerequisite. Its reduced thickness results in a greater percentage of melamine-impregnated plies, making its dimensional stability less than that of the heavier general purpose type. For this reason, its use is not recommended on surfaces exceeding 24" in width.

.025" *Cabir* s
intended fo -
faces. Its c(1
the facing -
face durab e
and preven ir
selection is k
and a few ne

.040" *Post* s
manufactur d
and bent tc r-
ties and uses are similar to 1/16" General Purpose Type.

A functional companion to the above facing material is the balancing or backing laminate sheet. Its purpose is to inhibit moisture absorption through the back or concealed surfaces, and also to attain structural balance. Several types are available. Proper selection and use are important and relate to the intended function of the item being manufactured. These backing types are:

.050" to .060" *Balancing Sheet Type.* This type, since it equals in thickness and approximates in construction the General Purpose Type, is the best balancing material and affords maximum structural balance and dimensional stability. Its use is recommended for pieces having large unsupported areas and wall paneling using .050" faces.

.040" *Backing Sheet Type.* This type is developed by removing the melamine face of regular .050" General Purpose Types whose face surfaces were impaired during the manufacturing process. Since its thickness approaches that of the .050" facing material, its balancing characteristics approximate those of the regular .040" Balancing Sheet Type.

.020" and .030" *Backing Sheet Type.* These types function to inhibit moisture absorption and do contribute some structural balance. Their use is recommended for small unsupported panels or components, or where the latter are solidly attached to other structural members. Since their thickness is close to that of the .030" Vertical Surface Type, they also function as an appropriate balancing sheet for this material.

FIGURE 3-31. Construction of Plastic Laminate.

FIGURE 3-32.
A merit award winner in the 1983 A.S.I.D./Wilsonart Design Competition shows the imaginative use of plastic laminate for an integrated fireplace/entertainment center in a waterfront home. This material is easy to maintain in a high humidity environment. The floor is travertine. (Designer: *William L. Vernon, A.S.I.D., Richard Plumer Interior Design;* photograph: *Dan Forer*)

Many manufacturers of high-pressure plastic laminates produce a fire-resistant type which, when applied with approved glues to a fire-resistant core, result in a wall paneling of Class 1 or "A" flame spread rating.

INSTALLATION. When plastic laminates are to be used on the wall, a 3/4 inch hardwood-faced plywood or particle board should be used as a core. The use of an expansion type joint or reveal is suggested (see Figure 3-33). To permit free panel movement and to avoid visible fastenings, AWI recommends that panels be hung on the walls, utilizing metal panel clips or interlocking wood wall cleats, as shown in Figure 3-34.

MAINTENANCE. Plastic laminates should be cleaned with warm water and mild soaps, such as those used for hands or dishes. Use of abrasive cleansers or "special" cleansers should be avoided because they may contain abrasives, acids, or alkalines. Stubborn stains may be removed with organic solvents or two-minute exposure to a hypochlorite bleach such as Clorox, followed by a clean water rinse.

Metallic laminate finishes can be easily cleaned with alcohol, glass cleaners, or ammonia. Standard metal cleaning agents should be avoided, as these may mar the surface beauty.

PORCELAIN ENAMEL

Porcelain enamel is fused (at temperatures above 800°F) to 28-gauge steel, laminated to 3/16 to 21/32 inch gypsum board or hardboard and comes in many colors and finishes for use in high-abuse public areas, such as hospitals and food processing and preparation areas. It is also available with writing board surfaces that double as projection screens. Widths are from 2 to 4 feet and lengths are from 6 to 12 feet. Weight varies from 1.60 to 2.75 pounds per square foot. This material is also used for toilet partitions in public restrooms.

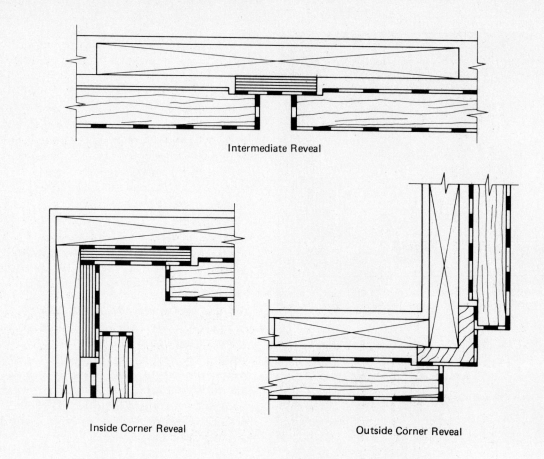

Intermediate Reveal

Inside Corner Reveal

Outside Corner Reveal

FIGURE 3-33. Reveals.
(Reproduced with permission of the Architectural Woodwork Institute)

MAINTENANCE. Same as for ceramic tile.

GLASS

In the past, glass has been used mainly for windows, permitting light and sun to enter the interior of a home or building. Currently, due to modern construction methods, glass is used for interior walls or partitions. Of course, one disadvantage of glass is that it is breakable, but there are products specially made to reduce this problem.

There are three methods of manufacturing glass. The first is for sheet or window glass, where the molten glass is drawn out and both sides are subjected to open flame. This type, which is not treated after manufacture, can show distortions and waviness. Plate glass has both surfaces ground and polished, rendering its surfaces virtually plane and parallel. Float glass is a more recently developed and less expensive process of manufacturing; molten glass is floated over molten metal and is interchangeable with plate glass.

Insulating glass consists of two or three sheets of glass separated by either a dehydrated air space or an inert gas-filled space, together with a **desiccant.** This insulating glass limits heat transference and, in some areas of the country, may be required by the building codes in all new construction for energy conservation purposes. It also helps to eliminate the problem of condensation caused by a wide difference in outside and inside temperatures.

There are various types of safety glass. The one with which we are most familiar is **tempered,** the kind used in entry doors or shower doors, where a heavy blow breaks the glass into small grains rather than sharp, jagged slivers. Another, which has a wire mesh incorporated into its construction, can break under a blow but does not shatter.

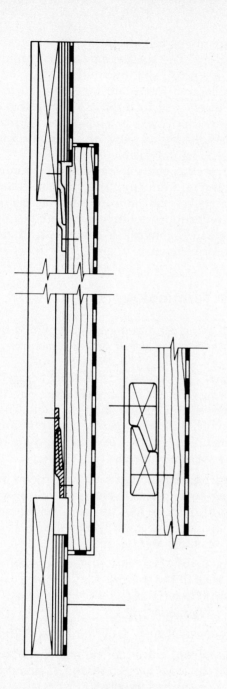

FIGURE 3-34. Hanging Methods.
(Reproduced with permission of the Architectural Woodwork Institute)

Laminated glass can control sound, glare, heat, and light transmission. It offers security and safety through high resistance to breakage and penetration. In interior areas where glass is desired, laminated acoustical glass is effective in reducing sound transmission. Where exterior sounds (traffic, airplanes, etc.) are present and distracting, laminated acoustical glass may be used. This glass may be clear or colored. See Figure 8-1 for custom etched smoked-glass panels. Another form of glass used for energy conservation is a laminated glass with a vinyl interlayer which, depending on the color of the interlayer, may absorb or transmit light in varying degrees. The tinted glass may have a bronze, gray, green, blue, silver, or gold appearance, and these tints cut down on glare in a manner similar to sunglasses or the tinted glass in an automobile. Where 24-hour protection is required, such as in jewelry stores, banks, and detention areas, a security glass with a high tensile polyvinyl butryal inner layer is highly effective. There are even bullet-resistant glasses on the market.

MIRROR

The mirrors used two thousand years ago by the Egyptians, Romans, and Greeks were highly polished thin sheets of bronze. Today, many of these metal mirrors may be seen in museums. The method of backing glass with a metallic film was known to the Romans, but it was not until 1507 that the first glass mirrors were made in Italy. Plate glass was invented in France in 1691, enabling larger pieces of glass to be manufactured. The shape of mirrors used in various periods of design should be studied by interior designers, but mirrors are no longer just accessories that are hung on the wall for utilitarian or decorative purposes. Walls are now completely covered with these highly-reflective surfaces. (See Figure 3-35 and as a backsplash covering in Figure 7-4).

Quality mirrors are made of float glass and are silvered on the back to obtain the highly-reflective quality. Also used under certain circumstances are the two-way mirrors, where from one side, the viewer can see out, but from the other side it appears to be an ordinary mirror. These two-way mirrors have many uses, such as in apartment doors, child observation areas, department stores, banks, and prison security areas.

Mirrors used on wall installations may be clear and brightly reflective or grayed or bronze hued. The

FIGURE 3-35.
Square mirror tiles in a grid design camouflage a low ceiling and add glamour and the illusion of space to a small entrance foyer in a luxury condominium residence. (Designer: *Ronald I. Noel, A.S.I.D.;* photographer: *Jerry Bushay)*

latter are not as bright, but do not noticeably distort color values. The surface may also be antiqued, producing a smoky, shadowy effect. Mirrored walls always enlarge a room and may be used to correct a size deficiency or to duplicate a prized possession, such as a candelabra or chandelier. Mirrored walls may also display all sides of a piece of sculpture or double the light available in a room.

Mirrors are available for wall installations in many sizes, ranging from large sheets to small mosaic mirrors on sheets similar to mosaic tile. Sometimes, a perfect reflection is not necessary and the mirrors may be in squares, **convex,** or **concave,** acid etched, engraved, or beveled.

Mirror Terminology

The following terminology was provided by the National Association of Mirror Manufacturers:

Acid Etch. A process of producing a specific design or lettering on glass, prior to silvering but cutting into the glass with a combination of acids. This process may involve either a frosted surface treatment or a deep etch. This process can also be done on regular glass as seen in Figure 8-1.

Antique Mirror. A decorative mirror in which the silver has been treated to create a smokey or shadowy effect. The antique look is often heightened by applying a veining on the silvered side in any one of a variety of colors and designs.

Backing Paint. The final protective coating applied on the back of the mirror, over copper, to protect the silver from deterioration.

Concave Mirror. Surface is slightly curved inward and tends to magnify reflected items or images.

Convex Mirror. Surface is slightly curved outward to increase the area that is reflected. Generally used for safety or security surveillance purposes.

Edge Work. Among numerous terms and expressions defining types of edge finishing, the five in most common usage are listed here:

> **Clean-cut Edge.** Natural edge produced when glass is cut. It should not be left exposed in installation.
>
> **Ground Edge.** Grinding removes the raw cut of glass, leaving a smooth satin finish.
>
> **Seamed Edge.** Sharp edges are removed by an abrasive belt.

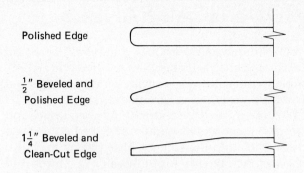

Polished Edge

$\frac{1}{2}''$ Beveled and Polished Edge

$1\frac{1}{4}''$ Beveled and Clean-Cut Edge

FIGURE 3-36. Mirror Bevels.

Polished Edge. Polishing removes the raw cut of glass to give a smooth-surfaced edge. A polished edge is available in two basic contours.

Beveled Edge. A tapered polished edge, varying from 1/4 of an inch to a maximum of 1 1/4 inches thick, produced by machine in a rectangular or circular shape. Other shapes or ovals may be beveled by hand, but the result is inferior to machine bevel. Standard width of bevel is generally 1/2 of an inch.

Electro-Copper-Plating. Process of copper-plating by electrolytic deposition of copper on the back of the silver film, to protect the silver and to assure good adherence of the backing paint.

Engraving. The cutting of a design on the back or face of a mirror, usually accomplished by hand on an engraved lathe.

Finger Pull. An elongated slot cut into the glass by a wheel, so that a mirrored door or panel, for instance, may be moved to one side.

First-Surface Mirror. A mirror produced by deposition of reflective metal on front surface of glass, usually under vacuum. Its principal use is as an automobile rear-view mirror or transparent mirror.

Framed Mirror. Mirror placed in a frame that is generally made of wood, metal, or composition material and equipped for hanging.

Hole. A piercing of a mirror, usually 1/2 inch in diameter and generally accomplished by a drill. Generally employed in connection with installations involving rosettes.

Mitre Cutting. The cutting of straight lines by use of a wheel on the back or face of a mirror for design purposes. Available in both satin and polished finishes.

Rosette. Hardware used for affixing a mirror to a wall. A decorative rose-shaped button used in several places on the face of a mirror.

Sand Blasting. Engraving or cutting designs on glass by a stream of sand, usually projected by air.

Shadowbox Mirror. Mirror bordered or framed at an angle on some or all sides by other mirrors, creating multiple reflections of an image.

Stock-Sheet Mirrors. Mirrors of varying sizes over 10 square feet, and up to 75 square feet, from which all types of custom mirrors are cut. Normally packed 800 to 1,000 square feet to a case.

Transparent Mirror. A first surface mirror with a thin film of reflective coating. To insure most efficient use, the light intensity on the viewer's side of the mirror must be significantly less than on the subject side. Under such a condition, the viewer can see through the mirror as through a transparent glass, while the subject looks into a mirror.

INSTALLATION. Both mastic and mechanical devices such as clips or rosettes should be used in order to install a mirror properly. Clips are usually of polished chrome, and are placed around the outside edges. Rosettes are clear plastic type fasteners and require a hole to be drilled several inches in from the edge, in order to accept the fastening screws and rosettes. Due to the fragile quality of mirror, use should be limited to areas where the likelihood of breakage is minimal.

INSTALLATION OF CERAMIC, METAL, AND MIRROR TILE. Due to the force of gravity, mortar cement cannot be troweled directly onto the wall without sagging. To prevent this sagging, a metal lath, similar to the one used for a plaster wall, is attached to the solid backing and then troweled with mortar. The metal lath acts as a stabilizing force. The backing may be wood, plaster, masonry, or gypsum board. This is equivalent to the thick-set method of floor installation. For wall use over gypsum board, plaster, or other smooth surfaces, an organic adhesive may be used. This adhesive should be water-resistant for bath and shower areas.

The *Handbook for Ceramic Tile Installation*, available from the Tile Council of America Inc., and also in Sweet's Catalogs, is the nationally accepted guideline for writing specifications, even for materials other than ceramic tile.

CERAMIC TILE

Ceramic tile is frequently used on walls when an easily cleaned, waterproof, and durable surface is desired. One use of ceramic is as a **backsplash** in the kitchen. When it is used for this purpose, the grout may be sealed by use of a commercial sealer or by using a lemon oil furniture polish. Ceramic tile is also used for the surrounds of showers and bathtubs, and for bathroom walls in general. These three uses are probably the most common ones, but ceramic tile may also be used on the walls in foyers and hallways, either plain, patterned, or in logos, and as a heat resistant material around fireplaces and stoves. Ceramic tile for counter tops will be discussed later.

If the walls are completely covered with ceramic tile, there will be no need of trim pieces. However, in bathrooms or kitchens, or any place where tiles will not be continued from wall to wall or from ceiling to floor, trim pieces must be added to cover the unglazed and uncolored side of the tile. These trim pieces are different in appearance, depending on the type of installations, thick or thin set.

A bullnose for thick-set installations has an overhanging curve piece, whereas a bullnose for thin-set is the same thickness as the surrounding tiles, but has a curved finished edge. For bath and shower installations, angle trims for the top and inside edges are used, and for walls meeting the floor, a cove is used (see Figure 2-20).

METAL

In the latter part of the 19th century, during the Victorian era, stamped tin panels were used on ceilings and dadoes of rooms. The dadoes even had a molded chair rail incorporated into them. Today, Pinecrest manufactures 26-gauge tin in 24 by 96 inch panels stamped with dies dating back to the Civil War. These panels are virtually indestructible and come with a silver tin finish. They may be painted with an oil base paint, if desired. Matching cornices are also available. Sheet brass can be seen in Figure 2-14 as a covering for the round columns in a bank.

ACOUSTICAL PANELS

Several manufacturers produce a mineral fiberboard or fiberglass panel, which, when covered with fabric, absorbs sound and also provides an attractive and individually designed environment (see Figures 3-7 and 3-37). Because of the textured, porous surface and the absorbent substrate, sound is absorbed rather than bounced back into the room. These panels may also be used as tack boards for lightweight pictures and graphics. In open plan areas, different colors can be used to direct the flow of traffic through an open office and to differentiate between work areas. In addition to the acoustical qualities of these panels, there are two other beneficial features. One is that the panels are fire retardant and the other is that, when installed on perimeter walls, there is an insulating factor that varies with the type of board used.

The panels may take the form of appliques in sizes of 2 by 4 feet, 2 by 6 feet, or they may cover the wall completely in panel sizes of 24 or 30 inches by 9 feet.

Vinyl or fabric faced acoustic panels may be designed for various types of installation. For use on an existing wall, only one side needs to be covered. For open-plan landscapes, both surfaces are covered to absorb sound from both sides. Some panels are covered on the two side edges for butted installation while another portable type is wrapped on all surfaces and edges.

INSTALLATION. As there are numerous types of acoustic panels, there is no one installation method that covers all panels. Depending on the type of panel as described in the paragraph above, panels may be attached to the wall by means of an adhesive and/or may have moulding concealing the seams. Manufacturers installation methods should be followed.

MAINTENANCE. Surface dirt is removed by vacuuming or light brushing. Spots can be treated with dry-cleaning fluid or with carpet shampoo.

FIGURE 3-37.
Horizontally padded and channeled fabric walls and an oak parquet floor set off the contemporary furniture. (Photograph courtesy Milo Baughman Design; furniture: *Thayer Coggin, Inc.)*

CORK

Cork tiles are available in 12 by 36 inches in 1/2, 3/4, 1, and 1 1/2 inch thicknesses and may be used in residential, commercial, educational, and institutional buildings. Due to its porous nature, cork can breathe and, therefore, can be used on basement walls or on the inside surface of exterior support walls without the risk of moisture difficulties. Due to the millions of dead-air spaces in the cork particles themselves, cork also has good insulating properties.

INSTALLATION. Panels are applied by using 1/8 by 1/8 inch notched trowel and the recommended adhesive.

MAINTENANCE. Dodge Cork Company recommends vacuuming periodically with the brush attachment. A light dust-free sealing coat of silicone aerosol spray will give dust protection; a heavier spray protects against dust and gives the surface a glossier finish, providing more light reflection. However, a heavy spray tends to close the pores of the cork, thus decreasing its sound deadening and insulating qualities. An alternate to the silicone spray is a 50-50 blend of clear shellac and alcohol.

Bibliography

Architectural Woodwork Institute. *Architectural Woodwork Quality Standards, Guide Specifications and Quality Certification Program.* Arlington VA: Architectural Woodwork Institute, 1978.

Hand, Jackson. *Walls, Floors and Ceilings.* New York: Book Division, Times Mirror Magazines, Inc., 1976.

Kicklighter, Clois E. *Modern Masonry.* South Holland IL: The Goodheart Willcox Co., 1977.

Percival, Bob. *The How-to-Do-It Encyclopedia of Painting and Wallcovering.* Blue Ridge Summit PA: TAB Books Inc., 1982.

Schumacher. *A Guide to Wallcoverings.* New York: Schumacher.

Time-Life Books. *Paint and Wallpaper.* New York: Time-Life Books, 1976.

Time-Life Books. *Walls and Ceilings.* Alexandria VA: Time-Life Books, 1980.

Glossary

Ashlar. Precut stone (see Figure 3-1).

Backsplash. The vertical wall area between the kitchen counter and the upper cabinets.

Beaded. Convex shape of the mortar joint (see Figure 3-4).

Beads. Rounded formed pieces of metal used in finishing the edges of gypsum wallboard.

Booked. Folding back of pasted wallcovering so that pasted sides are touching.

Casing. Exposed trim or moulding (see Figure 5-1).

Check. A small crack parallel to the grain of the wood.

Chinoiserie (French). Refers to Chinese designs or manner.

Cobble. Similar in appearance to fieldstone.

Compound curves. Curving in two different directions at the same time.

Compressive strength. Amount of stress and pressure a material can withstand.

Concave. Hollow or inward curving shape.

Convex. Arched or outward curving shape.

Coped. Shaped or cut to fit an adjoining piece of moulding.

Cramps. U-shaped metal fastenings.

Desiccant. Substance capable of removing moisture from the air.

Dimensional stability. Ability to retain shape regardless of temperature and humidity.

Dry wall. Any interior covering that does not require the use of plaster or mortar.

Evacuated. Air is removed.

Feathering. Tapering off to nothing.

Fieldstone. Rounded stone.

Flitch. Portion of a log from which veneer is cut.

Header. End of an exposed brick (see Figure 3-3).

Header course. Headers used every sixth course (see Figure 3-3).

Heads. Horizontal cross member supported by the jambs.

Jambs. Vertical member at the sides of a door.

Laminated glass. Breaks without shattering. Glass remains in place.

Mortar stain. Stain caused by excess mortar on face of brick or stone.

Mullions. Center vertical member of paneling (see Figure 3-29).

Nonferrous. Containing no iron.

Ogee. A concave and a convex curve in one moulding.

Osnaburg. Heavy cotton cloth.

Ovolo. A convex shaped moulding.

Plumbline. True vertical line.

Pre-trimmed. Selvages or edges have been removed.

Raking light. Light shining obliquely down the length of the wall.

Rubble. Uncut stone (see Figure 3-1).

Scratch coat. In three coat plastering, it is the first coat.

Shiplap. An overlapping wood joint.

Simple curve. Curving in one direction only.

Stile. Outside vertical member of paneling (see Figure 3-29).

Stretcher. Long side of an exposed brick (see Figure 3-3).

Struck. Mortar joint where excess mortar is removed by a trowel.

Suction. Absorption of water by the gypsum board from the wet plaster.

Tambours. Thin strips of wood, or other materials, attached to a flexible backing for use on curved surfaces. Similar in appearance to a roll-top desk.

Tempered glass. Glass toughened by heating and rapid cooling.

Toile-de-Jouy. Similar to the printed cottons made by Oberkampf in France during the 18th and 19th centuries.

Trompe l'oeil. French for fooling the eye. Also used on painted surfaces such as walls or furniture.

4

CEILINGS

CONTENTS

Early Greeks and Romans used lime stucco for ceilings, in which low, medium, and high **reliefs** were carried out. The Italians in the 15th century worked with plaster and Henry VIII's Hampton Court has very highly decorative plaster-work ceilings. In the Tudor and Jacobean periods, the plaster work for ceilings had a geometric basis in medium and high relief. This was followed by the classicism of Christopher Wren and Inigo Jones, an admirer of Palladio. In the latter part of the 18th century, the Adam brothers designed and used cast plaster ornaments with **arabesques, paterae,** and urns.

Stamped tin ceilings used in the 19th and 20th centuries disappeared from use in the 1930's but are now staging a comeback. In private residences, tin ceilings were occasionally used in halls and bathrooms. In commercial buildings, metal ceilings were used in order to comply with the early fire codes.

Today, the ceiling should not be considered as "just the flat surface over our heads, which is painted white." The ceiling is an integral part of a room, affecting space, light, heat, and sound and consideration should be given to making it fit the environment. There are many ways of achieving this integration, such as beams for a country or old world appearance, a stamped metal ceiling for Victorian, a wood ceiling for contemporary warmth, or acoustical for today's noisier environments. Ceiling treatments are only limited by the imagination.

PLASTER

There are times when the ceiling should be the unobtrusive surface in a room. When this is required, plastering is the answer. The surface may be smooth or highly textured or somewhere in between. A smooth surface will reflect more light than a heavily textured one of the same color.

The plaster for a ceiling is installed in the same manner as for walls, although it will require scaffolding so that the surface will be within working reach. It will take a longer period of time to plaster a ceiling when compared with a similar wall area, due to the overhead reach.

The ornately carved ceilings of the past are obtained today by using one of three means:

1. Precast plaster.
2. Molded polyurethane foam.
3. Wood mouldings, mainly used as **crown** mouldings.

The decorative ceiling shown in Figure 4-1, however, was made from plaster.

As these decorations are more applied mouldings than ceiling treatments, they will be covered under Chapter 5, Other Components—Mouldings.

GYPSUM WALLBOARD

The main difficulty with the installation of gypsum board for ceilings is the weight. It does require more labor and, again, scaffolding. The seams and screw holes are filled in the same manner as gypsum board walls. The surface may be perfectly smooth, lightly or heavily textured, with the smooth surface reflecting not only the most light, but also showing any unevenness of the ceiling joists.

Gypsum wallboard may also be applied in a curved manner as shown in Figure 3-8.

FIGURE 4-1.
*This very ornate ceiling was installed in the
Victorian era and is now part of the conference
room of a prestigious law office. The walls are
mahogany and were designed in keeping with the
formal appearance. As the office is on the top
floor of the building, a fireplace was installed
with a marble surround, a very typical material
for Victorian times. (Architects: DeLaMare-
Woodruff; project architect: Raymond N. Jones;
paneling: Fetzers, Inc.; photograph: Richard
Springgate)*

BEAMS

This is probably the oldest of ceiling treatments. Originally, the ceiling beams of the lower floor were the floor joists of the room above. The old New England houses had hand-hewn timbers that ran the length of the room; larger sized **summer beams** ran across the width. The area between the beams was covered either by the floor boards of the room above, or in the case of a sloped ceiling, the wood covering the outside of the roof timbers. Later these floorboards were covered with plaster and the timbers were left to darken naturally. The plaster in between the timbers had a rough or troweled surface.

Today, beamed ceilings are used for a country setting with an old world or contemporary feeling. The original beams were made of one piece of wood, 12 inches or more square, but today beams of this size are almost impossible to obtain.

If unavailable, there are several methods of imitating the solid heavy look of these hand-hewn beams.

First of all, a box beam may be built either as part of the floor joists or as a surface addition. In order to make a box beam appear similar to a hand-hewn beam, the surface must be treated to avoid the perfectly smooth surface of modern lumber.

Second, a precast polyurethane beam may be glued to a plaster ceiling. Usually, the author does not advocate imitation products, preferring the integrity of the real thing. However, some of these composition beams, if well made, have axe marks, saw marks, and wood grain which, together with the rough surface, provide a good imitation that is lightweight and easy to handle.

In contemporary homes, **laminated beams** are used. These consist of several pieces of lumber (depending on the width required) glued together on the wider flat surfaces. Because of the type of construction, laminated beams are very strong. Laminated beams are commonly referred to as "lam" beams (see Figures 3-2 and 4-2).

FIGURE 4-2.
Laminated beams are an integral part of the design of this home. The thick lam beams support the roof, creating an atrium effect of three stories high. Lower hall, landing, and stairs are of filled travertine and the walls on the left are fabric covered with flannel. The owners' art collection is well displayed by judicious design and lighting. (Architects: Max J. Smith and Norman Jaffee; photograph: Richard Springgate)

WOOD

A natural outgrowth of the beamed ceiling is using wood planks or strips to cover the ceiling joists. With the many types of wood available on the market today, wood ceilings are used in many homes, particularly contemporary ones.

Almost all types of strip flooring and solid wood for walls may be used on the ceiling (see Figure 3-6). Due to the darkness of wood, it is more suitable for a cathedral or shed ceiling as the color appears to lower the ceiling (see Figures 2-3 and 2-9).

Trysil, from Bangkok Industries, combines the appearance of wood with acoustic qualities. These low-density particle board panels may be faced with any of nine different wood veneers. The acoustic qualities are obtained by cutting a slot in the face which penetrates the 5/8 inch holes drilled the length of the core (see Figure 4-3).

FIGURE 4-3.
Using Trysil© from Bangkok Industries not only provides the appearance of wood but also has acoustical qualities. (Photograph courtesy of Bangkok Industries)

ACOUSTICAL CEILINGS

Residential Ceilings

Due to the fact that the ceiling is the largest unobstructed area in a room, sound is bounced off the surface without very much absorption. Just as light is reflected from a smooth, high gloss surface, so sound is reflected or bounced off the ceiling. This is the reason for the textured tiles on the market today, for both residential and commercial interiors. Uncontrolled reverberations transform sound into noise, muffling music and disrupting effective communication.

Acoustical ceilings, however, do not prevent the transmission of sound from one floor to another. The only answer to sound transmission is mass—the actual resistance of the material to vibrations caused by sound waves.

Sound absorption qualities may be obtained by using different materials and different methods. The best known is the acoustical **tile** (a 12 inch square) or **panel** (larger than one square foot) composed of mineral fiber board (see Figure 2-14). Other materials such as fiberglass, metal, plastic-clad fiber, and fabric may also be used. Sound absorption properties are produced by mechanical dies perforating the mineral fiber board after curing. Metal may also be perforated to improve its acoustical qualities if backed with an absorptive medium.

The residential ceiling system shown in Figure 4-4 has a patented clip which allows each panel to rotate 180°. The panels may be attached to a T-bar system or directly to PVC extrusions on a dry-wall ceiling.

The *Noise Reduction Coefficient* (**NRC**) is a measure of sound absorbed by a material and the NRC of different types of panels may be compared. The higher the number, the more sound reduction. When making a comparison, be sure tests are made at the same **Hertz** (Hz) range.

The *Sound Transmission Class* (**STC**) is a measure of the reduction of sound between two rooms due to transmission via the **plenum** path. The higher the STC value, the better the resistance to sound transmission. Another heading often found in acoustical mineral fiber board charts is *Light Reflectance* (**LR**) which indicates the percentage of light reflected from a ceiling product's surface. This LR varies according to the amount of texture on the surface and the value of the color.

FIGURE 4-4.
Hunter Douglas Designer Residential Ceiling has a patented clip that allows each panel to rotate 180°. It is available in brushed and metallic finishes and also three decorator colors, giving rooms a slick contemporary look. (Photograph courtesy of Hunter Douglas)

Some ceiling panels, like those of the Soft Look ceiling system, have a mineral fiber substrate with a needle-punched fabric surface (see Figures 4-5 and 4-6).

INSTALLATION. In private residences, two or three methods of installation are used. If the tiles are to be used over an existing ceiling, they may be cemented to that ceiling provided the surface is solid and level. Tiles have interlocking edges that provide a solid joining method as well as an almost seamless installation. If the existing ceiling is not solid or level, furring strips are nailed up so that the edges of the tile may be glued and stapled to a solid surface.

The third type of installation is the suspended ceiling which consists of a metal spline suspended by wires from the ceiling or joists. The tiles are laid in the spline so that the edges of the panels are supported by the edge of the T-shaped spline.

The splines may be left exposed or they may be covered by the tile. There are several advantages to using a suspended ceiling:

1. Panels damaged by water or abuse are easily replaced.
2. The height of the ceiling may be varied according to the size of the room or other requirements.

With an exposed spline, it is easy to replace a single panel; the damaged panel is merely lifted out. However, if the spline is covered, the damaged panel or panels are removed and when replacing the last panel, the tongue is removed.

MAINTENANCE. Celotex suggests that a soft gum eraser be used to remove small spots, dirt marks, and streaks. For larger areas, or larger smudges, a chemically treated sponge, rubber pad, or wallpaper cleaner is used. The sponge rubber pad or wallpaper cleaner must be in fresh condition. Nicks and scratches may be touched up with colored chalks. Dust is removed by brushing lightly with a soft brush or clean rag or by vacuuming with the soft brush attachment.

When tile is installed by the adhesive method, it may not be cleaned or painted for 90 days in order to

FIGURE 4-5.
Soft Look, a fabric surfaced 2 by 2 foot ceiling panel, has a sleek new grid of brushed aluminum called Soft Look Trimlok®. (Photograph courtesy of Armstrong World Industries, Inc.)

FIGURE 4-6.
A close-up of Soft Look used in Figure 4-5, showing the Soft Look Trimlok grid. (Photograph courtesy of Armstrong World Industries, Inc.)

allow time for the adhesive to set. The tile must not be excessively moistened or soaked with water. Washing is done by light application of a sponge dampened by a mild liquid detergent solution, about one-half cupful per gallon of water. After the sponge is saturated, it is squeezed nearly dry and then the surface to be cleaned is lightly rubbed. Long sweeping gentle strokes are used and cleaning is done in the same direction as the striations of texture, if tiles are ribbed or embossed.

Tiles may be repainted with a high hiding paint which, in one coat, will cover properly yet will not clog or bridge the surface openings. However, painting does lessen the acoustic characteristics.

Commercial Ceilings

Acoustical ceiling products have become a mainstay of commercial installations. Due to the flexibility of the movable office partitions, audio privacy is very necessary. In this day of electronic word processors and data processing equipment, the noise of an office has been somewhat reduced from the noisy typewriters of the past, but telephones and voices can still cause distracting sounds. Productivity is increased in a quieter environment, but a noiseless environment is easily disrupted. (See Figures 2-14, 4-7.)

The advantages of a residential suspended acoustical ceiling also apply in commercial installations, but the major reason for using a suspended ceiling in commercial work is the easy access to wiring, telephone lines, plumbing, and heating ducts.

The traditional approach is **luminaires** recessed at specific intervals into the acoustic ceiling. The fixtures are often covered by lenses or louvers to diffuse the light.

Today, not only lighting but also heating and cooling are incorporated into the installation. This is done in several ways. The heating and cooling duct may be spaced between the modules in one long continuous line or individual vents may be used. One interesting innovation is where the whole area between the suspended ceiling and the joists is used as a plenum area with the conditioned air entering the room below through orifices in the individual tiles.

OTHER CEILING MATERIALS

A vinyl coated, embossed aluminum, bonded to the mineral fiber substrate, results in an easily maintained, corrosion resistant, durable product. Grease vapor concentrations may be wiped clean with a sponge or a mild detergent solution, thus providing a suitable ceiling in commercial kitchens, laboratories, and hospitals.

Mirrors may be used on the ceiling, but due to the weight and fragile nature of mirror, it is not usually used except in residential applications (see Figure 2-15). However, a mirrored effect may be achieved by

FIGURE 4-7.
A tile-like or monolithic appearance can be achieved with Armstrong's new Suprafine 2 by 2 foot tegular lay-in ceiling panel available in five small scale geometric designs. (Photograph courtesy of Armstrong World Industries, Inc.)

using a mineral fiber core coated with a reflective aluminized film with a reflectivity of 92 to 95 percent. A special reflective spline gives the full effect of an overhead expanse of a mirrored surface. These mirrored panels expand the visual impact of displays and may be a major deterrent to shoplifting and pilfering in shops and stores.

The use of an acoustical mineral fiber board will also increase fire resistance. Custom-designed fiberglass core panels are used to acoustically upgrade existing ceilings as well as for new custom designed ceiling construction. This same material may be used for baffles constructed of 1, 1 1/2, or 2 inch thick panels. They are hung from the ceiling by means of wire attached to eyelets installed in the top edge. Vicracoustic® baffles are installed in existing spline systems using clips provided by the manufacturer. Quilted fiberglass banners may also be installed in a similar manner. (See Figure 4-8 for photograph of banners.)

When a sleek, uninterrupted expanse of sound-absorbing ceiling is desired, or when a ceiling that matches walls is called for, Vicracoustic Monolithic is the solution. It can be extended out to walls or can be installed so that it stops short of existing crown mouldings.

U.S. Gypsum manufactures ceiling tiles and panels that are backed with a special reflective aluminum foil which provides improved resistance on the back surface to breathing. Soiling and breathing (objectionable upward air travel due to positive room pressure) is reduced by the foil backing.

Lean-To™ is a luminous ceiling manufactured by Integrated Ceilings to express the feeling of a linear skylight. It can span between vertical surfaces or can be mounted as a cornice. Light is provided from above either by fluorescent strips alone or in combination with natural light. When used around the room perimeter, Lean-To can wash a wall with light, help plants grow, or highlight a merchandise display.

Integrated Ceilings's Pipe and Junction is an award winning approach to ceilings. This is a component parts system of pipes that are snapped or bolted together from up to six different directions. Pipe and Junction may be used alone or with fabric. The fabric may be stretched between the sections or hung from banners made of 100 percent cotton duck with a flame spread rating of 10.

Not all acoustic ceilings are flat. Many are *coffered* in 2 to 4 foot square modules. These panels may or may not include luminaires.

FIGURE 4-8.
Banners by Integrated Ceilings serve the dual purpose of being both an acoustical ceiling and an interesting and colorful treatment.
(Photograph courtesy of Integrated Ceilings)

Metal

Metal ceilings were originally introduced in the 1860's as a replacement for the ornamental plasterwork that decorated the walls and ceilings of the most fashionable rooms of the day. Once in place, it was discovered that these ceilings had other benefits. Unlike plaster, the metal could withstand rough-housing and could also be more easily maintained than plaster, which could flake, crack, and peel.

Stamped tin ceilings now come in 1 foot squares, 1 by 2, 2 by 4, or 2 by 8 feet and are installed by tacking the units to furring strips nailed 12 inches apart. These stamped tin ceilings are very suitable for Victorian restoration work (see Figure 4-9).

A contemporary metal ceiling is made up of 3 to 7 inch wide strips of painted or polished aluminum, which clip to special carriers. The polished metals also include bronze and brass finishes and can provide an almost mirrored effect. These ceilings may be used in renovations over existing sound ceilings or may be used for new construction (see Figure 2-25).

The metal strips may be installed as separate strips with the area between the strips left open to the plenum or the open space may be covered with an acoustical pad. They may also be covered with a joining strip on the face to form a flush surface, or on the back for a board-on-batten effect (see Figures 2-22 and 4-10).

Steel or aluminum panels, perforated or unperforated, are available in 12 inch squares or as large as 24 by 48 inch panels.

Another type of ceiling is shown on the cover and in Figure 3-7. This ceiling is actually the underside of the metal deck used for the poured concrete floor of the second level.

Ceramic Tile

For a ceiling that is easy to wipe clean, or in very moist areas such as bathrooms and showers, ceramic tile may be installed (see the kitchen in Figure 7-2).

FIGURE 4-9. A Close-Up of the Various Patterns Available in Stamped Metal Ceilings.
(Photograph courtesy Chelsea Decorative Metal Company)

FIGURE 4-10.
*A linear metal ceiling installed at different levels
and different angles creates an interesting design
in an airport waiting area. The floor is terrazzo
tile. (Architects: MHT, Inc.; photograph: Richard
Springgate)*

Bibliography

Hand, Jackson. *Ceilings,* A Popular Science Book. New York: Harper, 1976.

Rothery, Guy Cadogan. *Ceilings and Their Decoration.* London, England: T. Werner Laurie.

Schuler, Stanley. *The Floor & Ceiling Book.* New York: M. Evans & Co., 1976.

Time-Life Books. *Walls and Ceilings.* Alexandria VA: Time-Life Books, 1980.

Glossary

Arabesque. Elaborate scroll designs either carved or in low relief.

Coffered. Recessed panels in the ceiling. May or may not be decorated.

Crown moulding. The uppermost moulding next to the ceiling.

Hertz. Unit of frequency measurement. One unit per second. Abbreviation: Hz.

Laminated beam. Several pieces of lumber glued to form a structural timber.

LR. Light Reflectance. The amount of light reflected from the surface.

Luminaires. Lighting fixture, with all components needed to be connected to the electric power supply.

NRC. Noise Reduction Coefficient. The average percentage of sound reduction at various Hz levels.

Panel. A ceiling unit larger than one square foot.

Patera. A round or oval raised surface design. (See Adam fireplace in Figure 5-16.)

Plenum. Space between the suspended ceiling and the floor above.

Reliefs. A design that is raised above the surrounding area.

STC. Sound Transmission Class. A number denoting the sound insulating value of a material.

Summer beam. A main supporting beam in old Colonial homes; in the middle of the room resting on the fireplace at one end and a post at the other.

Tile. Ceiling tile (12 inch square).

5

OTHER COMPONENTS

CONTENTS

MOULDINGS

To an interior designer, trim and mouldings are what icing is to a cake; they cover, enhance, and decorate a plain surface. Basically, heavily carved or ornate trim is used in a traditional setting, whereas the simpler trim is used where a contemporary feeling is desired.

Materials for trim and mouldings should be constructed from easily shaped stock. Both pine and oak are used, providing details that are easily discernible and smooth. Trim should always be **mitered** at the corners; that is, the joint should be cut at a 45° angle.

Bases are universally used to finish the area where the wall and floor meet. There are several reasons for the use of a base or skirting. First, it covers any discrepancy or expansion space between the wall and the floor; second, it forms a protection for the wall from cleaning equipment; and third, it may also be a decorative feature. The word *base* is used to include all types of materials. *Baseboard* is the term used for wood bases only.

When a plain baseboard is used, the wood should be smoothly sanded on the face and particularly on the top edge to facilitate cleaning. The exposed edge should be slightly beveled to prevent breaking or chipping. The more traditional baseboard usually has a shaped top edge with the lower part being flat. This may be achieved with one piece of wood 3 1/2 to 7 inches wide or may consist of separate parts, the top being a base moulding above a square-edged piece of lumber. A base shoe may be added to either type. Traditional one-piece baseboards are available as stock mouldings from the better woodworking manufacturers (see Figure 5-l).

For residential use, windows come prefabricated with the **brickmold** or exterior trim attached. The interior **casing** (the exposed trim) may be flat or molded and is applied after the window and walls have been installed and the windows **caulked,** the latter step being extremely important in these days of energy conservation. The interior casing usually matches the baseboard design, although the size may vary as seen in Figure 5-l.

Doors, particularly for residential use, come prehung and, after installation of the door frame, the space between the jamb and the wall is covered by a casing. This casing matches the profile of the one used around the windows, with the width of the casing being determined by the size, scale, and style of the room.

Crown and **bed** mouldings are used to soften the sharp line where the ceiling and walls meet. Cove mouldings also serve the same purpose, the difference being that crown mouldings are more intricately shaped and cove mouldings have a simple curved face. Cove mouldings may be painted the same color as the ceiling, thus giving a lowered appearance to the ceiling.

Cornice mouldings may be very ornate and made up of as many as 10 separate pieces of wood as seen in Figures 5-2 and 5-3.

Chair rails are used in traditional homes to protect the surface of the wall from damage caused by the backs of chairs. These rails may be simple strips of wood with rounded edges or have shaped top and bottom edges depending again upon the style of the room (see Figures 2-10 and 5-1). The installed height should be between 30 and 36 inches. When trim is to be painted, it should be made of a hard, close-grained wood. If it is to be left natural, it should be of the same material and should be finished in the same manner as the rest of the woodwork.

When plywood panels are used on the walls, the edges are sometimes covered with a square edge batten or, in more traditional surroundings, a molded batten is used.

Picture mouldings, as the name implies, were used to create a continuous projecting support around the walls of a room for picture hooks. The picture moulding has a curved top to receive the picture hook. Of course, when pictures are hung by this method the wires will show, but this method is used in older

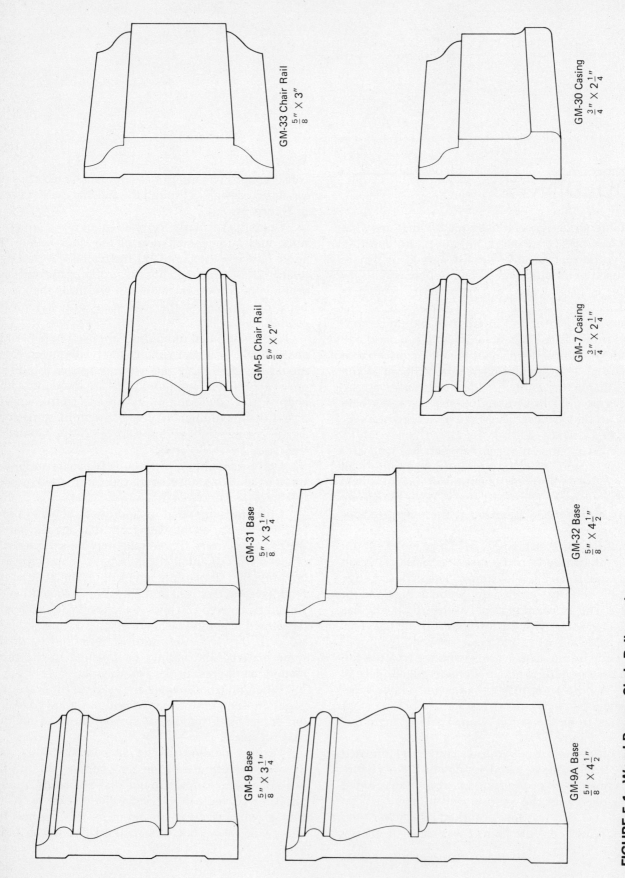

GM-33 Chair Rail
$\frac{5}{8}"\times 3"$

GM-30 Casing
$\frac{3}{4}"\times 2\frac{1}{4}"$

GM-5 Chair Rail
$\frac{5}{8}"\times 2"$

GM-7 Casing
$\frac{3}{4}"\times 2\frac{1}{4}"$

GM-31 Base
$\frac{5}{8}"\times 3\frac{1}{4}"$

GM-32 Base
$\frac{5}{8}"\times 4\frac{1}{2}"$

GM-9 Base
$\frac{5}{8}"\times 3\frac{1}{4}"$

GM-9A Base
$\frac{5}{8}"\times 4\frac{1}{2}"$

FIGURE 5-1. Wood Bases, Chair Rails, and Casings.
(Courtesy of Granite Mill)

FIGURE 5-2.
This Southern Colonial mansion has a very decorative 11-piece wooden ceiling cornice. (Photograph courtesy of Driwood Period Mouldings)

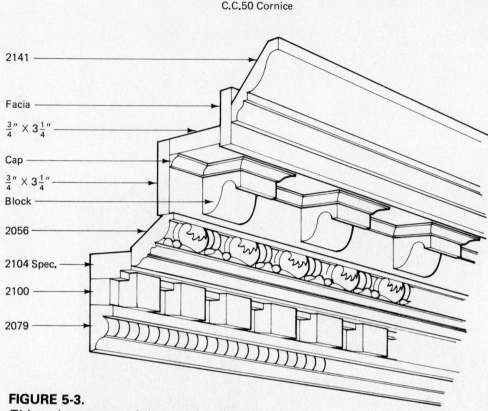

C.C.50 Cornice

2141

Facia

$\frac{3}{4}'' \times 3\frac{1}{4}''$

Cap

$\frac{3}{4}'' \times 3\frac{1}{4}''$

Block

2056

2104 Spec.

2100

2079

FIGURE 5-3.
This enlargement of the cornice shown in Figure 5-2 shows the 11 individual pieces which go to make up this elaborate yet authentic moulding. Drawing courtesy of Driwood Period Mouldings.

homes, museums, and art galleries where frequent rearranging is required. No damage is done to the walls as with the more modern method of hanging paintings by means of concealed wires. The picture moulding is placed either just below or several inches below the ceiling. Wherever the placement, the ceiling color is continued down to the top of the moulding.

There is an infinite variety of patterns that may be used for mouldings. Some are stock shapes and sizes; others may be custom ordered; and a third may be shaped to the designer's specifications by the use of custom-formed shaper blades. This latter method is the most expensive, but does achieve a unique moulding.

Wood mouldings may also be covered with metal in many metallic finishes, including bright chrome, brass, copper, or simulated metal finishes for use as picture frame moulding, interior trim, and displays.

All the mouldings discussed thus far have been constructed of wood but, when a heavily carved cornice moulding is required, the material may be a **polymer.** Focal Point, Inc., makes a polymer moulding by direct impression from the original wood, metal, or plaster article. This direct process gives the reproduction all the personality, texture, and spirit of the original, but with several pluses. The mouldings are much less expensive than the hand carved originals. They are lighter weight and, therefore, are easier to handle; they may be nailed, drilled, or screwed; and

FIGURE 5-4.
*The Innkeeper's Room at the Raleigh Tavern in
Colonial Williamsburg, Virginia, contains the
original dentil moulding from Focal Point®
WILLIAMSBURG™ moulding Number 133 CW
Raleigh Tavern was reproduced. (Photograph
courtesy of Focal Point)*

FIGURE 5-5.
An enlargement of the reproduction of the original moulding shown in Figure 5-4. (Photograph courtesy of Focal Point)

are receptive to sanding. Another feature is that, in many cases, the original moulding consisted of several pieces, but modern technology has produced these multiple mouldings in a one piece strip, thus saving on installation costs. (See Figures 5-4 for original and 5-5 for reproduction.)

Polymer mouldings are factory primed in white; however, if a stained effect is desired, the mouldings may be primed beige and stained with Carver Tripp's wood stain. Careful brush strokes will simulate grain and, when installed 8 to 10 feet up, the effect is very convincing.

In Chapter 4, ceiling medallions were mentioned as a form of ceiling decoration. Originally, when these medallions were used as **backplates** for chandeliers, they were made from plaster but, again, the polymer reproductions are lightweight and easy to ship. The medallions are primed white at the factory, ready to paint. The use of a medallion is not limited to chandeliers, but is also used as a backplate for ceiling fans.

Other materials used in ornate ceiling cornices are gypsum with a polymer agent which is reinforced with glass fibers for added strength. Or, a wood fiber combination may also be used.

Other reproductions from the past include the dome and the niche cap. When first designed, they were made of plaster or wood, which was then hand carved. These domes and niche caps can provide a touch of authenticity needed in renovations; in fact, many of Focal Point's designs have been used in restoration of national historical landmarks (see Figure 5-6). Niche caps have a shell design and form the top of a curved recess that usually displays sculpture, vases, flowers, or any other prized possession (see Figure 5-7).

Stair brackets are another form of architectural detail and are placed on the finished stringer for a decorative effect.

FIGURE 5-6.
This dome from Focal Point® provides an elegant ceiling treatment for a traditional home. The dome shown requires an interior depth of 14 1/2 inches. The smaller version requires only 8 inches. (Photograph courtesy of Focal Point)

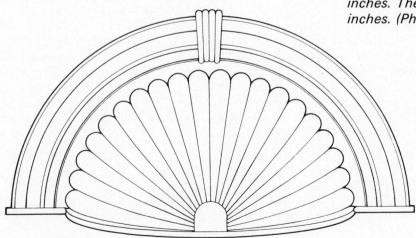

Niche Cap

FIGURE 5-7. Niche Cap.

DOORS

Doors for residential use are commonly constructed of wood, although metal may also be used. In commercial applications, however, doors are more likely to be made of metal or laminate due to fire codes and ease of maintenance.

Wood Doors

Flush doors are perfectly flat and smooth with no decoration whatsoever (see Figure 5-10). There are several methods of construction. A hollow core is used for some interior residential flush doors. The core of the door is made up of 2 to 3 inch wide solid wood for the rails and 1 to 2 inches of solid wood for the stiles, with an additional 20 inch long strip of wood called a *lock block* in the approximate hardware location. The area between the solid wood is filled with a honeycomb or ladder core. In less expensive doors, this is covered by the finish veneer. More expensive doors have one or two layers of veneer before the finish veneer is applied. Thus, a flush door may be of three-, five-, or seven-ply construction.

A solid flush door may be constructed with a lumber core, also known as *staved wood*, where wood blocks are used in place of the honeycomb or ladder core of the hollow core door. The staved or lumber core may or may not have the blocks bonded together. With staved core doors, the inside rails and stiles are narrower because this type of construction is more rigid.

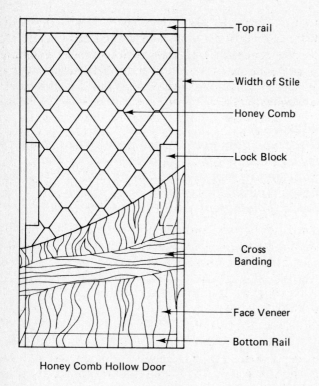

Honey Comb Hollow Door

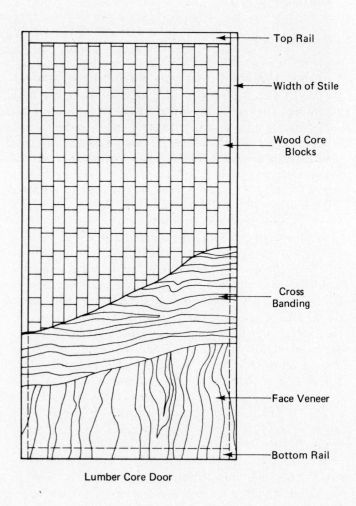

Lumber Core Door

FIGURE 5-8. Door Construction.

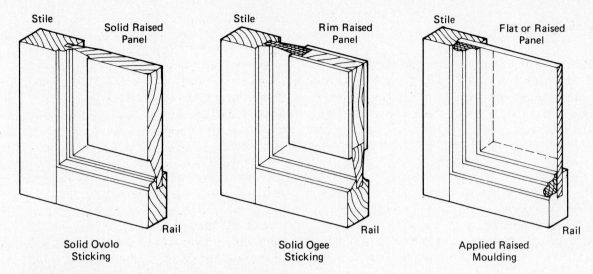

| Stile | Solid Raised Panel | Stile | Rim Raised Panel | Stile | Flat or Raised Panel |

Rail

Rail

Rail

Solid Ovolo Sticking

Solid Ogee Sticking

Applied Raised Moulding

FIGURE 5-9. Paneled Door Construction.
(Reprinted with permission from the Architectural Woodwork Institute)

Another method of construction utilizes a particle board or flakeboard core with a crossband veneer to which the face veneer is attached. A particle board frame panel may also be dropped into a perimeter frame but not attached or glued to the frame. Pre-manufactured plywood skins on hardboard are bonded to assembly (see Figure 5-8).

Flush doors for commercial installations may have a high pressure decorative laminate (HPDL) as the face veneer or, for low maintenance, a photogravure or vinyl covering similar to the paneling discussed in the chapter on walls may be used.

There are three methods of achieving the paneled look in doors. One is by using a solid ogee **sticking;** in other words, the stiles and rails are shaped so that the moulding and stile or rails are all one piece of wood. The second method is the same as above only using an ovolo sticking. The third method uses a dadoed stile and rail and the joining of panel and stile is covered by a separate applied moulding. If the panel is large, it will be made of plywood and a moulding used; but, if under 10 inches in width, it may be of solid wood. (See Figure 5-9.) Paneled doors reflect different periods, as do paneled walls. When period paneling is used, the doors should be of similar design (see Figures 5-10 and 5-16).

Dutch doors for residential use consist of an upper and a lower part. Special hardware joins the two parts to form a regular height door or, with the hardware undone, the top part may be opened to ventilate or give light to a room, with the lower part remaining closed. Dutch doors are sometimes used commercially as a service opening and, in this case, a shelf is attached to the top of the bottom half (see Figure 5-10).

Louvers are used in doors where ventilation is needed, such as in cleaning or storage closets or, to aid in air circulation. Louvers are made of horizontal slats contained within stile-and-rail frames. Louvers may be set into wood or metal doors, with the louver being either at the top and/or bottom, or the center may be all louvered. Some louvers are vision-proof, some adjustable, and others may be lightproof or weatherproof (see Figure 5-10). One of the most common residential uses for a louvered door is in a bifold door for a closet. Bifold doors consist of four panels, two on each side with a track at the top. The center panel of each pair is hung from the track and the outer panels pivot at the jamb (see Figure 5-10).

A pocket door or recessed sliding door requires a special frame and track that is incorporated into the inside of the wall. The finished door is hung from the track before the casing is attached. The bottom of the door is held in place by guides which permit the door to slide while preventing sideways movement (see Figure 5-10).

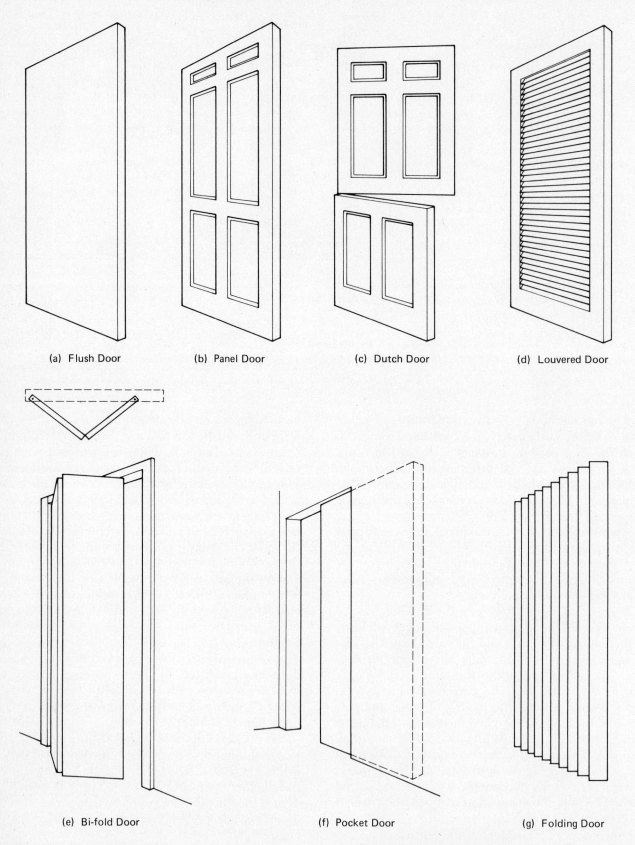

(a) Flush Door   (b) Panel Door   (c) Dutch Door   (d) Louvered Door

(e) Bi-fold Door   (f) Pocket Door   (g) Folding Door

FIGURE 5-10. Types of Doors.

(a) Flush, (b) Paneled, (c) Dutch, (d) Louvered, (e) Bifold, (f) Pocket, (g) Folding.

For an Oriental ambience, fixed or sliding Shoji panels are available which are wood framed with vellum or synthetic vellum inserts.

Folding or accordion doors are used where space needs to be temporarily divided. These folding doors operate and stack compactly within their openings. The panels may be wood veneered lumber core or particle board core with a wood grained vinyl coating. Each panel is 3 5/8 inches or under in width, and the folding doors are available in heights up to 16 feet 1 inch. Folding doors operate by means of a track at the top to which the panels are attached by wheels. The handle and locking mechanism is installed on the panel closest to the opening edge (see Figure 5-10).

Glass Doors

Sash doors are similar in construction and appearance to the panel door except one or more panels are replaced with glass. French doors are often used in residences to open out onto a balcony or patio. They have wood frames and may consist of one sheet of plate glass or may have multiple **lights** in each door. French doors are most often installed in pairs and usually open out.

When French doors or other styles of doors are installed in pairs, one of them is used as the primary door. The second one is stationary with a flush bolt or special lock holding it tight at the top and bottom. To cover the joining crack between the pair of doors and to make them more weathertight, an **astragal** is attached to the interior edge of the stationary door. If required, both doors may be opened to enlarge the opening.

Glass doors for residential use may have a wood or metal frame and may pivot on hinges or have one sliding panel with the second panel being stationary. Whenever full length glass is used, by law it must be tempered or laminated.

Commercial glass doors must also be made of tempered or laminated glass and are subject to local building codes. The door may be all glass, framed with metal at the top and/or bottom, or framed on all four sides. Due to the nature of a glass door, the most visible design feature is the hardware.

Specialty Doors

When X-ray machines are used, special doors must be specified. These flush panel doors have two layers of plywood with lead between; then a face veneer of wood, hardboard, or laminate is applied.

Firedoors have an incombustible material core with fire-retardant rails and stiles covered by a wood veneer or high pressure decorative laminate. These doors are rated according to the time they take to burn. Depending on materials and construction, this time will vary between 20 minutes to 1 1/2 hours.

Metal Doors

Most metal doors are made of steel, although some are available in aluminum. In the past, metal doors had a commercial or institutional connotation, but today many interior and exterior residential doors and many bifold doors are made of metal. Exterior metal doors were shunned in the past because wood exterior solid core doors had better insulating qualities. The use of polystyrene and polyurethane as a core has now provided a residential metal exterior door with similar insulating qualities, plus it is not as susceptible to temperature changes as is the wood door.

Metal doors are available coated with a rust-resistant primer for finishing on the site, or they may be prefinished with a heavy baked-on coating.

Exterior Doors

For exterior use, a wood door must be of solid construction. Handcarved doors are available for exterior use, but manufacturer's specifications must be studied carefully because a door that appears to be handcarved may actually be molded to imitate handcarving at less expense but with less aesthetic appeal.

Specifications for Doors

Most doors are available prehung, that is, assembled complete with frames, trim, and sometimes hardware. For prehung doors, door hand is determined by noting hinge location when the door opens away from the viewer, i.e., if the hinge jamb is on his/her right, it is a right-hand door. In the case of a pair of doors, hand is determined from the active leaf in the same way. If prehung doors are specified, door handing should be included.

The following additional information should be provided when specifying doors:

Manufacturer.

Size including width, height, and thickness.

Face description—species of wood, type of veneer, rotary or sliced. If not veneer, laminate, photogravure, vinyl coating, or metal.

Construction—crossbanding thickness, edge strips, top and bottom rails, stiles, and core construction.

Finishing—prefinished or unfinished.

Special detailing includes specifying **backset** for hardware and any mouldings. Special service such as glazing, fire doors.

Warranty—differs whether for interior or exterior use.

Door Hardware

HINGES. A *hinge* is a device permitting one part to turn on another. The two parts consist of metal plates known as **leaves** and are joined together by a pin that passes through the **knuckle** joints. These pins may be **loose, nonrising** loose, nonremovable loose pins, or **fast** pins. Hinges are available in brass, bronze, stainless steel, and carbon steel.

A loose pin hinge enables a door to be easily removed from the frame by merely pulling out the pin. A loose pin type of hinge is used for hanging less expensive residential doors. One problem with a loose pin is that the pin has a tendency to raise with use.

A nonrising loose pin has the same advantage as the loose pin but without the "rising" problem. If the pin of the loose pin hinge is visible, a locked door can be removed from its frame by simply removing the pin.

In a nonremovable loose-pin hinge, however, a setscrew in the barrel fits into a groove in the pin, thereby preventing its removal. The setscrew is inaccessible when the door is closed.

The fast (or tight) pin is permanently set in the barrel of the hinge at the time of manufacture.

The tips of the pins may be finished in different styles. Shapes include flat button, oval head, steeple, or ball tip. Hospital and fast riveted pins are other types of pin or tip styles. Flat button tips are standard for the majority of hinges. Oval head tips are used only on hinges with loose pins and no plugs. Steeple tips are used on colonial hinges. Ball tips are available by special order. On hospital types, the ends of the barrel are rounded for added safety as well as cleanliness. Fast riveted pins have both ends **spun** which makes the pin permanent.

Butt hinges are mortised into the edge of the door. A **gain** is cut in the jamb and also in the edge of the door, resulting in the leaves being flush with the surfaces of the door and jamb. Butt hinges are used on most doors. **Countersunk** holes are predrilled in the leaves. **Template** hardware has these holes drilled so accurately as to conform to standard drawings, thus assuring a perfect fit. Template butt hinges have the holes drilled in a crescent shape. (See a full mortise hinge in Figure 5-11.)

The number of hinges per door depends on the size and weight of the door and, sometimes, on conditions of use. A general rule recommends two butt hinges on doors up to 60 inches high; three hinges on doors 60 to 90 inches high; and four hinges on doors 90 to 120 inches high.

With a full mortise hinge, the leaves are flush with the door and the frame and only the knuckles are visible when the door is closed. When a half mortise hinge is used, one leaf is mortised in the door edge and the other leaf is surface mounted on the jamb. A half surface hinge is the opposite with the surface mounted part being on the door and the mortise on the jamb. Thus, it is the type of installation on the door itself that provides the name. On full surface hinges, both leaves are surface mounted.

Swing clear hinges are designed to swing doors completely clear of the opening when the door is opened 90° to 95°. This type is very expensive and is used almost exclusively in hospitals, institutions, or public buildings.

Bearings may be ball, oil impregnated, or antifriction. Ball bearing hinges are packed with grease to assure a quiet long-life hinge. These types of bearings should always be specified for doors equipped with door closers.

Concealed hinges are used on doors when the design precludes the use of visible hinges. With concealed hinges, one side is mounted on the inside of the frame and the second side is mortised into the door. These hinges are available in 90 to 100° openings or 176°. (See Soss hinge, Figure 5-12.)

Concealed hinges for cabinets are different in construction. They are not visible from the outside of the cabinet, but are surface mounted on the inside of the cabinet door. (See Grass America, Figure 5-12.)

Spring hinges are used when automatic closing of doors is required. The tension is adjustable.

LOCKS. The needs of the client and the expected usage of a lock will determine which lock will be se-

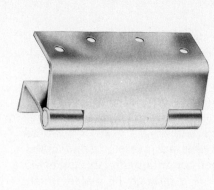

Full Mortise Swing Clear

Pivot Reinforced

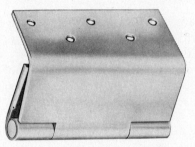

Half Mortise Swing Clear

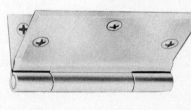

Full Surface Swing Clear

Half Surface Swing Clear

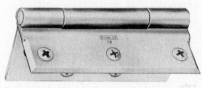

Half Mortise

Half Surface

Full Mortise

Full Surface

FIGURE 5-11. Types of Hinges.
(Photos courtesy of Stanley Hardware Division)

FIGURE 5-12.
Shown above is the Soss Invisible Hinge which can only be seen when the door or lid is open. (Photograph courtesy of Universal Industrial Products). Below is a concealed cabinet hinge from Grass America which opens 176° and is self-closing. (Photograph courtesy of Grass America)

lected. For residential uses, security is probably the foremost criterion, whereas for a commercial installation, heavy usage will necessitate not only a secure lock but also one built to withstand constant use.

There are three weights or grades of locks. The most expensive is the heavy duty, then standard duty, and the least expensive is the light duty or builders grade. The first two types are made of solid metal with a polished, brushed, or antique finish; however, the light duty grade has a painted or plated finish that may be removed with wear.

The **Door & Hardware Institute** describes the four types of locks and bolts as follows:

Bored Type

These types of locks are installed in a door having two round holes at right angles to one another, one through the face of the door to hold the lock body and the other in the edge of the door to receive the latch mechanism. When the two are joined together in the door they comprise a complete latching or locking mechanism.

Bored type locks have the keyway (cylinder) and/or locking device, such as push or turn buttons, in the knobs.

The assembly must be tight on the door and without excessive play. Knobs should be held securely in place without screws and a locked knob should not be removable. **Roses** should be threaded or secured firmly to the body mechanism. The trim has an important effect in this type of lock because working parts fit directly into the trim.

Regular backset for a bored lock is 2 3/4 inches, but may vary from 2 3/8 to 42 inches.

Preassembled Type

The preassembled lock is installed in a rectangular notch cut into the door edge. This lock is one that has all the parts assembled as a unit at the factory and, when installed, little or no disassembly is required.

Preassembled locks have the keyway (cylinder) in the knobs. Locking devices may be in the knob or on the rose or **escutcheon.**

Regular backset is 2 3/4 inches. The lock is available only in heavy duty weight.

Mortise Lock

A mortise lock is installed in a prepared recess (mortise) in a door. The working mechanism is contained in a rectangular shaped case with appropriate holes into which the required components, cylinder, knob,

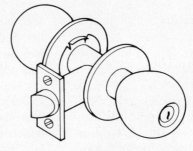

Bored Lock

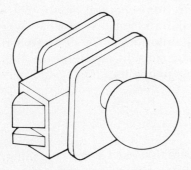

Pre-assembled Lock

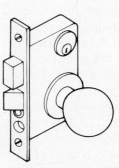

Mortise Lock

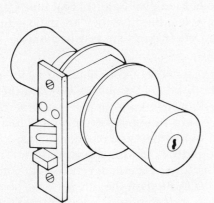

Integral Lock

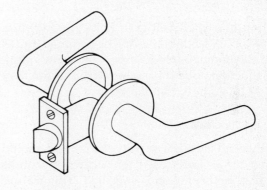

Bored Lever Handle Lock

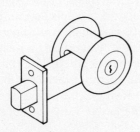

Bored Deadbolt

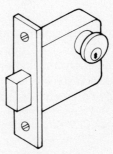

Mortised Deadbolt

FIGURE 5-13. Types of Locks.

and turnpiece spindles are inserted to complete the working assembly.

Regular backset is 2 3/4 inches. These locks are available in heavy duty and standard duty weights. **Armored** fronts are also available.

In order to provide a complete working unit, mortise locks, except for those with **dead lock** function only, must be installed with knobs, levers, and/or other items of trim as described in the section on door knobs and handles.

Integral Lock

An integral lock is a mortise lock with a cylinder in the knob. It is installed in a prepared recess (mortise) in a door. A complete working unit consists of the lock mechanism and selected trim (knob, rose, escutcheon). Roses or escutcheons are bolted together through the lock case.

Regular backset is 2 3/4 inches. These locks are available only in heavy duty weight.

The lock achieves its function by means of various types of bolts. The bolt is a bar of metal that projects out of the lock into a strike prepared to receive it.

Latch Bolts

The function of a latch bolt is to hold the door in a closed position. A latch bolt is spring actuated and is used in all swinging door locks except those providing **dead bolt** function only. It has a beveled face and may be operated by a knob, handle, or turn.

Auxiliary Dead Latch

An auxiliary dead latch is a security feature and should be required on all locks used for security purposes unless a dead bolt function is specified. This feature deadlocks the latch bolt automatically and makes it virtually impossible to depress the latch bolt when the door is closed.

Dead Bolt

A dead bolt has no spring action and is activated by a key or by a turn. It must be manually operated. Dead bolts provide security and, when hardened steel inserts are used, the security is greater. The minimum throw should be 1/2 of an inch but today most throws are 1 inch.

Lock Strikes

A **lock strike** is a metal plate mortised into the door jamb to receive and to hold the projected latch bolt and, when specified, the dead bolt also, thus securing the door. It is sometimes called a *keeper*. The proper length lip should be specified so that the latch bolt will not hit the door jamb before the strike.

A wrought box should be installed in back of the strike in the jamb. This box will protect the bolt holes from the intrusion of plaster or other foreign material, which would prevent the bolt from projecting properly into the strike.

Electric Strike

This is an electromechanical device that replaces an ordinary strike and makes possible remote electric locking and unlocking of a door. When a control mechanism actuates the electric strike, this allows the door to be opened without a key and relocked when closed.[1]

Rim Locks

Rim locks were first used at the beginning of the 18th century and are attached to the inside of the door stile. They are used today in restoration work or in new homes of Medieval English, Salt Box, Cape Cod, or Colonial styles. Because they are exposed to view, the case and other parts are finished brass.

The simplest type of door hardware is the passage set where both knobs are always free and there is no locking mechanism. An example would be the door between a living or dining room and a hallway. A **springlatch** holds this type of door closed.

Bathroom doors require a privacy lock. This type is locked from the inside in several ways. Some have a push button located on the interior rose, some have a turn button in the interior knob, while still others have a turnpiece that activates a bolt. In the case of an emergency entrance, all privacy locks have some means of opening from the outside, either by use of an emergency release key or by using a screwdriver.

When the type of use has been decided upon, the style of handle, rose, and finish is selected. There are many shapes of knobs from ball, round with a semiflat face, to round with a concave face, which may even be decorated. Knobs may be made of metal, porcelain, or wood. Grip handle entrance locks combine the convenience of button-in-the-knob locking with traditional grip handle elegance. Grip handles should be

---

[1]"Basic Builders' Hardware." (McLean VA: Door & Hardware Institute, 1969, 1981), pp. 8-9.

of cast brass or cast bronze. Interior Colonial doors may have a thumb latch installed on the stile surface.

Natural finishes take the color of the base metal in the product and may be either high or low luster. Applied finishes result from the addition by plating of a second metal, a synthetic enamel, or other material.

Polished brass and bronze finishes are produced by buffing or polishing the metal to a high gloss before applying synthetic coating. Satin brass and natural bronze finishes are obtained by dry buffing or scouring and the resultant finish is then coated.

The most popular of the plated finishes are the chromiums, both polished and satin.

A lever handle must be specified when used by a handicapped person. When blind persons have access to areas that might be dangerous, such as a doorway leading to stairs, the knob must be knurled or ridged to provide a tactile warning.

Roses used to cover the bored hole in the door may be round or square and may also be decorated. Locks, which include all operating mechanisms, come with numerous finishes including brass, bronze, chrome, and stainless steel in bright polish, satin, antique, or oil rubbed.

Some locks, particularly the mortise type, have escutcheon plates instead of roses. These are usually rectangular in shape.

In addition to security, there are several other features that have to be considered. One is door handing. The following rules are suggested by Baldwin Hardware Manufacturing Corp. The hand of a door is determined from the outside only. If the hinges are on the right, it is a right-hand door and if the hinges are on the left, it is a left-hand door. The door that opens in is a regular bevel door but, if the door opens out, it is a reverse bevel door. While some locks are reversible and may be used on a right- or left-hand door, others are not, and proper door handing must be specified (see Figure 5-14).

The outside of an exterior door is the street or entrance door and the outside of a room door is the hall side. The outside of a single communicating door is the side from which the hinges are not visible when the door is closed. The outside of a closet door is the room or hall side.

In residential use, door stops protect the wall from damage caused by the knob or handle hitting the wall. These stops may be attached to the wall and consist of a metal-framed rubber cushion or they may be metal rods with a rubber tip at the end, attached to the floor, base, or even door hinge.

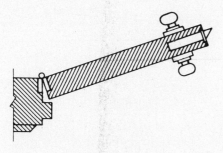

Left Hand Hand Lock

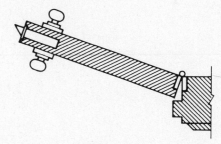

Right Hand Lock

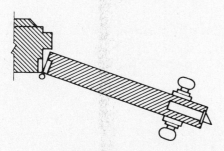

Left Hand Reverse Bevel Lock

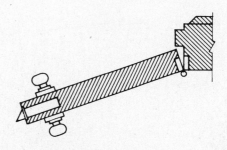

Right Hand Reverse Bevel Lock

FIGURE 5-14. Door Handing.

Door controls used in commercial installations may be overhead closers (either surface-mounted or concealed) or floor-type closers. These devices are a combination of a spring and an oil-cushioned piston that dampens the closing action inside a cylinder. Surface-mounted closers are more accessible for maintenance but concealed closers are more aesthetically pleasing. Overhead installations are preferred as dirt and scrub water may harm the operation of a floor-type closer (see Figure 5-15). A three second delay is required to provide safe passage for a handicapped person.

In public buildings, all doors must open out for fire safety. Either a push plate is attached to the door or a fire exit bar or panic bar is used. Slight pressure of the bar releases the rod and latch. For use by the handicapped, this bar should be able to be operated with a maximum of 8 pounds of pressure.

Door opening may also be accomplished by the use of an electronic eye where, when the beam is broken, the door opens. For areas requiring special security, doors are opened by the use of a specially coded plastic card, similar to a credit card, or a numbered combination may be punched in. The combination may be easily changed, thus eliminating the re-issuing of keys.

These security systems are being used more and more in restrooms of office buildings and other special areas where accessibility is restricted to certain personnel.

To eliminate having to carry several keys for residential use, all the locksets for exterior doors may be keyed the same. This may be done when the locks are ordered or a locksmith can make the changes later but at a greater expense.

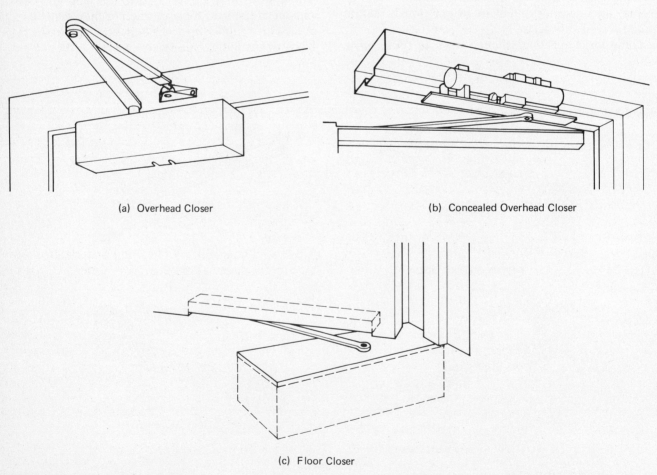

(a) Overhead Closer

(b) Concealed Overhead Closer

(c) Floor Closer

FIGURE 5-15. Door Controls.

When specifying locksets, the following information must be provided: manufacturer's name and style number, finish, style of knob and rose, backset, wood or metal door, thickness of door, and door handing.

Installation should be performed by a professional locksmith or carpenter to insure correct fit with no door rattles or other misfitting problems.

FIREPLACES

In earlier times, the fireplace was not only the source of heat for the home, but also served as a source of heat for cooking. The fireplace is the focal point in a room and furniture is arranged around the fireplace. Of all the design features in a room, it is the fireplace that most sets the mood; therefore, it is important for designers to recognize the different mantel styles (see Figure 5-16). If the mantel is wood, the fireplace surrounding it must be fireproof with 8 inches between fireplace opening and the mantel (see Figure 3-27).

A fireplace is actually a very inefficient means of providing heat as there is a large amount of heat lost up and through the chimney, and this is the reason many architects suggest placing the fireplace on an inside wall. Thus, heat that escapes from the fireplace itself will then be given off to the interior rather than lost to the outdoors.

Fireplaces consist of a noncombustible base, a **firebox,** and a **flue.** Traditionally, they were constructed by brickmasons but today many fireplaces are prefabricated, where the base, firebox, **smoke chamber,** flue, and **damper** come preassembled. Many house fires are started from improperly built or installed fireplaces. Most areas of the country have strict building codes covering the construction of fireplaces.

The *hearth,* which is constructed of incombustible material, is the base of the fireplace and projects into the room and extends to each side. These measurements are controlled by local building codes. The **fireback** of a fireplace is lined with **firebrick** which is resistant to the high temperatures of a fire. The *damper* is a metal plate that controls the amount of air entering the fireplace. In other words, it controls the draft. If, when a fire is lit in the fireplace, smoke billows into the room, it is because the damper has not been opened. It is the damper that keeps the warm air in the house in the winter when the fire is out, but it is also the reason for loss of heat. As long as there is any burning material in the fireplace, the damper must be left open.

Thus, after the fire has gone out in the early hours of the morning, the damper will remain open and heated air from the house, obeying the laws of physics, will rise and be lost out the flue. Automatic dampers that close after a certain temperature has been reached are available today.

The *smoke chamber* is the area directly over the fireplace; it tapers upward to fit into the flue. The *flue* is the means by which the smoke is vented to the outside. In a masonry fireplace, the flue lining is a heat resistant tile but, in many of the prefabricated fireplaces, the flue is a metal pipe.

This metal pipe must be double walled if it is enclosed in a wall. Single pipe may be used, if permitted by fire codes, where the flue is exposed to view but, wherever metal flues pass through any wood construction, the pipe must be insulated to prevent heat from being transferred to the combustible wood. Exterior chimneys should extend 3 feet above the nearest roof area. When the wind blows the smoke back into the room, the most common reason is that the chimney is not high enough.

One of the conveniences that may be built into a fireplace is an ash pit where the ashes from the fire are collected and are removed from the outside of the house instead of filling a bucket and carrying it through the house.

Today, in contemporary homes, free-standing prefabricated fireplaces are being used instead of the more expensive built-in fireplaces that require a masonry chimney. The free-standing fireplaces usually have an exposed flue that radiates heat in the exposed area. They are available in matte black or colored enamel finishes.

Fireplace Accessories

Screens prevent sparks or burning material from leaving the fireplace. There are many different types on the market. One type is a metal mesh drawstring screen that is drawn by a cord similar to a traverse rod. This type is custom ordered to the exact measurements of the fireplace opening. Also custom ordered are tempered glass doors that allow the flickering flames to be visible but prevent sparks from being a fire hazard. Glass doors also prevent the loss of heat caused by an open damper. The base of the glass doors has a metal grille to allow some passage of air for combustion purposes.

More traditional screens are similar in shape to a bay window and may be black metal mesh with either a polished brass or plain black frame. Another type

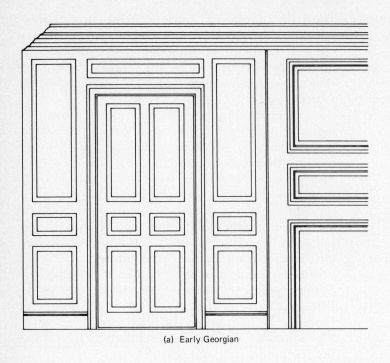

(a) Early Georgian

FIGURE 5-16. Mantels.

(b) Late Georgian

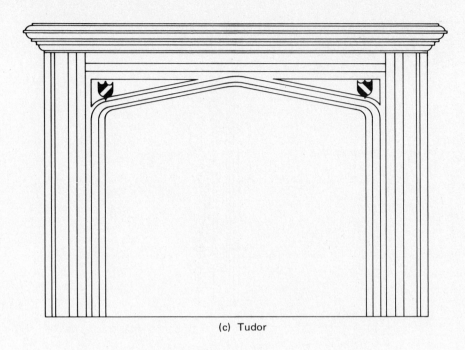

(c) Tudor

(d) Adam

(e) Louis XV

of fire prevention accessory is the brass fender—a low metal railing with a solid base that prevents live coals from rolling beyond the hearth.

Andirons are used in English and Colonial homes. These pairs of metal supports with legs hold the logs above the hearth to aid in combustion. They may also be called **firedogs.** The utilitarian part of the andiron is made of cast iron, but the top of the front legs may, according to style, be crowned by a brass finial or ball. Others may be made of all cast iron.

Several accessories may be used with Colonial fireplaces and the following would add to the ambience. A **bedwarmer** is a polished brass pan with a hinged perforated lid that is attached to a turned wooden handle. The bedwarmer was originally filled with glowing coals from the fire and moved around between the top and bottom sheets of the bed in days before central heating. Today, they stand alongside the fireplace with the brass pan down and the handle resting on the wall. The large Colonial fireplaces were used for cooking and an arched recess or oven was built into the back of the chimney. In order to reach into this fairly deep oven and remove the bread, a **peel** was used. A peel is a large wooden spadelike tool similar to a modern pizza tool but with a longer handle. Also used in these large Colonial fireplaces was a chimney or fireplace crane from which was hung handled cast iron pots for heating water and cooking food.

Whatever type of fireplace accessories are chosen, they must be the correct style for the fireplace—English, French, American, or modern.

STOVES

In the 18th century, Benjamin Franklin perfected his Franklin stove and for many years stoves were used as a heat source in the home. Today, cast-iron stoves have come back into fashion due to the increasing cost of utilities. Instead of burning coal, most of these stoves burn wood, a renewable resource. They are quite energy efficient due to the primary and secondary draft controls. These controls slow down the burning of the wood, yet the cast-iron stove continues to radiate heat. However, there is one problem with a slow burning wood stove and that is the buildup of creosote in the stove and in the flue. Creosote is a black tarry substance caused by slow combustion, is very flammable, and can be the cause of chimney fires. Chemicals are available to rid the stove and flue of this build-up.

Sizes of stoves vary considerably from 12 inches wide by 24 inches long to as large as 30 inches wide and 36 inches long or even larger. They may be black cast iron or may have a baked on enamel finish.

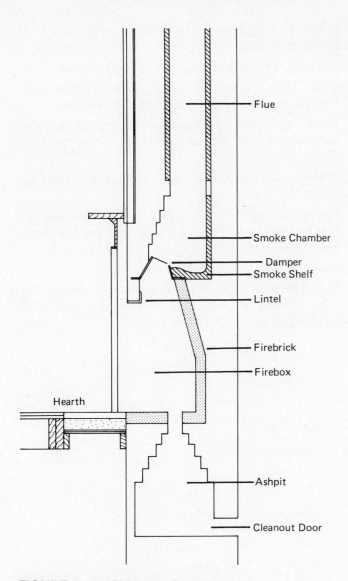

FIGURE 5-17. Chimney Components.

Flue

Smoke Chamber

Damper

Smoke Shelf

Lintel

Firebrick

Firebox

Hearth

Ashpit

Cleanout Door

Bibliography

Ortho Books. *Finish Carpentry Techniques.* San Francisco: Chevron Chemical Company, 1983.

Time-Life Books. *Doors and Windows,* Home Repair & Improvement. Alexandria VA: Time-Life Books, 1978.

Glossary

Astragal. Vertical strip of wood with weatherstripping.

Andirons. Fireplace accessory. A pair of decorative columns attached to iron bars to hold logs above the level of the hearth.

Armored. Two plates are used to cover the lock mechanism in order to prevent tampering.

Backplate. An applied decorative moulding used on ceilings above a chandelier or ceiling fan.

Backset. The horizontal distance from the center of the face-bored hole to the edge of the door.

Base. Baseboard or skirting. Material placed against wall at the floor area to protect base of the wall from damage (see Figure 5-1).

Bed moulding. Cornice moulding.

Bedwarmer. Fireplace accessory. A long-handled, polished brass pan with a perforated hinged lid.

Brickmold. Exterior wood moulding to cover gap between door or window frame.

Butt hinges. Two metal plates joined with a pin, one being fastened to the door jamb or frame and the other to the door (see Figure 5-11).

Casing. Exposed trim moulding, either interior or exterior (see Figure 5-1).

Caulk. Filling a joint with resilient mastic. Also spelled *calk.*

Chair rail. Strip of wood or moulding that is placed on the wall at the same height as the back of a chair to protect the wall from damage (see Figure 5-1).

Countersunk. Hole prepared with a bevel to enable the tapered head of a screw to be inserted flush with the surface.

Damper. Device used to regulate draft in the flue (see Figure 5-17).

Deadbolt. Hardened steel bolt with a square head operated by a key or turn piece (see Figure 5-13).

Door and Hardware Institute. DHI representing the industry.

Escutcheon. Plate which surrounds the keyhole and/or handle.

Fast pin. Pin is permanently in place. Nonremovable.

Fireback. The back lining or wall of the fireplace (see Figure 5-17).

Firebox. The area where combustion takes place (see Figure 5-17).

Firebrick. Special brick constructed to withstand high temperatures; used to line firebox.

Firedogs. Another name for andirons.

Flue. Fire resistant passage by which smoke escapes to the outside (see Figure 5-17).

Gain. Area cut away on door or jamb into which leaves of hinges are set.

Knuckle. Cylindrical area of hinge enclosing the pin.

Leaves. Flat plates of a pair of hinges (see Figure 5-11).

Lights. Small panes of glass, usually rectangular in shape.

Lock strike. A plate fastened to the door frame into which the bolts project.

Loose. Able to be removed.

Mitered. Cut at a 45° angle to form a right angle (see Figure 6-2).

Nonrising. Pins that do not ride up with use.

Peel. Fireplace accessory. Flat, long-handled, wooden, spadelike instrument with which bread was originally removed from 17th and 18th century ovens.

Polymer. A high-molecular weight compound from which mouldings are made.

Prehung. Frame and door are packaged as one unit.

Rose. The plate, usually round, that covers the bored hole on the face of the door (see Figure 5-13).

Smoke chamber. The transition areas above the firebox, between the damper and the flue (see Figure 5-17).

Springlatch. Latch with a spring rather than a locking action (see Figure 5-13).

Spun. Moving the metal by means of a spinning action and applied pressure which changes the shape of the metal.

Sticking. The shaping of moulding.

Template hardware. Hardware that exactly matches a master template drawing, as to spacing of all holes and dimensions (see Figure 5-13).

6

CABINET CONSTRUCTION

CONTENTS

In order to properly select or design well-made cabinetwork, it is necessary to become familiar with furniture construction. By studying the casework joints, specifiers will be able to compare and contrast similar items and be able to make an informed decision on which piece of furniture, or which group of cabinets, is the most value for the money expended.

When designing casework and specifying materials, there are several parts that need definition. According to AWI, exposed surfaces include all surfaces visible when doors and drawers are closed. Bottoms of cases more than 4 feet above the floor are considered exposed. All visible members in open cases or behind glass doors are also considered exposed surfaces.

Semi-exposed portions of casework include those members behind opaque doors, such as shelves, divisions, interior faces of ends, case backs, drawer sides, backs and bottoms, and the back face of doors. Tops of cases 6 feet 6 inches or more above the floor are considered semi-exposed. Concealed portions include **sleepers, web frames, dust panels,** and other surfaces not usually visible after installation.

JOINTS

The stile and rail joinery may use one of the following three methods: **Mortise and tenon,** where the stile has a mortise or hole and the rail has the tenon or tongue. **Dowel joints** consist of holes for the dowels being drilled in the stile and dowels being inserted in corresponding places on the rail. A **stub tenon** is similar to a tongue-and-groove joint except that the rounded tongue-and-groove has been squared off. A **spline** joint is used for gluing plywood in width and length. Since the spline serves to align faces, this joint is also used for items requiring on-site assembly. (See Figure 6-2.)

French dovetail joints are used for joining drawer sides to fronts when fronts conceal metal extension slides or overlay the case faces. Conventional dovetail is the traditional joint for joining drawer sides to fronts and backs, and eliminates, due to its interlocking nature, any possibility of the drawer sides and front separating. Conventional dovetail joints are usually limited to **flush** or **lipped** drawers. A drawer lock joint also joins the drawer sides to the fronts and is usually used for flush installations, but can be adapted to lip or **overlay** drawers.

Wood may also be joined together with a **butt joint**—merely placing the two pieces of wood at right angles to each other. This type of joint is only found in cheap furniture. Another method of joining two pieces of wood at right angles is to miter the adjoining edges. A mitered joint is frequently used when con-

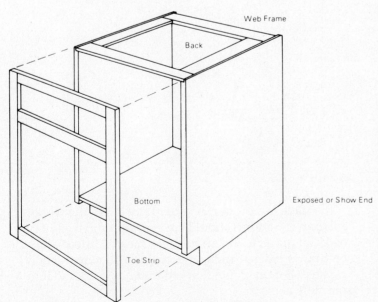

FIGURE 6-1. Casework Construction.

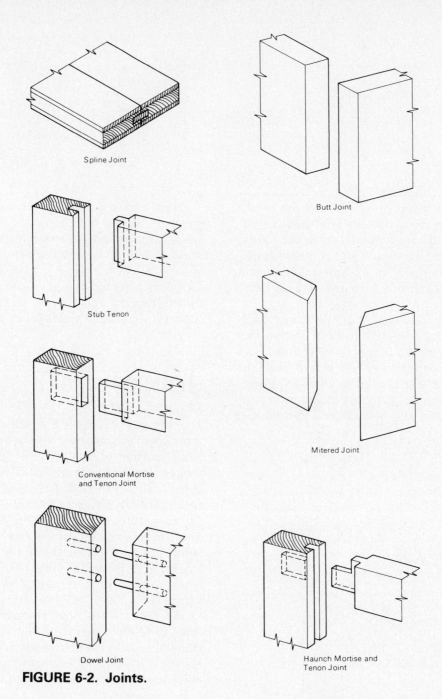

Spline Joint

Butt Joint

Stub Tenon

Conventional Mortise
and Tenon Joint

Mitered Joint

Dowel Joint

Haunch Mortise and
Tenon Joint

FIGURE 6-2. Joints.

structing picture frames. It may also be used in furniture construction, sometimes in conjunction with a spline.

Premium grade has some form of dovetail to attach the backs of the drawers to the sides. In custom grade, the shouldered lock joint may be used at the front and back.

A **dado** is a groove or square slot cut in the wood. All drawer bottoms should have a minimum thickness of 1/4 of an inch and should be inserted into dadoes on drawer sides, fronts, and backs. This construction creates a bottom panel that is permanently locked into position.

Edge banding is required when materials other than solid wood are used. This edge treatment is used

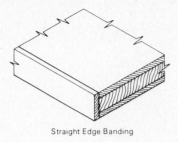

Straight Edge Banding

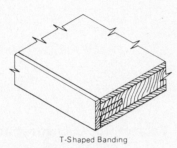

T-Shaped Banding

FIGURE 6-3. Edge Banding.

for case body members and shelves but varies according to the grade of the work. For premium grade, the visible edges should be banded with lumber or standard veneer edgings, glued under pressure with no nails allowed. Species should match the face veneers of plywood, but may be of any species on particleboard. Visible edges are eased by sanding. Custom grade is the same as premium except edges must match face if a transparent finish is to be used (see Figure 6-3).

DRAWERS/DOORS

Drawers or doors may be of one of the three following design categories.

1. (a) Exposed Face Frame—Flush.
   (b) Exposed Face Frame—Lipped.
2. Flush Overlay
3. Reveal Overlay

Exposed face frame—flush (also often known as *conventional flush construction*) is the design most basic to architectural woodwork. The drawer and door faces are flush with the face frame. This design is highly functional and allows the use of different thicknesses of wood for doors and drawer fronts. The exposed face frame has the advantage of providing a solid surround for the operating doors and drawers which keeps them aligned. This type of construction is recommended for hard-service applications because of its superior strength and rigidity. It is, however, a more expensive design, due to the necessity of careful fitting and alignment of the doors and drawers, and the close tolerances required by the exposed joinery in the face frame. For these reasons, this design does not lend itself to the economical use of plastic laminate covering.

Exposed face frame—lipped design has most of the advantages and is similar in construction to the flush design. Provided that edge banding is not required on the doors, the lipped design is a more economical style since the fitting tolerances of the doors and drawers are less critical.

Flush overlay is becoming increasingly popular. It offers a very clean, contemporary design since only the door and drawer fronts are visible on the face of the cabinet and a matched grain effect can be achieved, if specified, by having all the doors and drawer fronts cut from the same panel. It also lends itself ideally to the use of laminated plastic for the exposed surfaces. Heavy-duty hardware is required with a flush overlay design. The absence of a face frame requires careful site preparation and installation to maintain the proper alignment of the doors and/or drawers to one another.

Reveal overlay, a variation of the flush overlay design, presents a "raised panel" effect. Although it requires a face frame, it is for the most part concealed and, as with a lipped design, requires less demanding fitting tolerances. The **reveal** between the doors and drawer fronts reduces the problem of alignment. It incorporates most of the advantages of the flush overlay and exposed face frame designs. The architect or designer has the option of utilizing the reveals vertically and/or horizontally, and the width of the reveal is variable (see Figure 6-4).

The stock for doors is 3/4 of an inch thick provided the doors are not over 26 inches wide and, depending on the grade of installation, the height varies from 48 inches for premium grade to 54 inches in height for custom grade. Specifications for flush type doors are contained in Section 400-A of Architectural Woodwork Quality Standards, Guide Specifications and Quality Certification Program of the AWI.

When doors are covered with a high pressure laminate, a **balancing** laminate must be used on the reverse side of the substrate.

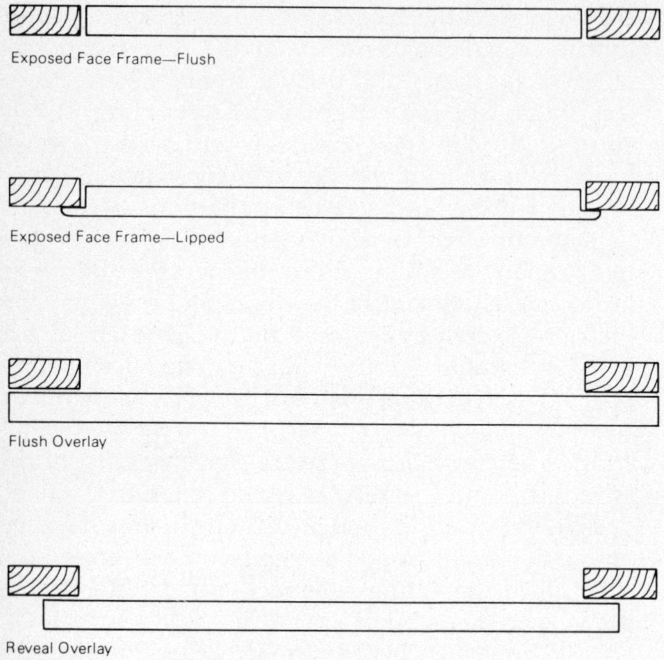

Exposed Face Frame—Flush

Exposed Face Frame—Lipped

Flush Overlay

Reveal Overlay

FIGURE 6-4. Cabinet Door Construction.

For shelves, or when the case body is exposed, the following construction methods are used: Through dado is the conventional joint used for assembly of case body members, the dado is usually concealed by application of a case face frame. Blind dado has an applied edge "stopping" or concealing the dado groove and is used when case body edge is exposed. Stop dado is applicable when veneer edging or solid lumber is exposed. A 3/4 of an inch thickness may be used for shelves under 36 inches wide but, for exposed shelving unsupported for a length exceeding 36 inches, the minimum thickness is 1 inch. (For dados see Figure 6-5.)

Drawer guides are an important feature of well-made casework. They may be constructed of wood or metal. If wood is selected, it should have both male and female parts made of wood. Wood drawer guides are usually centered under the drawer, but they may also be attached to the side of the case with the drawer sides being dadoes to accommodate the wood guide. The reverse procedure may also be used with the guide being attached to the drawer side and the frame dadoes to receive the guide. Paste wax should be applied to the wood guides to facilitate movement.

When an exposed face frame with a flush drawer front is designed, a **stop** must be incorporated in order to prevent too much inward travel. As has been mentioned before, flush doors and drawers are the most expensive form of design because of the tolerances and hand-fitting of such extras as drawer stops.

Kitchen cabinets and some furniture use metal guides attached to the case and drawer sides. The drawers slide out on metal or nylon rollers running in the guide track. Kitchen drawers often employ the use of self-returning slides. In other words, when the drawer is pulled out to its fullest extent, it remains open but, when pushed in approximately half-way, the rollers continue to close without more pressure being applied to the drawer front. This is a useful feature that prevents unsightly and unsafe half-open drawers in the kitchen. All drawer guides are installed with a very slight inward tilt.

A toe space is required for such items as kitchen cabinets and dressers, thus providing a recessed space for toes under the doors or drawers. This toe strip is usually 4 inches high and 2 1/2 inches deep. These measurements vary slightly with the European kitchen cabinets having a height of 5 7/8 inches (see Figures 7-l, 7-2, 7-3, and 7-10).

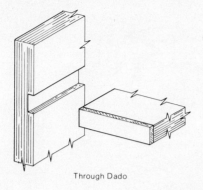

Through Dado

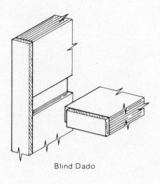

Blind Dado

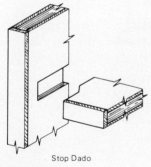

Stop Dado

FIGURE 6-5. Dados.
(Reprinted with permission from the Architectural Woodwork Institute)

CABINET HARDWARE

The type of hardware selected will depend upon the design category. With an exposed face frame and a flush door, heavy-duty **exposed hinges** may be used or they may be concealed. **Concealed hinges** are recessed into the door, attached to the side of the frame, and hidden from view when the cabinet door is closed (see Figure 5-12). A half-mortise or half-surface hinge with a decorative end to the pin may be used where a semiconcealed hinge is desired. Lipped doors are hung by means of a semiconcealed hinge. Flush overlay and reveal overlay doors may be hung by using semiconcealed or concealed hinges. **Pivot hinges** are often used for fitting doors to cabinets without frames. Pivot hinges are particularly useful on plywood and particle board doors. Only the pivot shows from the front when the door is closed. (See Figure 5-11 for a pivot hinge.) A piano hinge or continuous hinge is used on drop leaf desks and on the doors of some fine furniture. Because they are installed the whole length of the edge, they support the weight of the door in an efficient manner.

Cabinet doors and drawers may be designed without pull hardware by having a finger pull either as part of the door or drawer construction or by the addition of a piece of shaped wood, plastic, or metal to the front of the door (see Figures 7-1, 7-7, 7-8, and 7-9). It is necessary to design these finger pulls in such a manner that the doors or drawers are opened easily without breaking fingernails.

Cabinet pull hardware may be knobs, rounded or square, or handles ranging from simple metal strips to ornately designed ones. The material from which this hardware is constructed may be wood, porcelain, plastic, or metal. It is necessary to select hardware that is compatible with the design of the cabinets or furniture. For traditional or period cabinets, authentic hardware should be chosen (see Figure 7-10).

In order to hold cabinet doors shut, some form of catch is needed. There are five different types: **friction,** roller, magnetic, **bullet,** and touch catch. A friction catch, when engaged, is held in place by friction. The roller catch has a roller under tension that engages a recess in the **strike plate.** The magnet is the holding mechanism of a magnetic catch and, in a bullet catch, a spring-actuated ball engages a depression in the plate. A touch catch releases automatically when the door is pushed. Many of these catches have elongated screw slots that enable the tension of the catch to be adjusted. (See Figure 6-6.)

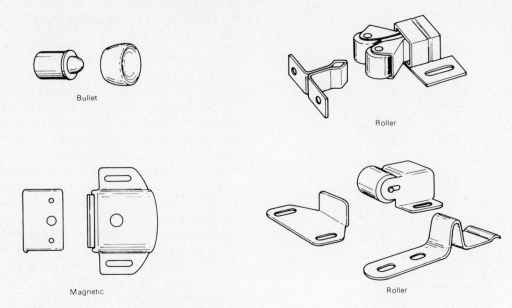

Bullet

Roller

Magnetic

Roller

FIGURE 6-6. Cabinet Catches.

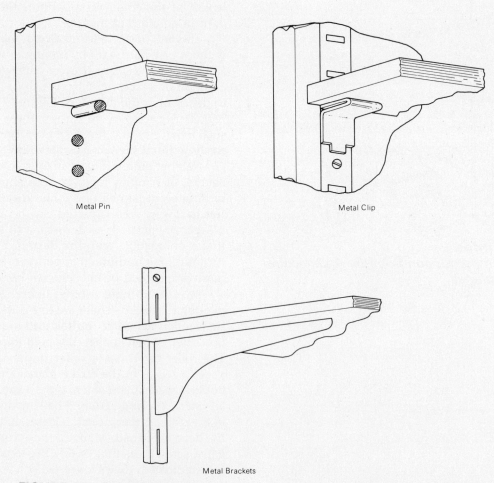

Metal Pin

Metal Clip

Metal Brackets

FIGURE 6-7. Shelf Supports.

Shelves

Shelves may be made of several materials. If solid 3/4 inch wood is used, the span must be no more than 42 inches.

When shelves are to be permanently installed, some form of dado may be used for positioning. The type used depends upon the frame construction. Another permanent installation uses a wood quarter round at the desired height.

If, however, the shelves are to be adjustable there are several methods of support. The type used in fine china cabinets is a metal shelf pin. A number of blind holes, usually in groups of three, are drilled 5/8 of an inch apart in two rows on each interior face of the sides. The metal shelf pins are then inserted at the desired shelf level.

Metal shelf standards have slots every inch, with two standards on each side running from top to bottom of the shelf unit. Four adjustable metal clips are inserted at the same level into these slots. The metal strips may be applied to the inside surface of the shelf unit or they may be dadoed into the interior face.

When metal brackets are used, the shelf standards are attached to the back wall surface instead of to the sides. (See Figure 6-7.)

Bibliography

Architectural Woodwork Institute. *Architectural Woodwork Quality Standard, Guide Specifications and Quality Certification Program.* Alexandria VA: Architectural Woodwork Institute, 1978.

Ortho Books. *Finish Carpentry Techniques.* San Francisco: Chevron Chemical Company, 1983.

Glossary

Balancing sheet. In plastic laminate doors, the lighter weight laminate on the interior face.

Bullet catch. A spring actuated ball engaging a depression in the plate (see Figure 6-6).

Concealed hinge. All parts are concealed when door is closed (see Figure 5-12).

Dado. A groove cut in wood to receive and position another member (see Figure 6-5).

Dowel joint. A joint usually right angle, using dowels for positioning and strength (see Figure 6-2).

Dust panel. Thin panel between two drawers of a chest. Prevents dust from settling through (see Figure 6-1).

Exposed hinge. All parts are visible when door is closed (see Figure 5-11).

Flush. Door and frame are level and frame is completely visible when door is closed (see Figure 6-4).

Friction catch. When engaged, catch is held in place by friction (see Figure 6-6).

Lipped door. A door with an overlapping edge. Partially covers the frame (see Figure 6-4).

Overlay door. The door is on the outside of the frame and, when closed, the door hides the frame from view (see Figure 6-4).

Pivot hinge. Hinge leaves are mortised into the edge of door panel and set in frame at jam and top of door. Some pivot hinges pivot on a single point. (See Figure 5-11.)

Reveal. The small area of the frame that is visible when door and/or drawer is closed.

Stop. A metal, plastic, or wood block placed so as to position the flush drawer front to be level with the face frame.

Strike Plate. Metal plate attached to the frame, designed to hold roller catch under tension.

Sleeper. Middle member of base frame running from front to back—used for reinforcement.

Web Frame. The four-sided top frame of a cabinet.

KITCHENS

CONTENTS

The kitchen has undergone many changes over the years. In the Victorian era, the cast-iron cookstove was the main source of cooking and heating and, although an improvement over the open fire of Colonial days, it still required much time and labor to keep it operating. The coal or wood had to be carried into the house and the stove itself required blacking to maintain its shiny appearance. In the winter, the welcome heat radiating from the cookstove heated the kitchen and made it a gathering place for the family. But, in summer, in order to use the top for cooking and the oven for baking, the fire had to be lit, causing the kitchen to resemble a furnace.

In the kitchens of the past, besides the cookstove, the only other pieces of furniture were tables and chairs and a sink. All food preparation was done on the table or on the draining board next to the sink. There were no such things as counters as we know them today and no such things as upper storage cabinets. All food was stored in the pantry or in a cold cellar. Today, the kitchen has once again become a gathering place for the family and much of the family life is centered around the kitchen, not only for food preparation but also for entertaining and socializing. Regardless of the type of kitchen desired, there are some basic requirements necessary for all kitchens.

The work areas or appliances most used in a kitchen are the refrigerator for food storage, stove for cooking, and the sink for the washing area. The **work triangle** connects these three areas and the total distance should not be over 22 feet and may be less than that in some smaller kitchens. The distance between the refrigerator and the sink should be 4 to 7 feet, with 4 to 6 feet between sink and stove and 4 to 9 feet between stove and refrigerator.

The type of kitchen desired depends upon availability of space, life style, and ages and number of family members. Expense and space are the limiting factors in kitchen design and best utilization of that space will create a functional and enjoyable working area.

Life style involves several factors. One is the manner of entertaining. Formal dinners require a separate formal dining room, while informal entertaining may take place just outside the work triangle with guest and host/hostess communicating while meals are being prepared. If entertaining is done outside of the home of a working host and/or hostess, then the kitchen may be minimal (see Figure 7-1).

FIGURE 7-1.
This compact kitchen has cabinets with durable laminate fronts with integrated shell grips in solid oak, reflecting function plus beauty. (Zeiloplan cabinet designs from Allmilmö® Corporation)

A young couple with a beginning family might require a family room within sight of the parents. Teenagers like to be near food preparation areas and have easy access to refrigerator and snacks. All of these factors need to be taken into consideration when planning a kitchen.

FLOOR PLANS

There are several basic layouts for kitchens as described below; however, there is no limit to the variations that can be created. The simplest of all kitchen floor plans is the one-wall, otherwise known as **pullman, strip,** or **studio.** Here, all appliances and counter space are contained on one wall and, when required, folding doors or screens may be used to hide the kitchen completely from view. This is a minimal kitchen not designed for elaborate or family meals.

The **corridor** or two-wall plan utilizes two parallel walls and doubles the available space over the one-wall plan. The major problem with this design is through traffic. If possible, for safety's sake, one end should be closed off to avoid this traffic. The width of the corridor kitchen should be between 8 and 10 feet. A narrower width prevents two facing doors from being opened at the same time. For energy conservation, refrigerator and stove should not face each other directly.

In an L-shaped kitchen, work areas are arranged on two adjacent walls rather than on two opposite walls, the advantages being there is no through traffic and all counter space is contiguous. The L-shaped kitchen may also include an island or a peninsula. This island may be simply an extra work surface, contain the sink or stove, and/or may also include an informal eating area.

The U-shaped kitchen is probably the most efficient design. There is no through traffic and there are three walls of counter space and, depending on location of the window, at least two walls or more of upper cabinets. The work triangle is the easiest to arrange with the sink usually at the top of the U, the refrigerator on one side, and the range on the other. The refrigerator is always placed at the end of the U to avoid breaking up the counter space and also to be more easily accessible to the eating area. The stove, range, or cooktop is on the opposite side but more centered in the U. See Figure 7-5 for kitchen floor plans.

When planning any kitchen, thought should be given to the activities of each area. The sink area serves

FIGURE 7-2.
These white cabinets have chrome pulls. Ceramic tile covers the countertops, floor, backsplashes, and even the ceiling. Cabinets are Zeilodesign Edelweiss from Allmilmö Corporation of Fairfield, N.J., and West Germany. (Photograph: *Reed Kaestner)*

a dual purpose. First, it is used for food preparation such as washing and cleaning fruits and vegetables. Second, after the meal it is used for cleanup. In the age of the electric dishwasher, the sink area is generally only used for preliminary cleaning but, in the event of a large number of dishes, sufficient space should be provided next to the sink for a helper to dry the dishes.

The refrigerator or cold food storage should be at the end of one side of the counter and, regardless of the type of design, there must be at least 16 inches of counter on the handle side of the refrigerator.

The cooking area is considered to be the cooktop area. Many wall ovens are now located in separate areas from the cooktop. The cooktop may be gas or electric.

FIGURE 7-3.
This imported kitchen from Poggenpohl has white cabinets with natural ash accents. Note the round sinks and also that the toe strip is higher than those under American kitchen cabinets. (Photograph courtesy of Poggenpohl)

FIGURE 7-4.
A remodeled L-shaped kitchen has two sinks from Kohler, one diagonally in the corner and one in the island. The innovative design of the island permits a raised eating area for quick snacks. Mirrored backsplashes and baseboard visually enlarge the kitchen. The custom designed floor and counter tops are ceramic tile from American Olean Tile Company. A Jenn-Air® range and wall oven by Thermador™ complete the kitchen. (Designer: Tom Mooney-Seib Enterprises, Inc.)

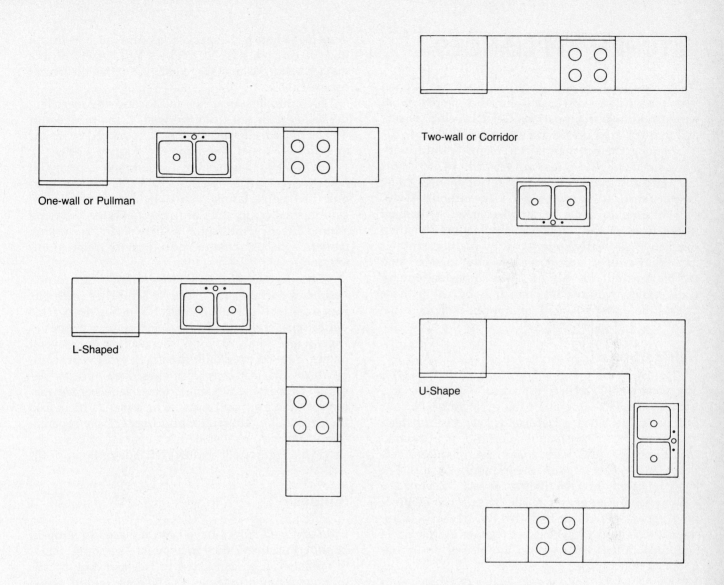

Two-wall or Corridor

One-wall or Pullman

L-Shaped

U-Shape

FIGURE 7-5. Kitchen Floor Plans.

KITCHEN APPLIANCES

Only those appliances that are necessary to a kitchen floor plan will be discussed—in other words, what we consider major appliances. Others such as mixers and toasters are outside the scope of this textbook.

Major appliance manufacturers must comply with a law enacted by Congress in 1975 (P.L. 94-163). This law provides that energy costs for appliances must be calculated on so much per **kilowatthour** (kwh). This information must be supplied on a tag attached to the front of the appliance. Consumers can then calculate their yearly energy cost by finding out their local kwh rate. It is important to bear in mind that the higher the local rate the more important energy conservation features become. It is by using these figures that comparison shopping can be done.

Refrigerators

The most costly kitchen appliance to purchase and the most costly to operate is the refrigerator. For our purposes, the word *refrigerator* will be used instead of refrigerator/freezer combination as it is presumed that all refrigerators have some form of freezer section. This freezer section is commonly on top, but some refrigerators have the freezer section below the regular food storage area. Side-by-side refrigerators have separate vertical doors for the freezer and refrigerator sections. Other exterior features include panel adaptor kits that are used on the face of the refrigerator to match other appliances.

For larger families, an ice water dispenser with cubed and/or crushed ice that is accessible without opening the door may conserve energy and justify the additional expense. One manufacturer even has a third door for access only to the ice cube compartment.

The most common features found in refrigerators include meat keepers, vegetable storage, unwrapped food sections, and adjustable shelves. Other interior features might include egg storage, handy cheese and spread storage, and glass shelves that prevent spilled liquids from dripping onto other shelves, although these solid glass shelves may prevent full air circulation. The shelves on the doors may be fixed or adjustable.

Some manufacturers specialize in energy conservation with greatly improved efficiency over the past 15 years. A self-defrosting refrigerator consumes more energy than a manual defrost but is much more convenient. Others have specialty features such as frozen juice can dispensers, ice makers and, newly on the market, an ice cream maker contained within the freezer compartment.

Nylon rollers are provided for moving or rolling the refrigerator out from the wall. If the refrigerator is to be moved sideways, it should be moved by means of a **dolly** to avoid damaging the floor covering.

Refrigerators are sold by their storage capacity, in other words by cubic feet of space. It is interesting to note that while families and kitchens generally are getting smaller, the size of the refrigerator is staying around 16 to 17 cubic feet. This may be due to working parents with less time to shop or more frequent entertaining.

The average size for refrigerator/freezer combinations is 66 1/2 inches high, 35 3/4 inches wide (fits into a 36 inch space), and 30 1/2 inches deep. This depth measurement means that the door of the refrigerator extends beyond the counter for several inches. Sub-Zero has built-in refrigerator-freezer combinations that are only 24 inches deep and are designed to accept removable exterior panels of any material on the front and sides, which blends them into the decor. The refrigerator and freezer have separate doors and may be installed in separate places if desired (see Figure 3-11 and the left side of Figure 7-9).

Ranges

Old-fashioned stoves have been replaced by **drop-in** or **slide-in** units or they may be free-standing. Slide-in models can be converted to **free-standing** by addition of optional side panels and a backguard. Some ranges contain the cooking units, microwave, and/or oven in one appliance, or the oven and cooktop may be in two separate units, often in two separate locations in the kitchen. For ranges with cooking units and ovens see Figures 7-1, 7-3, and 7-7. For separate units see Figures 7-2, 7-8, and 7-9.

A free-standing range has finished sides and is usually slightly deeper than the 24 inch kitchen counter. This type of range may be considered if a change of residence will take place in the near future. The drop-in or slide-in units are designed for more permanent installation and are usually placed between two kitchen cabinets. The cooking medium may be either gas or electricity. Some ranges have the cooking surface flush with the counter, while others are lowered an inch or so. The only difference is that, if several large or wide pans are used at the same time, such as during canning or for large parties, the lowered surface is more restricting. The flush surface permits the overhanging of the larger pans.

ELECTRIC RANGES. In order to obtain the most efficiency, all cooking utensils used on an electric range must be flat bottomed to allow full contact with the cooking unit. There are three types of electrical elements: One is the conventional circular or coil element and the second is the smooth top or **glasstop.** The third is also a smooth top but the method of heating is induction which operates on the basis of electromagnetic induction.

This third method requires some elaboration. Because a magnet is involved in this method, magnetic cookware such as iron, iron with porcelain enamel, tri-ply, or cast iron must be used. When turned on, the surface units are activated by this magnetic attraction. The surface unit itself does not get hot. The only heat the glasstop may retain is absorbed from a hot pan.

Some cooktops are modular with interchangeable coil elements, smooth top, induction, **griddle, grill, shish kebab rotisserie,** wok, and wok-canning units (see Figure 7-4). Other electric cooktops such as Amana's Temp-Assume™ elements provide unmatched electric control. A simmer stays a simmer without scorching. Some ranges have units that adjust to the size of the pan.

Controls for ranges are usually at the back along with timer controls. On separate cooktops, controls are in the front or at the side of the cooktop.

Many 30 inch ranges now come with a second oven above the cooktop surface. This may be another **conventional oven** or a **microwave.** An exhaust fan is incorporated beneath some of the microwave ovens (see Figure 7-4).

Free-standing ranges vary from 21, 30, and 40 inches wide with slide-in ranges usually measuring 30 inches.

GAS RANGES. One advantage of using gas is that it is easier to moderate the temperature changes and the required temperature is reached more rapidly. Gas means an open flame which can cause a fire quicker than an electric element and also gas may discolor the bottom of the cooking pans especially those that are copper clad (see Figures 7-8 and 7-9).

Some of the gas cooktops and ovens have a pilotless ignition.

One of the trends of the 1980's seems to be the use of the multiburner commercial gas range with six or even eight burners. These ranges are free-standing and are very useful when catering for a large crowd.

Ovens

Electric ovens come in two types, self-cleaning, **(pyrolytic)** or continuous cleaning **(catalytic).** Self-cleaning ovens have a special cleaning setting that is activated by the timer for the required length of time. This cleaning cycle runs at an extremely high temperature and actually incinerates any oven spills, leaving an ash residue. One of the excellent byproducts of a self-cleaning oven is that, due to the high temperatures required to operate the cleaning cycle, the oven is more heavily insulated than is customary and, thus, when baking the oven retains the heat longer and uses less energy.

The continuous-cleaning oven features a special porous ceramic finish that disperses and partially absorbs food spatters to keep the oven presentably clean. Oven-cleaning products available at the grocery store may not be used on the continuous-cleaning surface.

Ovens cook by one of three methods: The first is the conventional radiant baking method that is used in most ovens. The second is by convection where streams of heated air flow round the food, resulting in less cooking time with more natural juiciness. The last method is microwave, which is treated separately.

Built-in ovens are required when using a separate cooktop. These may be single conventional oven units, or double oven units with one a conventional type and the other a microwave.

Electric ovens may have a solid door, porcelain enamel door with a window, or may have a full black glass window door. The porcelain enamel is available in many colors as well as white. A glass door may be seen in Figures 7-2, 7-4, 7-7, and 7-9.

Microwave Ovens

Today, most microwave ovens are operated by means of touch controls that electronically control the amount of energy from full power to a warming setting or defrost cycle. Some microwaves have rotating glass dishes to spread out the microwaves and avoid hot spots. Others such as the Amana microwave **convection oven** cook by microwave, convection, or a combination of the two, so you have the speed of a microwave with the browning of a convection oven.

Microwave ovens may be programmed to cook whole meals on a delayed time basis. Some even have recipes that are available at a touch. A temperature probe is another optional accessory. This probe turns off the microwave when the desired internal temperature is reached (see Figure 7-7).

Exhaust Fans

Exhaust fans are used above the cooking surface. They may be vented with a vertical or horizontal discharge or may be ductless. Vertical discharge takes up some of the space in the cabinet above the range. A horizontal discharge vents to the outside, which requires locating the range on an outside wall. Ductless hoods have a **charcoal filter** that filters out odors, and washable grease filters. Jenn-Air® manufactures a surface unit with a built-in charcoal filter exhaust fan that vents down to the outdoors, thereby eliminating an overhead hood.

Dishwashers

Usually, the dishwasher is built in adjacent to the sink so that the plumbing connections are easily made. Dishwashers discharge the dirty water through the sink containing the garbage disposal. For older style kitchens with no under counter space for a dishwasher, movable models are available that connect directly to the faucet in the sink and discharge directly into the sink.

Available features in dishwashers include a heavy-duty cycle for cleaning heavily soiled pots and pans, a regular cycle for normal soil, rinse and hold for a small number of dishes requiring rinsing, and low-energy wash cycles.

Dishes may be dried by the heated cycle or, for energy efficiency, a no-heat drying cycle may be programmed. Most dishwashers require little or no scraping of soiled dishes as a soft food disposer is built-in to newer models. Racks may be adjustable in some models, allowing for large size dishes. (Dishwashers may be seen adjacent to the sink in Figures 7-7 and 7-9.)

Kitchen Sinks

Kitchen sinks are constructed of stainless steel, enameled cast iron, or Corian®. Each material has its own pros and cons. Stainless steel sinks give a very contemporary look to a kitchen and are less likely to break dishes that are accidentally dropped into them. However, any water spots will leave a ring on the shiny surface. Also, heat from the hot water dissipates more rapidly with a metal sink than with a porcelain enamel one. When selecting a stainless steel sink, the lower the number of the gauge, the thicker the metal (see Figures 7-7, 7-8, and 7-9).

Porcelain enamel sinks do show stains more easily and a scouring powder is usually required to remove such stains. The porcelain may become chipped when hit with a heavy object. However, enameled cast iron sinks do provide a colorful touch in the kitchen.

Some kitchen sinks, such as the stainless steel ones and those designed to be used with a metal rim, are flush with the counter. Any water spilled on the counter may be swept back into the sink. However, the self-rimming type are raised above the surface of the counter and any water spilled on the counter must be mopped up. (See a self-rimming sink in Figure 7-4).

Kitchen sinks come bored with three holes standard or four holes for a spray or soap dispenser.

There are several options as to size and shape in selection of kitchen sinks. Both stainless steel and porcelain enamel sinks are available with one, two, or three bowls. Single compartment models should only be installed where there is minimum space. One bowl models do not provide a second disposal area if the bowl is in use. Two bowl models may be of the same size and depth or one bowl may be smaller and shallower.

In triple bowl sinks, one of the bowls is usually shallower and smaller than the other two and may contain the garbage disposal unit. The size of a kitchen sink varies between 25 and 43 inches wide.

Corian, when used as a material for kitchen sinks, may or may not be an integral part of the counter and is discussed on page 184 under Counters.

Eljer and American Olean have cooperated to produce Cerámica Coordinates, a line of sinks and ceramic tile that blend.

Kitchen Faucets

Faucets should be constructed of all chrome-plated steel. Faucets that appear to be all chrome-plated steel may, upon closer examination, have a chrome type plating over plastic and that surface will gradually peel off. A mixing type of valve, where hot and cold may be blended with one handle, enables one-handed operation which is useful when holding something in the other hand (see Figure 7-9). One problem is that the handle may be accidentally turned on when in the hot position and a burn can occur.

Moen makes a chrome plated solid brass faucet called the Riser™. Simply lift and the spout locks into

its high-rise position more than 10 inches above the top of the sink. This extra height is useful for filling tall buckets and tall vases, and washing hair. (See Figure 7-6.)

Another type of faucet with a higher spout than normal is the gooseneck. This type may be used for the kitchen sink, but is more frequently used in a bar sink. (See Figure 7-6 and note the chrome blade handles.)

There are several hot water dispensers on the market that provide very hot water (about 190°) for use in making hot drinks and instant soups.

Trash Compactors

Trash compactors reduce trash volume by 80 percent in less than one minute. Most have some form of odor control and use a compacting ram with the force of approximately 3,000 pounds. In today's society, where trash disposal has become a very expensive service, trash compactors do reduce the volume of trash considerably. Trash compactors vary in width from 12 to 18 inches wide.

FIGURE 7-6. Kitchen Faucets.
Chrome kitchen faucet with spray, gooseneck spout, aerator outlet, chrome blade handles, and escutcheons on 8 inch centers. The Decorative Series by Chicago Faucet. The Riser faucet from Moen provides extra convenience with its adjustable heights. (Photo courtesy of Moen Division, Stanadyne Corp.)

KITCHEN CABINETS

Kitchen cabinets come in 3 inch increments, usually starting at 15 inches wide, and may be as wide as 48 inches. The depth of lower cabinets is 24 inches and the depth of upper cabinets is 12 inches. Filler strips are used between individual cabinets to make up any difference in measurements. When double doors are used, the doors must have either an interlocking edge or a center stile to ensure a tight fitting door.

Kitchen cabinets may be made of steel or wood. St. Charles manufactures the best steel kitchen cabinets made in this country. The door and drawer fronts are of furniture grade steel using a **double-pan** construction. The result of this type of construction is a strong durable quiet door that cannot be matched by any other product for long life and also provides a quiet solid door unlike the flimsy utility cabinets found in bargain basements.

Steel cabinets are of flush overlay design and have semiconcealed pivot hinges. Doors open 180° and are held closed by specially designed built-in plastic catches that close quietly. Due to the structural strength of steel cabinets, no supportive mullion is required for cabinets up to 42 inches in width. This provides unobstructed access to the entire width of the cabinet. With steel drawers, the side and bottom are formed from one piece of steel, thus providing for easy cleaning.

The St. Charles steel cabinets are rust proofed with a process called Bonderizing. The coating is applied to the steel and the primer is then applied and subjected to high temperature baking which fuses the primer to the prepared steel to form an ideal base for

FIGURE 7-7.
St. Charles Tri-color steel chassis kitchen cabinets have Formica plastic laminate faces and Le Mans extruded pulls. The upper cabinets are coffee colored with terra cotta counter tops and almond bases. Appliances are from General Electric. (Photograph courtesy of St. Charles Manufacturing Company)

the succeeding finish coating. All components of each individual kitchen are finished at the same time to ensure uniformity.

St. Charles also manufactures other types of kitchen cabinets, including wood and plastic laminate. These materials are used for doors and drawer fronts and are attached to a steel frame. The wood doors are solid lumber core with a veneer cross banding of poplar wood. All wood exteriors are cut from large panels for vertical grain matching within individual cabinets. This makes the grain continuous from one drawer through the other doors and drawers below. Fronts are all overlay design.

Plastic laminate doors have a core of dense particleboard with decorative plastic laminate bonded under pressure to the front and back, resulting in a fully balanced construction (see Figures 7-7, 7-8, and 7-9).

Other kitchen cabinet manufacturers make their cabinets in all wood or wood with plastic laminate doors. Some use a high density particleboard for the case and shelves and the edges are banded with a wood veneer that matches the door and drawer fronts.

Wood cabinets may have flush overlay, reveal overlay or, for more traditional styles, an exposed frame with a lipped door. The face surface of the door may be plane, have a flat or raised panel, or have mouldings applied for a traditional approach. Contemporary kitchens have not only flush overlay doors, but flush overlay in combination with linear metal or wood decorative strips that also function as drawer and door pulls (see Figures 7-3, 7-4, and 7-7).

The award-winning kitchen by Stewart Skolnick shown in Figures 7-8 and 7-9 has high gloss Wilsonart® laminate for not only the face of the cabinets and countertops, but also the refrigerator, dishwasher, bookcase, and tabletop.

Shelves in all cabinets should be fully adjustable to accommodate the height and needs of the user.

There are many special features that may be ordered for the custom-designed kitchen. These will add to the cost of the installation but may be ordered to fit the personal and budgetary needs of the client.

Base sliding shelves make all items visible, which eliminates getting down on hands and knees to see what is at the bottom of a base unit. A bread box may be contained within a drawer with a lid to help maintain freshness. A cutting board, usually made of maple, that slides out from the upper part of a base unit is convenient and will help protect the surface of the counter from damage.

Lazy susans in corner units or doors with attached swing-out shelves both utilize the storage area of a corner unit. Another use for the corner unit is to install a 20 gallon hot water heater, thus providing instant hot water for the kitchen sink and the electric dishwasher. A second hot water heater can then be installed close to the bathrooms for energy conservation and to avoid those long waits for the hot water to reach the kitchen faucet.

Dividers in drawers aid in drawer organization and vertical dividers in upper or base units utilize space by arranging larger and flat items in easily visible slots, thus avoiding nesting.

Bottle storage units have frames to contain bottles. Spice storage may be attached to the back of an upper door or specially built into a double-door unit. Hot pads may be stored in a narrow drawer under a built-in cooktop.

Wire or plastic coated baskets for fruit and vegetable storage provide easily visible storage. A wastebasket, either attached to a swing-out door or slid out from under the sink, also provides a neat and out-of-sight trash container.

COUNTER MATERIALS

Counters may be of the following materials: plastic laminate, wood, ceramic tile, marble, travertine, Corian, stainless steel, granite, or slate.

Plastic Laminate

Plastic laminate is the most commonly used counter material. The construction is exactly the same as the material used for walls. For countertop use, two thicknesses are available; a choice of one or the other depends on the type of counter construction. For square-edged counters, the general purpose grade is used but, if it is necessary to roll the laminate on a simple radius over the edges of the substrate, a postforming type is specified. The postforming method eliminates a seam at the edge of the counter.

Wilsonart makes a laminate for postforming installations with a simulated oak edge that gives a customized look without the expense of real wood. Also available is a striped edge in a contrasting color from the main countertop. The postforming type may be installed with a **waterfall** edge or a **no-drip** edge which is similar to the waterfall but with a slightly raised front lip. Wilsonart also has a postforming solid color plastic laminate called SOLICOR®.

INSTALLATION. Postformed countertops must be constructed at the plant rather than at the job site as heat and special forming fixtures are used to create the curved edge. The counter may be manufactured as a single unit or each postformed side may be manufactured separately. By manufacturing each side separately, any discrepancy in the alignment of the walls can be adjusted at the corner joints.

Self-edged counters may be constructed on the job site in the following manner: A particle board, plywood, or flakeboard substrate is cut to cover the countertop area. An equal thickness strip is glued to the underside of the front edge of the counter top to build up the counter thickness. Narrow strips of laminate are then cut slightly wider than the edge. An adhesive (contact cement) is spread on both the counter edge and the back of the strips and allowed to dry according to instructions on the adhesive container. The strips are then carefully positioned so that the lower edge is flush with the bottom and the top edge extends slightly above the edge of the counter. As bonding is immediate, it is important that the two surfaces do not touch until properly aligned. A router

is then used to cut away the excess laminate. The color of the laminate may be the same as the top surface as shown in Figures 7-7, 7-8, and 7-9, or contrasting.

As the flat surface of the counter is very large, a slightly different method of application is used. The counter area and the back of the laminate are covered with the recommended adhesive. When the adhesive is dry, dowels are placed on top of the counter area, and the laminate is carefully positioned on top of the dowels. When properly placed with the front edge extending over the previously installed edge, the dowels are carefully removed and the counter and laminate become bonded. A secure bond is established by applying firm pressure with roller or hard wood blocks and hammer. The excess at the front is then trimmed with the router.

A plastic laminate surface is durable but is neither a cutting surface nor a heatproof one. The surface will also chip if heavy objects are dropped onto it.

For areas where chemical spills or other destructive or staining substances may be used, a chemical and stain resistant laminate may be specified. Specific

FIGURE 7-8.
This kitchen was a first prize winner in the 1983 A.S.I.D./Wilsonart Design competition in the existing application category. This renovation/addition of a kitchen-breakfast area in a turn-of-the-century mansion shows a 4 feet wide by 18 feet long curved work island. The risers on the stairs in the background are covered in a laminate and the lowered ceiling soffit is also covered in laminate. (Designer: Stewart R. Skolnick of Stewart R. Skolnick & Associates; photograph: *Rick Barnes)*

FIGURE 7-9.
A view of the kitchen in Figure 7-8 taken from the other end of the work island, showing the glass block wall on the right. Custom designed cabinetry has recessed drawer and door pulls that do not interrupt the smooth surface of the high-gloss laminate. (Designer: Stewart R. Skolnick of Stewart R. Skolnick & Associates; photograph: Rick Barnes)

uses are chemistry laboratory tops, photographic lab tops, medical and pathology labs, and clinics.

For high use and heavy wear areas such as fast food countertops, supermarket checkout stands, or bank service areas a .125 inch thickness of plastic laminate is available.

MAINTENANCE. Plastic laminate may be cleaned with warm water and mild dish soaps. Use of abrasives or "special" cleansers should be avoided because they may contain abrasives, acids, or alkalines. Stubborn stains may be removed with organic solvents or two minutes' exposure to a hypochlorite bleach such as Clorox followed by a clean water rinse. Consult laminate manufacturers for specific instructions and recommendations.

Wood

Wood counters are usually made of a hardwood such as birch or maple and are constructed of glued up strips of wood that are then usually sealed and coated with a varnish. Unsealed wood will permanently absorb stains. Wood counters should not be used as a cutting surface as the finish will become marred. Any water accumulating around the sink should be mopped up immediately as the surface can become damaged from prolonged contact with moisture (see Figure 3-11).

Wood counters may be installed in a curved shape by successively adding a bent strip of wood, gluing, and clamping it. When dry, another piece is added.

Ceramic Tile

Ceramic tile has become a very popular material with which to cover kitchen counters. To facilitate cleaning, the **backsplash** may also be covered with tile. Ceramic tile is a very durable surface, but the most vulnerable part is the grout which will absorb stains. A grout sealer or lemon furniture oil will seal the surface of the grout so that stains will not penetrate. Due to the hard surface of the tile, fragile items that are dropped on the counter will break and, if heavy objects are dropped, the tile may be broken or cracked. Always order sufficient tile for replacements. (See Figures 2-3 and 7-4 for ceramic tile counters. Figure 7-2 shows a ceramic tile counter with a wood edge.)

INSTALLATION. When installing a ceramic tile counter, it is recommended that an exterior grade plywood be used as the substrate. The remaining installation procedure is the same as for floors and walls.

MAINTENANCE. Same as for ceramic tile floors.

Marble

In the past, marble was used as a material for portions of the countertop but today, in some expensive installations, marble may be used for the whole counter area. Some people like to use a marble surface for the rolling out of pastry or the making of hand dipped chocolates. As was seen in the marble floor section, marble may absorb stains resulting in unsightly blemishes on the counter. Heavy items dropped on a marble surface will crack it.

MAINTENANCE. Stain removal is the same as for marble floors.

Travertine

When travertine is used as a counter material, it must be filled. Maintenance is the same as for marble.

Corian

This man-made material from DuPont is similar in appearance to marble with the color and pattern clear through, yet is tougher and more stain resistant. There are many imitation marbles on the market, but the quality of Corian is far superior. Corian is available in 1/4, 1/2, and 3/4 inch thicknesses in a variety of lengths. Also available is a kitchen counter top with integral cast-in single or double bowl sinks, designed to accept standard food disposers and faucets (see Figure 7-10). Corian in a bathroom setting is shown in Figure 8-2.

The edge of Corian may be shaped like wood. Figure 7-11 shows some of the many ways in which the edge of a Corian counter may be finished.

MAINTENANCE. Most stains just wipe right off with household detergent and water. Even abrasive household cleansers may be used for stubborn stains due to the solid composition of Corian. Corian, like other counter materials, is not made to be used as a cutting board but, should any cuts occur, fine sandpaper may be used to repair the damage. This fine sanding should be followed by rubbing with a Scotch-Brite® pad using

FIGURE 7-10.
This Du Pont Corian® integral countertop with durable sink eliminates hard-to-clean crevices that catch dirt. (Photograph courtesy of E. I. DuPont de Nemours & Company)

a gentle circular motion to blend repaired area to surrounding gloss. Paint remover, paint brush cleaners, acid drain cleaners, and certain brands of nail polish and nail polish removers may harm Corian.

Stainless Steel

All commercial kitchens have stainless steel counters because they can withstand scouring, boiling water, and hot pans. Stainless steel counters can be installed in private residences, if desired, providing a high-tech look.

MAINTENANCE. One of the problems with stainless steel is that the surface shows water spots and may scratch. However, scratches gradually blend into a patina and water spots may be removed by rubbing the damp surface with a towel. Apart from the spots and possible scratches, stainless steel is extremely easy to maintain.

Granite and Slate

Both these stones may be used as counter materials if desired, although construction of the cabinets must be strong enough to support the extra weight. As was mentioned in the floor chapter, these stones vary in porosity and care should be taken to prevent stains from penetrating the surface.

MAINTENANCE. The same as for granite walls and slate floors.

FLOORS

Kitchen floors may be ceramic tile, quarry tile, wood, or any of the resilient floorings. The choice of flooring will depend on the client's needs and personal wishes. Some people find a hard-surfaced floor to be tough on the feet, while others are not bothered at all. Ceramic tile on the floor is shown in Figures 7-1, 7-2, 7-3, 7-4, 7-8, and 7-9. Wood floors need to be finished with a very durable finish that will withstand any moisture which may be accidentally spilled. Resilient flooring may be vinyl, cushioned or not, or some of the new rubber sheet flooring currently on the market.

WALLS

Walls should be painted with an enamel that is easily cleansed of any grease residue. The backsplash may be covered with the same plastic laminate used on the counter, either with a cove or a square joint (see Figure 7-7). Ceramic tile may be used in conjunction with a ceramic tile counter (see Figures 7-1, 7-2, 7-3)

BULL NOSE EDGE

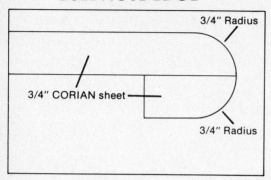

CORIAN® WITH WOOD STRIP INSERT

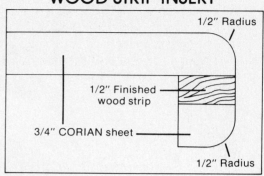

ROUTED TOP WITH WOOD EDGE

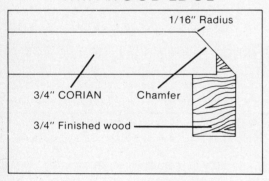

CORIAN® TOP WITH WOOD APRON

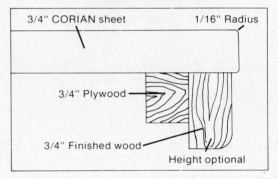

CORIAN® TOP WITH APRON AND BOTTOM TRIM

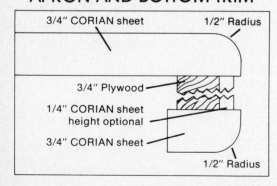

CORIAN® WITH ACRYLIC INSERT

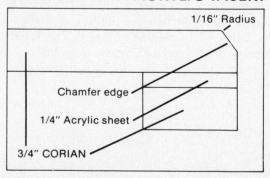

FIGURE 7-11. Edge Treatments for Corian® Countertops.

(Photograph courtesy of E.I. DuPont de Nemours & Company)

or it may be used with a plastic laminate. Mirror may also be selected for walls as shown in Figure 7-4. In this figure also, mirror was used as a base for the cabinets. This, of course, provides reflected light and visually enlarges the appearance of the floor and counter space. A completely scrubbable wallcovering may also be used for the backsplash.

CERTIFIED KITCHEN DESIGNERS

A *certified kitchen designer* **(CKD)** is a professional who has proved knowledge and technical understanding through a very stringent examination process conducted by the Society of Certified Kitchen Designers, the licensing and certification agency of the American Institute of Kitchen Dealers. A CKD has technical knowledge of construction techniques and systems regarding new construction and light exterior and interior remodeling which includes plumbing, heating, and electrical.

A CKD will provide a functional and aesthetically pleasing arrangement of space with floor plans and interpretive renderings and drawings. In addition to designing and planning the kitchen, the CKD also supervises the installations of residential-style kitchens.

An interior designer would be well advised to work with a CKD who will not only aid in the design but also the installation details.

Bibliography

Harrison, Molly. *The Kitchen in History.* New York: Charles Scribner's Sons, 1972.

Time-Life Books. *Kitchens and Bathrooms.* Alexandria VA: Time-Life Books, 1977.

Glossary

Backsplash. The wall area between the top of the base cabinet and the base of the upper unit.

Catalytic. A porous ceramic finish that accelerates the dispersion of food splatters.

Charcoal filter. A frame that contains charcoal particles that filter the grease from the moving air.

Convection oven. Heated air flows around the food.

Conventional oven. Food is cooked by radiation.

Corridor kitchen. Two parallel walls with no contiguous area.

Dolly. A 2- or 4-wheel cart used for moving heavy appliances.

Double-pan. Shaping and bending of the steel to provide a strong frame.

Drop-in range. Ranges designed to be built in to the base units.

Free-standing range. Ranges having finished sides.

Glasstop. A smooth ceramic top used as a cooking surface in electric ranges.

Griddle. A unit with a flat cooking surface used for cooking pancakes.

Grill. A unit specially for broiling food.

Kilowatthour. A unit of energy equal to 1,000 watt hours. Abbreviation: kwh.

Microwave oven. Heat is generated by the activation of the molecules within the food by the microwaves.

No-drip counter edge. The front two inches of the counter are raised above the level of the rest of the counter.

Pullman kitchen. A one-wall kitchen plan (see Figure 7-5).

Pyrolytic action. An oven that cleans by extremely high heat, incinerating any residue to an ash.

Rotisserie. An electrical accessory that rotates the food on a spit or skewer.

Shish Kebab. A rotisserie accessory combining alternate small pieces of meat and vegetables on a skewer or spit.

Slide-in range. Similar in construction to a drop-in range except that the top edges may overhang the sides and, therefore, this type must be slid in rather than dropped in.

Strip kitchen. One-wall kitchen plan (see Figure 7-5).

Studio kitchen. Also a one-wall kitchen plan (see Figure 7-5).

Waterfall. A rounded front edge to the countertop.

Work triangle. An imaginary triangle drawn between the sink, refrigerator, and cooking area.

8

BATHROOMS

CONTENTS

The Greeks had many large public baths where one could take a hot and cold bath and then get a rubdown with olive oil. Public bathing was also practiced by the Romans. The Romans used aqueducts to bring the water to the people of Rome. After the influence of the Romans was lost, very few people bathed in the Dark Ages. In the 1800's and early 1900's one often reads of the ritual of the Saturday night bath, where a metal tub was brought into the heated kitchen and hot water was poured in by hand. The last 25 years have produced almost 90 percent of all the progress in bathrooms.

It was the American hotels that started the idea of bathing rooms and the first one was built at the Tremont House in Boston in 1829. The idea proved very popular and spread to other hotels and private homes throughout the country. As a nation, Americans take more baths and showers than any other people in the world. The realities of the 1980's, however, include both energy and water conservation.

As all bathrooms have the same three basic fixtures, it is the designer's challenge to create a bathroom that is not only unique but functional. A knowledge of the different materials used in these fixtures and the variety of shapes, sizes, and colors will help meet this challenge.

PLANNING A BATHROOM

Eljer has the following suggestions for planning a better bathroom. First, the size of the family needs to be considered. The more people who will use a bathroom, the larger it should be. There should also be more storage, more electrical outlets and, perhaps, more fixtures. If the bathroom is to be used by several people at the same time, compartmenting can often add to utility.

The family schedule should also be considered. Where several people depart for work or school at the same time, multiple or **compartmented** bathrooms should be considered. Two **lavatories** will allow a working couple to get ready for work at the same time.

The most economical arrangement of fixtures is against a single **wet wall**. Economy, however, is not the only factor to be considered. Plumbing codes, human comfort, and convenient use require certain minimum separation between, and space around, fixtures. The minimum size for a bathroom is approximately 5 by 7 feet, although, if absolutely necessary, a few inches may be shaved off these measurements. Deluxe bathrooms may be very large and incorporate an exercise room and/or **spa.**

In a corridor-type bathroom, there should be 30 inches of aisle space between the bathtub and the edge of the counter or fixture opposite. The bathtub should never be placed under the window as this will create too many problems—lack of privacy, drafts, condensation on the window, and possible damage to the wall when using a shower.

There should be a minimum of 24 inches in front of a toilet to provide knee room. When there are walls on either side of the toilet, they should be 36 inches apart. If the lavatory or bathtub is adjacent to the toilet, then 30 inches is sufficient.

The lavatory requires elbow space. Five feet is the recommended minimum length of a countertop with two lavatories. The lavatories should be centered in the respective halves of the counter top. For a sit-down **vanity,** make the counter 7 feet long and allow 24 inches between the edges of the lavatories for greatest comfort. Six inches minimum should be allowed between the edge of a lavatory and any side wall.

All bathroom fixtures, whether tubs, lavatories, toilets, or **bidets,** come in white and pastels, with some manufacturers offering darker colors—even black. Generally, only lavatories are offered in bright accent colors. Care should be taken not to select the "fad" colors as they will become dated and bathroom fixtures are both difficult and expensive to replace when

FIGURE 8-1.
The popular concept of the master bedroom suite is carried to the ultimate in this bathroom design. Separated from the bedroom beyond by custom etched smoked-glass panels, the bathroom is an integral part of the suite's design. (Photograph courtesy of Eljer Plumbingware)

remodeling. Colored fixtures cost slightly more than white. In order to obtain a perfect match, all fixtures should be ordered from the same manufacturer as colors, even white, vary from one manufacturer to another.

The location of the door is extremely important. The door should be located in such a manner that it will not hit a fixture or anyone already in the bathroom, because it can eventually cause damage both to the door and the fixture. A sliding pocket door may have to be used to prevent this from happening. A bathroom door should *never* be placed at the end of a hall where the fixtures may be visible.

Floors

Bathroom floors should be of a type that can be easily cleaned, particularly in the area of the bathtub, shower, and toilet. Ceramic tile may be used but should not be highly glazed as this type, when used on a floor, can be very slippery when wet. Other types of flooring material for the tub area can be wood with a good finish or any of the resilient flooring materials.

Carpeting may be used in the master bath, but it is not suggested for a family bath because of a like-

lihood of excessive moisture, causing possible mold and mildew.

Walls

The bathroom is an area in the house where wallcoverings are often used. Vinyls or vinyl-coated wallcoverings are suggested because they are easy to wipe dry and maintain. Again, due to the moisture mentioned above, the walls should be treated for possible mildew (see Chapter 3, page 83).

Only semigloss paints or enamels that can withstand moisture should be used on bathroom walls.

If an acrylic shower and tub surround is not used, ceramic tile is installed because of its vitreous quality.

Bathtubs

The average bathtub is 5 feet long, 30 inches wide and, in less expensive styles, only 14 inches deep. However, 6 foot long tubs are available for those who like to soak and the height, measured from the floor, may also be 15, 16, or even 22 inches. When bathing children, the lower height is more convenient. However, the depth figures are the outside measurements and, making allowance for the **overflow** pipe, the 14 inches does not permit the drawing of a very deep bath. Many state laws require that all bathtubs installed today have a **slip resistant** bottom. Many tubs also come with a handle on one or both sides, which is extremely useful for the elderly or infirm. (See Figure 8-1.)

The straight end of the bathtub contains the drain and the plumbing, such as faucets or **fittings** as they are sometimes called, and the overflow pipe; therefore, location of the bathtub must be decided before the order is placed. Bathtubs may be ordered with left or right drain, all four sides enclosed, enclosed on the front and two sides, front and one side, or for a completely built-in look, a drop-in model may be specified.

The drop-in model is sometimes installed as a sunken tub and, while this may present a luxurious appearance, thought must be given to the problem of getting into and out of a tub that is low. Thought must also be given to maintenance. Cleaning a sunken tub means lying flat on the floor to reach the interior. Another danger of a sunken or partially recessed tub is that small children may crawl into the bathtub and hurt themselves or, at the worst, drown.

CONSTRUCTION. Bathtubs are manufactured of several materials. The old standby is the porcelain enameled cast-iron tub. This was originally a high-sided bathtub raised from the floor on ball-and-claw feet with the underside exposed. This style is still available today in a slightly modernized version. The porcelain enamel is approximately 1/16 of an inch thick, but this finish can be chipped if a heavy object is dropped onto it. Therefore, bathtubs should be kept covered with a blanket or a special plastic liner may be used until construction has been completed.

A cast-iron bathtub is the most durable bathtub available but it is expensive and heavy, about 500 pounds. Therefore, the floor should be constructed strongly enough to bear the combined weight of the tub, a tub full of water, and the bather.

Formed steel tubs with a porcelain enamel finish were developed to provide a lightweight (about 100 pounds) tub that would be less expensive than cast iron. They are ideally suited for upper story installations or for remodeling because they are easier to move into place. A formed steel tub is noisier than the cast-iron, but a sound-deadening coating may be applied to the underside at extra cost. Or, if the bathtub does not come with an insulated coating on the outside, a roll of fiberglass insulation can be wrapped around the tub which not only helps the fixture retain the heat longer, but also helps reduce the noise of a steel tub. Due to the properties of the steel, formed steel bathtubs may flex and, therefore, they do not have such a thick layer of porcelain enamel as do cast-iron tubs.

One of the newer materials for bathtubs is heavy-duty polyester reinforced with fiberglass and surfaced with a **gel** coat. In specifying this type of tub, it is important to select a name brand. As there are currently many poor quality units on the market produced by a process that does not require a large investment, this field has many manufacturers, not all of whom are conscious of quality. Consequently, the tubs can crack easily and lose their surface fairly rapidly. Good maintenance practices and avoidance of abrasive cleansers is mandatory. Should the gel coat surface become dull in appearance, some manufacturers suggest using a coat of marine wax or a good automotive wax to restore the shine.

Another type of lightweight bathtub is acrylic reinforced with fiberglass with the color throughout. This type of bathtub does not have such a high gloss as the gel coated ones but, on the other hand, are easier to maintain and the color does not fade.

There are several advantages to this new material. First, it is much lighter weight than steel or cast iron, but not as durable. Second, the tub **surround** can be cast as an integral part of the bathtub and can include such features as a built-in seat, soap ledges, and grab bars. This latter type can be installed only in new construction as the tub and surround are too large to be placed in a remodeled bathroom. For remodeling, there are molded tub units with wall surrounds in two, three, or four pieces that pass easily through doorways and join together in the recessed bathtub area to form a one-piece unit.

Soaking tubs are also made from reinforced fiberglass. Instead of sitting or lying in the tub, one sits on a molded, built-in seat and the tub is filled to the requisite depth. Some soaking tubs are recessed into the floor and one steps over the edge and down into the tub; others are placed at floor level and require several steps to reach the top. Soaking tubs should not be installed in every bathroom in the house, as bathing small children is impossible and the elderly or infirm will find entering and leaving a soaking tub too dangerous. A regular bathtub should be installed in at least one bathroom in the house.

Whirlpool baths are generally bathroom fixtures; they must be drained after each use. Jacuzzi® Whirlpool Bath has a high gloss acrylic, fiberglass reinforced whirlpool bathtub with built-in patented jets.

FIGURE 8-2.
Easy-clean, Corian® on tub facing, decking, and molded vanity complement the clean lines of the chrome and mirrored surfaces. (Photograph courtesy of E.I. DuPont de Nemours & Company)

(See Figure 8-3.) These whirlpool jets create a circular pattern of bubbles as the air/water mixture flows into the tub, providing luxurious, deeply penetrating massage. Jacuzzi Whirlpool Baths come in one-person sizes (60 to 72 inches long by 29 1/2 to 42 inches wide, and 18 to 20 inches high) and two-person or family sizes (61 1/2 to 72 inches long by 48 to 66 inches wide by 20 to 23 1/2 inches high). Most major manufacturers produce similar whirlpool-type tubs.

Spas are similar to whirlpool baths but need not be drained after each use. They are equipped with heat and filtration systems. Since the same water is recirculated, daily testing and maintenance of the proper water chemistry is required. Spas may be installed outside in warmer climates or in an area other than the bathroom. They have the same features of the whirlpool baths but are larger, being 64 to 84 inches long by 66 to 84 inches wide and 28 to 37 inches

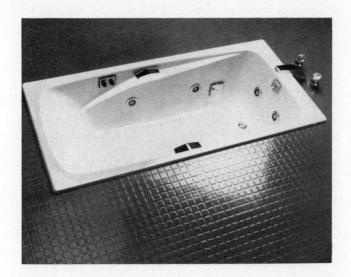

FIGURE 8-3.
A Jacuzzi® Whirlpool Bath from the imported Lumière Collection features a double contour backrest, angled armrests, slip-resistant bottom, and convenient grip handles. It is made of enameled cast-iron in lengths of 5 and 6 feet. (Photograph courtesy of Jacuzzi Whirlpool Bath)

high. Spas come with factory installed redwood skirts and rigid covers.

Tub surrounds and shower enclosures may also be of reinforced fiberglass, as mentioned previously, or they may be of plastic laminate, ceramic tile, solid ABS, or solid acrylic. Many of these have integrated tubs with built-in whirlpool systems. The all-in-one type eliminates the need to caulk around the area where the tub and surround meet. Failure to install and caulk the tub surround properly is the major cause of leaks in the tub area. When designing a bathroom, the bathtub should be placed where an access panel can be installed to facilitate future plumbing repairs. Access must also be provided to the whirlpool equipment to facilitate future maintenance.

Ceramic tile is installed as described in the chapter on walls. The substrate must be exterior grade plywood or a special water-resistant grade of gypsum board. The backer board mentioned in Chapter 2 also makes a suitable substrate. Particular attention must be paid to the application of the grout, as it is the grout that makes ceramic tile a waterproof material. Sometimes, particularly when a cast-iron tub is used, the extra weight may cause a slight sagging of the floor and any space caused by this settling should be filled immediately.

Showers

Showers may be installed for use in a bathtub or they may be in a separate shower stall. There should always be at least one bathtub in a house, but stall showers may be used in remaining bathrooms. When used in conjunction with a bathtub, the tub spout contains a **diverter** that closes off the spout and diverts the water to the shower head. A bathroom with a shower instead of a tub is designated as a three-quarter bath.

The standard height of a shower head is 66 inches for men and 60 inches for women, which puts the spray below the hairline. These measurements also mean that the plumbing for the shower head must break through the tub or shower surround. Therefore, it is recommended that the shower **feed-in** be 74 inches above the floor. When placed at this height, the shower head should be adjustable so that it can be used for hairwashing or hit below the hairline.

A hand-held shower can easily be installed in any bathtub, provided the walls are covered with a waterproof material. These showers come with a special diversion spout and the water reaches the shower head by means of a flexible metal line. One type of shower head is hung on a hook at the required height. The second type is mounted on a 5 foot vertical rod and attached to the water outlet by means of a flexible hose. This full range sliding spray holder or grab bar locks at any desired height. The spray holder is both adjustable and removable. There are several positive attributes of the hand-held shower. One is that it can be hung at a lower level for use by children, and the hand-held unit can be used to rinse the hair of young children without the complaint of "the soap is getting in my eyes." A second factor is that the hand unit may be used to more easily clean and rinse the interior of the bathtub.

Stall showers are 34 by 32 inches wide or a slightly larger 36 inch square is recommended if space is available. These are the minimum requirements and, of course, the deluxe shower may be 48 inches or even 60 by 32 inches wide and usually has a seat. Stall showers may be constructed entirely of ceramic tile; in other words, the slightly sloping base and walls are all made of tile. When installing a shower area made from ceramic tile, particular attention should be paid to the waterproof base and installation procedures supplied by the manufacturer or the Tile Council of America. Other stall showers have a **preformed base** with the surround touching the top of the 5 to 6 inch deep base. This preformed base is less slippery than a base of tile but not quite as aesthetically pleasing. Shower walls may be constructed of Corian (see Figure 8-2).

The water is kept within the shower area by several means. One is the shower curtain which is hung from rings at the front of the shower. A shower curtain is a decorative feature but, unless care is taken to ensure the placement of the shower curtain inside the base when using the shower, water may spill over onto the floor and cause a slippery area. Glass shower doors are also used, the type depending upon the local building codes (see Figure 8-2). All have tempered glass, but some codes require the addition of a wire mesh. These glass doors may pivot, hinge, slide, or fold. The major maintenance problem with glass doors is removing the soap and hard water residue from the glass surface and cleaning the water channel at the base of the door.

Some bathtub/shower units are designed with close fitting doors that completely enclose the front of the unit and become steam systems with the **sauna** effect.

Kohler produces a Masterbath Series, personal and programmable retreats that combine the soothing elements of sun, sauna, steam, shower, and warm breezes with the added relaxation of a spacious whirlpool bath. The overall size of the unit measures 91 by 52 by 82 inches with the whirlpool bath measuring 66 by 19 1/2 by 33 inches. The luxury Environment™ features an upholstered deck, 24-carat gold trim, and genuine teakwood interior—the ultimate in sybaritic pleasure. The Habitat™ Masterbath has the same functional features as the Environment Masterbath, but the interior is acrylic instead of teak, has chrome interior trim, and comes in 16 Kohler colors. The padded deck is optional.

Tub and Shower Faucets

The old-fashioned type of faucet is ledge mounted, where the fitting is mounted on the edge of the tub or tub enclosure, usually with an 8 to 18 inch **spread.**

Tub/shower combinations may be of five different types. Two of them are wall mounted, including the single control which is operated by pulling to turn on, pushing to turn off, and twisting to regulate the temperature. The single control may be operated with one hand. The other wall mounted type has separate handles for hot and cold water. An 8 inch spread is standard.

Diverters include the diverter-on-spout where, when the water temperature is balanced, the diverter is pulled up to start the shower. To stop the flow of water to the shower head, the diverter is pushed down. The handle diverter design has three handles and, by twisting the middle handle, the water is diverted to the shower head. The two other handles control the hot and cold water. This handle diverter has 8 inch **centers.** The button diverter is often found on single control faucets where, by merely pushing the button, water is diverted.

For stall showers, the controls may be single control similar in action to the single control bath type. The second design has two separate hot and cold handles with a standard 8 inch spread.

Most shower heads are adjustable and change the flow of water to drenching, normal, or fine spray. Some shower heads have a pulsating flow that provides a massaging action.

Water-saving shower heads limit the flow of water to a maximum of three gallons per minute while still delivering drenching, satisfying showers. Conventional shower heads use from 6 to 8 gallons per minute.

Lavatories

Lavatories come in many sizes and shapes, according to personal and space requirements. Some are **pedestal** lavatories and may be as streamlined or decorative as desired (see Figures 8-1 and 8-4). Most are made of vitreous china, but some pedestals are even sculpted out of marble. Besides being made out of china, lavatories may be made from enameled cast iron, enameled formed steel, or Corian.

Lavatories are usually round or oval but may also be rectangular, or even triangular, for corner installations. Sizes range from 11 by 11 inches for powder rooms, to 38 by 28 inches for hairwashing and other washing chores.

The pedestal lavatories are the latest style of lavatory to be used, but are probably more suitable in a

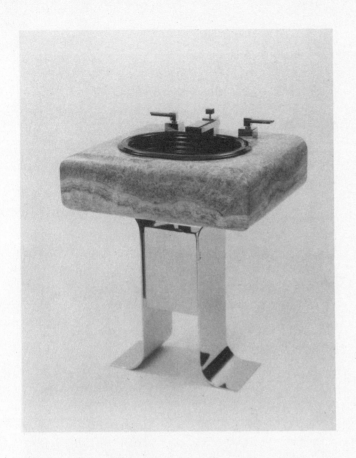

FIGURE 8-4.
This magnificent onyx lavatory, hand-carved from a solid block of stone, rests on a curved stainless steel pedestal that artfully conceals the plumbing. A ridged gleaming black porcelain washbasin points up the natural tones of the onyx whose gently rounded corners subtly enhance this architecturally inspired design. (Photograph courtesy of Sherle Wagner International, Inc.)

master bathroom because they lack an adjacent counter area, which is needed in family bathrooms. To overcome this lack, some pedestal lavatories come as large as 44 by 22 inches, with a wide ledge surrounding the bowl area.

Built-in lavatories may be one of six types. First, they may be self-rimming, where a hole is cut into the counter smaller than the size of the lavatory and the bowl is placed in such a manner that the edge is raised above the level of the counter. With a self-rimming sink, water cannot be swept back into the bowl but must be mopped up.

Second, for a flush counter and bowl installation, the lavatory may be installed with a flush metal rim. This is a popular and inexpensive style but does cause a cleaning problem at the junctures of the rim with the countertop and the lavatory.

Third is the integral bowl and counter such as those made of Corian. With this type, there is no joint between counter and bowl.

A fourth type is the more old-fashioned wall-hung installation that is quite often used in powder rooms. The fifth type is installed under the counter and is generally used with a tile, marble, or synthetic counter top. This type does require more maintenance to clean the area immediately below the edge of the counter. Under-the-counter installations require that the fittings be mounted through the countertop (see Figure 8-6).

The sixth type is grouted flush with the ceramic tile counter and is produced by cooperation of Eljer Plumbingware and American Olean Tile Company.

A specialty item in the way of a lavatory is the solid brass self-rimming bowl, which adds a special elegant look to a bathroom. For a unique lavatory, a self-rimming painted ceramic washbasin may be used.

All lavatories come punched with at least three holes. With single control fittings and 4 inch centerset fittings, the third hole is for the **pop-up** rod. However, in wide-spread fittings, the third hole is used for the mixed water.

Some lavatories are punched with one or two extra holes. These are for use as a shampoo lavatory and have a retractable spray unit. The second extra hole is used for a soap or shampoo dispenser. These shampoo lavatories are extremely useful for a family with children as the bowl is usually installed in a 32 inch high **vanity** as compared to 36 inches with a kitchen **sink**. Some styles even have spouts that swing away.

FIGURE 8-5.
This bathroom, designed for a restoration project, retains the old-fashioned feeling by using the traditional octagonal and square ceramic tile pattern on the floor. The remainder of the bathroom has been updated by use of dual self-rimming sinks with a ceramic tile counter on the left, and by the use of a large whirlpool bath and striped wallcovering. The ceiling was painted in a dark gloss paint to aid in maintenance and reduce the apparent height of the ceiling. The color is also repeated in the other design accents. (Architect: *John E. Pace, A.I.A.;* interior designer: *Bert Vieta;* photograph: *Richard Springgate)*

FIGURE 8-6.
This luxury hotel bath utilizes a heavily patterned marble on floors, walls, and counter top. Here the lavatory is set below the marble top and the faucets are mounted on the ledge. A large soaking tub with dual sets of fittings completes the look of luxury. Note Roman faucets on the bathtub. (Photograph: *Richard Springgate)*

FIGURE 8-7.
This marble bathroom is very different in appearance from the bathroom in Figure 8-6. Marble has been used throughout the bathroom of this custom designed home. The marble squares on the floor are laid with a parallel pattern. Large vertical panels were custom sized for the tub surround. (Buehner Concrete & Marble Co; designer: R.E. Dansie; photograph: Richard Springgate)

FIGURE 8-8.
A field of poppies in vivid natural colors adorns this handpainted ceramic washbasin with overlapping rim. The coordinated faucet set has porcelain levers and is also available in 24-carat gold-plate or a variety of other finishes. (Photograph courtesy of Sherle Wagner International, Inc.)

Lavatory Faucets

There is also a wide choice of lavatory faucets. For the past few decades, **center-fit** faucet fittings have been used. With this unit, the two handles and spout are in one piece, with the spread being 4 inches. The single control unit with a 4 inch spread has a central control that regulates both temperature and rate of flow (see Figure 8-9). This single control unit may also work by means of a lever which, when pulled up, increases the flow of water and, when pushed down, decreases the flow. Temperature is controlled by moving the lever to the right for cold and to the left for warmer or hot water. The lever is easier to operate for arthritis victims who cannot grasp and turn the knob type. Regaining popularity is the idea of the spread-fit fittings that have the hot and cold handles and the spout independent of each other. In order to make installation and choice of faucet sets easier, the fittings should be joined by means of flexible connectors. If these flexible connectors are not used, your selection of faucets may be limited to the spread of the holes that come in the selected lavatory. When the center-fit fittings are used, the plate covers the center hole. But, when a spread-fit fitting is used, the center hole accommodates the spout.

Faucets may be chrome or gold plated, and have chrome plated, translucent, or a combination of translucent and metal handles. Translucent and metal handles have slight indentations in order to provide a nonslipping surface. Other handles may be of the lever type (see Figure 8-8 for porcelain levers). The traditional shape for spouts is being replaced by the more delicately curved shape which is popular in Europe.

For use by the handicapped are the **wrist control** handles that do not require turning or pulling but are activated by a push or pull with the wrist rather than the fingers.

Toilets

In Europe the toilet is often called the *water closet* and the plumbing trade frequently uses the term *water closet* or *closet* when referring to what the layman calls a toilet. In some areas of the country, it may also be referred to as a commode. We will use the word "toilet" in the text as this is the more common word but, when talking to a plumber, "closet" is more correct.

Toilet bowls are constructed of vitreous china and, in most instances, so are the tanks. However, some tanks may be made of other materials. Only vitreous china can withstand the acids to which a toilet is subjected. Most toilets are designed with water saving devices that are important considerations, both economically and environmentally.

There are two basic shapes to a toilet: the regular or round-bowl and the elongated bowl. Toilets do not come with a toilet seat and, therefore, it is important to know the shape of the toilet before ordering a seat. Another design feature of the elongated bowl is that more space, usually 2 inches, is required for installation. Consult your local building codes.

Toilets may be wall hung, which leaves the floor unobstructed for easy cleaning, or floor mounted. Wall-hung toilets have a wall outlet; in other words, they flush through a drain in the wall. In order to support the weight of a wall-hung toilet, 6 inch studs must be used and an L-shaped unit called a *chair carrier* must be installed.

Floor-mounted toilets flush either through the floor or wall. For concrete floor construction, wall outlets are suggested to eliminate the extra cost of slab piercing.

Another choice in the design of toilets is whether the tank and bowl should be a **low profile,** one-piece integral unit, or whether the tank and bowl should be in two pieces (see Figure 8-1 for an elongated bowl). For space saving in powder rooms or bathrooms, a corner toilet, an Eljer exclusive, is available. The nostalgia of the past can be created by using an overhead wall-hung tank with the traditional pull chain. In areas where condensation on the toilet tank is a problem, an insulated tank may be ordered.

All toilets are required to have a visible water turn off down near the bowl on the back wall in case of a faulty valve in the tank.

Toilets for the elderly and infirm have an 18 inch high seat, while regular toilets have 15 1/2 inch high seats. This higher toilet may also have a set of metal rails or armrests for extra support. The height of the seat on the one piece toilets may be even lower.

Toilets have different flushing actions. The washdown is the least expensive but is also the least efficient and the noisiest of toilet flushing actions. The most expensive of the siphon-action toilets is the reverse trap, where the rush of water when flushed creates a siphon action in the trapway, assisted by a smaller water jet at the trapway outlet. More of the bowl is covered by water, so it stays cleaner. The siphon-jet that is used on almost all newer toilets is much quieter and more efficient but usually more expensive. However, most of the interior of the bowl is covered by water, thus aiding in cleaning.

A maximum of 3 1/2 gallons of water is mandated by most codes, but some water-saving toilets are designed to flush with a lesser amount, a savings that

FIGURE 8-9.
A triplated chrome lavatory gooseneck faucet has separate faceted acrylic handles. (Photograph U.S. Brass). Lower left, there is a single control lavatory mixer with temperature/volume adjustment. (Designer: Arne Jacobsen; photography courtesy of Kroin Architectural Complements). Lower right, Sherle Wagner combines malachite and stainless steel in a sculptured design to create a new art form for the home. (Photograph courtesy of Sherle Wagner International, Inc.)

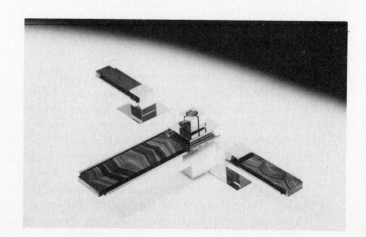

could add up substantially for an average family of four.

Bidets

While common in Europe, bidets are only now becoming an accepted fixture in American bathrooms and then only in the more sophisticated types of installations. A bidet is generally installed as a companion and adjacent to the water closet or toilet and is used for cleansing the perineal area. Bidets do not have seats. The user sits astride the bowl, facing the controls that regulate water temperature and operate the pop-up drain and transfer valve. Water enters the bidet via the spray rinse in the bottom of the bowl; or the water can be diverted by the transfer valve to the flushing rim. A bidet may also be used as a foot bath when the pop-up drain is closed. (See Figures 8-1 and 8-7 for bidets.)

Counter Tops

The term *vanity cabinet* is not technically used in the architectural profession, but ready-made bathroom cabinets containing the lavatory are so often called and sold by this name that this term will be used for the prefinished cabinet with doors underneath the counter top. Vanity cabinets may be ordered with or without the finished counter top and, with this design, the lavatory is purchased separately. Other types of vanities may come with the counter top and bowl molded in one, such as those constructed of Corian.

A ready-made vanity is between 29 and 30 inches in height. For a master bathroom in a custom designed house, the counter can be raised to suit personal requirements; however, at least one of the vanities in the house must be at the lower height.

Most custom designed bathrooms have specially designed cabinets containing the lavatory with a storage area beneath. A bathroom counter top may be made of the same materials as a kitchen counter, though marble is more frequently used in bathrooms than kitchens. (See Figure 8-5 for ceramic tile counter, and Figure 8-6 for a marble counter.)

Accessories

There should be 22 inches of towel storage for each person. Towels should be located within convenient reach of the bath, shower, and lavatory. Soap containers may be recessed into the wall, such as those used in the tub area. For the lavatory with a counter, a soap dish can be a colorful accessory. A toilet tissue dispenser should be conveniently located adjacent to the toilet.

Electrical outlets should also be provided for the myriad of electrical gadgets used in the bathroom. All switches should be located so that they cannot be reached from a tub or shower area. This is usually required by the local codes.

Mirrors may be on the door of a built-in medicine cabinet or they may be installed to cover the whole wall over the counter area. When used in the latter manner, they visibly enlarge the bathroom. The top of the mirror should be at least 72 inches above the floor.

The materials selected for floors, walls, and ceilings should be compatible with the moist conditions that prevail in most bathrooms.

PUBLIC RESTROOMS

The bathrooms previously discussed were designed to accommodate one or two people at the most. However, in public restrooms, conditions and location may necessitate designing an area to be used by many people at the same time. This not only includes people who can walk, but also those confined to wheelchairs.

Public restrooms receive much physical abuse, most of which is not premeditated, but occurs through normal wear and tear. Unfortunately, vandalism is a major problem and, therefore, the types of fixtures and selection of materials must be based on durability. Naturally, the two-stall restroom in a small restaurant and the multistall restrooms in a huge recreational facility will have to be designed with this factor in mind.

Another factor in selection of materials and fixtures is maintenance. Floors are almost always made out of ceramic tile or similar material and require a floor drain, not only for an emergency flooding problem, but also to facilitate the cleaning and disinfecting of the floor.

Lavatories

To aid in cleaning the counter areas of public restrooms, vitreous china lavatories with flush metal rims are most frequently specified. This provides quick cleaning of any excess water on the counter. White sinks are usually selected in restrooms for two reasons: first, they are cheaper and, second, cleanliness is more easily visible.

Lavatories come with the normal three holes punched in the top, but soft or liquid soap dispensers may be installed in a four hole sink. Or, the powder soap dispenser may be attached to the wall above each lavatory or between two adjacent ones.

For free-standing applications, wall-hung vitreous china lavatories may be specified.

For those who are confined to wheelchairs, a specially designed lavatory must be installed that enables the seated person to reach the faucet handles. Again, a wrist control handle or a push button that requires 5 pounds or less pressure should be specified. Because some wheelchair occupants are paraplegic, it is necessary to take some safety precautions that include either turning down the temperature of the water to 110° or wrapping the waste pipe with some form of insulation. These measures will prevent inadvertent burns.

Faucets

Some companies specialize in faucets designed to be used in public restrooms. These faucets are available with **metering devices,** usually of the push-button type, that can be field-adjusted to flow for 5 to 15 seconds. This, of course, conserves both energy and water and prevents accidental flooding.

Toilets

Wall-hung toilets are quite often used in public restrooms to facilitate cleaning. To aid in quicker maintenance and to avoid vandalism, toilets in public restrooms do not usually use the conventional tank, but have a **flushometer** valve. This valve requires greater **water pressure** to operate but uses less water and is easier to maintain. This type of valve is not used in private residences because it is too noisy.

There are several different types of **urinals** that may be used in the men's room. All are constructed of vitreous china and all have integral flushing rims. The first type is the stall urinal mounted on the floor. The second type is the wall-hung unit. This second type may have an elongated lip for use by those in wheelchairs.

Stall Partitions

There are many different styles of stall dividers and many different materials from which to select. The **pilasters** may be floor mounted with overhead bracing, floor supported, or ceiling hung. The latter type minimizes maintenance but also requires structural steel support in the ceiling. Doors for regular stalls are 24 inches wide and open into the stall. The actual width of the stall is determined by the width of the pilasters. Stalls for the handicapped have wider, outswinging doors, that must meet applicable codes. The handicapped stall is usually placed at the end so that passers-by are not hit when the door is opened from the inside (see Figure 8-10).

The materials used for construction of the partitions may be galvanized steel that has been primed and finished with two coats of baked enamel, stainless steel, seamless high pressure plastic laminate, or even marble (see Figure 8-10). All of these come in a variety of colors and may be coordinated with the colors used for washroom accessories, vanity centers, shelves, and countertops.

When the design of restrooms dictates, entrance screens for privacy should be used. It is important to consider the direction the door opens and placement of mirrors to ensure privacy.

Another screen used in men's rooms is the urinal screen. These may also be wall hung, floor anchored, ceiling hung, or supported by a narrow stile going from floor to ceiling, in a similar manner to the stall partitions. They are placed either between each urinal or between the urinal area and other parts of the restroom (see Figure 8-10).

Accessories

As was mentioned previously, soap dispensers may be installed in the lavatory rim itself. This type is probably preferable as any droppings from the dispenser are washed away in the bowl; the dry powder type usually leave a mess on the counter area. Paper towel dispensers should be within easy reach of the lavatory, together with the towel disposal containers. Sometimes these two accessories come in the same wall hung or wall recessed units. Another method of hand drying is the heated air blower where, at the push of a button, heated air is blown out and the hands are rubbed briskly. This type of hand dryer obviates the necessity of having the mess of paper towel disposal, but is a problem if the dryer breaks down.

FIGURE 8-10.
Dividers in this commercial men's restroom are Marblstal® from the Georgia Marble Company. Note the end stall is for wheelchair patrons. The outswinging door and handrail is shown. (Photograph courtesy of the Georgia Marble Company)

Each toilet compartment requires a toilet tissue dispenser; an optional accessory is the toilet seat cover dispenser. Necessary in each toilet stall in a ladies room is a feminine napkin disposal and outside, near the toilet stalls, a napkin and tampon vending machine is required. Optional in a toilet stall is a hook for hanging pocketbooks and jackets. The preferred location is on the handle side of the door so that no personal items are left behind. Another optional accessory in the ladies toilet stalls is a flip-down shelf that holds packages off the floor area.

In handicapped stalls, stainless steel grab bars are required by law to be mounted on the wall nearest the toilet. They are 1 1/2 inches in diameter and 1 1/2 inches from the wall and 33 to 36 inches from the floor. Local codes vary from city to city and state to state, so it is important to consult these codes for exact measurements.

There are two methods of transfer for wheelchair bound people, depending upon their abilities. Those who are able to stand with support can pull themselves upright by means of the grab bars. Others have to use the side transfer method, where the arm of the wheelchair is removed and the person leans across the toilet and pulls himself/herself onto the seat. The side transfer method requires a larger stall, as the chair must be placed alongside the toilet; the front transfer only requires the depth of the chair, plus standing room in front of the toilet.

Bibliography

Eljer Plumbingware. *Expressions.* Pittsburgh PA: Eljer Plumbingware, Wallace Murray Corporation, 1983.

Galvin, Patrick. *Remodeling Your Bathroom.* Popular Science Skill Book. New York: Harper & Row, 1980.

Ortho Books. *How To Design and Remodel Bathrooms.* San Francisco: Chevron Chemical Company, 1982.

Time-Life Books. *Kitchens and Bathrooms.* New York: Time-Life Books, 1977.

Time-Life Books. *Plumbing.* New York: Time-Life Books, 1976.

Glossary

Bidet. A sanitary fixture for cleansing the genito-urinary area of the body (see Figure 8-7).

Center-fit. Two handles and one spout mounted on a single plate.

Centers. Another way of saying on centers; in other words, the measurement is from the center of one hole to the center of the second hole.

Compartmented. Bathroom divided into separate areas according to function and fixtures.

Diverter. Changes flow of water from one area to another.

Feed-in. Where the rough plumbing is attached to the fittings.

Fittings. Another word for the faucet assembly; a term used by the plumbing industry.

Flushometer. A valve designed to supply a fixed quantity of water for flushing purposes (see Figure 8-10).

Gel coat. A thin, outer layer of resin, sometimes containing pigment, applied to a reinforced plastic moulding to improve its appearance.

Lavatory. The plumbing industry's name for a bathroom sink.

Low profile. A one-piece toilet with almost silent flushing action having almost no dry surfaces on the bowl interior.

Metering device. A preset measured amount of water is released when activated.

Overflow. A pipe in bathtubs and lavatories used to prevent flooding. The pipe is located just below the rim or top edge of these fixtures.

Pedestal. A lavatory on a base attached to the floor rather than set into a counter surface. Base hides all the waste pipes that are usually visible.

Pilaster. Vertical support member, varying in width.

Pop-up rod. The rod that controls the raising and lowering of the drain in the bottom of the lavatory.

Preformed base. Shower pans or bases of terrazzo or acrylic.

Sauna. A steam bath of Finnish origin.

Slip-resistant. Special material on the bottom of the tub to prevent falls.

Spa. Whirlpool-type bath for more than one person, with a heating and filtration system. Frequently installed outside in warmer climates.

Spread. Distance between holes of a bathtub or lavatory.

Surround. The walls encircling a bathtub or shower area (see Figures 8-2, 8-6, and 8-7).

Urinals. Wall-hung vitreous plumbing fixtures used in men's rooms, with a flushometer valve for cleaning purposes (see Figure 8-10).

Vanity. Layman's term for a prefabricated lavatory and base cabinet.

Water pressure. Measured as so many pounds per square inch. Usually 30 to 50 psi.

Wet wall. The wall in which the water and waste pipes are located.

Wrist control. Long lever handles operated by pressure of the wrist rather than with the fingers.

A

MANUFACTURERS & ASSOCIATIONS

S ome materials such as the stones do not have manufacturers and these materials may only be found through the Yellow Pages. For information on other manufacturers not listed in the Yellow Pages, write to the addresses in Appendix B.

It must be remembered that the names listed are just a few of those manufacturing that particular product. As far as possible, the listed names are nationally distributed items, but there are many local products that may be similar in quality.

Associations and Institutes represent their members in sales promotions and informational services only. They do not sell products, but many can provide a list of suppliers in your area.

Chapter 1

*Paints**

P.P.G. Industries

Sherwin Williams

Glidden Coatings Systems

*Stains**

Olympic Stain

*Danish Oil**

Watco Dennis Corp.

Chapter 2

Associations and Institutes

American National Standards Institute (ANSI) sets the codes and standards based on consensus of their membership.

*Denotes that the local distributor may be found in the Yellow Pages under the brand name or the manufacturer's name.

American Parquet Association represents some of the parquet manufacturers and prints a brochure listing the manufacturers and the types of patterns each company produces.

American Society for Testing and Materials (ASTM) sets the standard for all types of products.

Marble Institute of America represents the marble industry. They have a booklet, *How to Keep Your Marble Lovely*, which is available for $1.25 from the address in Appendix B.

National Oak Flooring Manufacturers Association (NOFMA) sets the standards by which wood flooring should be installed.

National Terrazzo and Mosaic Association, Inc., represents the terrazzo industry.

The Tile Council of America, Inc. publishes the *American National Standard Specifications for Ceramic Tile* annually. These specifications cover all types of tile installations and are a guide for the tile industry.

Strip

Longstrip Plank™, Harris-Tarkett, Inc.

Random Plank

Andersen Hardwood Floors

Kentucky Wood Floors, Inc.

Parquet

Dura Park™, Harris-Tarkett

Bruce® Hardwood Floors

Chickasaw Memphis Hardwood Flooring Co.

Kentucky Wood Floors, Inc.

Pattern-Plus™, Hartco, Tibbals Flooring Co.

Peace Flooring Co., Inc.

Acrylic Impregnated

Gammapar®, Applied Radiant Energy Corp.

Hartco, Tibbals Flooring Co.

PermaGrain® Products

Foam Backed Parquet

Hartco, Tibbals Flooring Co.

Prefinished and Packaged

Kahrs, Bangkok Industries

Prefinished

Squar-Edge™, Masonite Corp.

Mesquite

Du Bose Architectural Floors

Kentucky Wood Floors

End Grain

Du Bose Architectural Floors

Worthwood, Oregon Lumber Co.

Inlaid Border

Architectural Brasada Embellishments

Bangkok Industries

Kentucky Wood Floors

Laminated Wood Floors for Below-Grade Installations

Karpawood© and Asian Rosewood©, Bangkok Industries

Marble*

Carthage Marble Corp.

Georgia Marble Co.

Marble Veneers

Marble Technics Ltd.

Tejas Architectural Products, Inc.

Agglomerate

Terrazzo & Marble Supply Co.

Granite*

Granite Veneers

Marble Technics Ltd.

Flagstone*

Slate*

Buckingham-Virginia Slate Corp.

Structural Slate Co.

Ceramic Tile*

American Olean Tile Corp.

Florida Tile, Division of Sikes Co.

Dal-Tile Corp.

Marazzi USA, Inc.

Villeroy & Boch USA, Inc.

Ceramic Mosaic Tile

American Olean Tile Co.

Dal-Tile Corp.

Pregrouted Ceramic Tile

Redi-Set®, American Olean

Flexi-Set, Dal-Tile

Conductive Tile Vinyl

Flexco

Quarry Tile

American Olean Co.

Summitville® Tiles, Inc.

Mexican Tile*

Glass Tile

Emaux de Briare, Imported by The Briare Company, Inc.

Glass Block

Vistabrick®, Pittsburgh Corning Corp.

Monolithic Terrazzo*

Terrazzo

Dynasty Corp.

Fritztile, Fritz Chemical

Brick

Perma Brick®, PermaGrain Products, Inc.

Floor Maintenance

Hillyard Chemical Co.

Vinyl Asbestos (Composition)

Azrock Floor Products Division

Kentile® Floors

Vinyl Tile

Azrock Floor Products Division

Kentile® Floors

Vinyl and Rubber Bases

Burke Flooring Products

Johnson Rubber Co.

Kentile® Floors

Rubber Tile and/or Sheet

Jason/Pirelli, Jason Industrial, Inc.

Nora Flooring

R.C.A. Rubber Co., an Ohio Corp. of Akron, Ohio

Roppe Rubber Co.

Sheet Vinyl

Armstrong Floor Division

Congoleum Corp.

Mannington Mills Inc.

Tarkett

Cork

Designer Cork™, PermaGrain Products, Inc.

Vinyl Coated Fabric

Fabritile, PermaGrain Products, Inc.

Plastic Laminate

Wilsonart® Perma-Kleen™, Ralph Wilson Plastics Co.

Chapter 3

Associations and Institutes

The Architectural Woodwork Institute (AWI) is a non-profit organization devoted to the elevation of industry standards, to continuing research into new and

better materials and methods, and to the publication of technical data helpful to architects and specification writers in the design and use of architectural woodwork. Write for their price list covering all the books mentioned in this book as well as many others.

The National Association of Mirror Manufacturers promotes the many uses of mirror and produces a compilation of outstanding mirror ideas by leading interior designers.

*Granite**

*Marble**

Marble Technics Ltd.

Tejas Architectural Products Inc.

*Travertine**

*Brick**

*Concrete Block**

Glass Block

ARGUS®, VISTABRICK®, Pittsburgh Corning Corp.

*Plaster**

Gypsum Wallboard

Georgia-Pacific

Gold Bond Building Product

SHEETROCK®, U.S. Gypsum Co.

Vinyl-Surfaced Gypsum Wall Panels

Eternawall®, Georgia-Pacific

Gold Bond Building Product

U.S. Gypsum Co.

Wallpaper

Anaglypta®, Crown Decorative Products

Katzenbach & Warren

Schumacher

Albert Van Luit & Co.

Commercial Wallcoverings

Realwood®, Bangkok Industries

Bolta Wallcoverings

Vicrkleen™, Vicrtex, L.E. Carpenter & Co.

Tedlar®, E.I. DuPont de Nemours & Company

Acousticord, Eurotex, Inc.

Flexwood®, Flexible Materials

B.F. Goodrich Wallcoverings Products

Tambour, National Products

Primeline™, Ralph Wilson Plastics Co.

Redwood*

California Redwood Association

Solid Wood Strips

Potlatch Corp.

Profilewood®, Osterman & Scheiwe USA

Plywood Paneling*

Consult a member of the Architectural Woodwork
Institute

Bangkok Industries

Prefinished Plywood

Champion International Corp.

Georgia Pacific

Hardboard

Marlite®, Monoplank®, Peg-Board®, Masonite
Commercial Division

Plastic Laminate

Formica Corp.

Wilsonart®, Ralph Wilson Plastics Co.

Metal Laminates

METTLE MICA®, The October Co.

Homopal, The Diller Corp.

Plastic Laminate Wall Panels

Miami Carey

Tambours

National Products

Primeline®, Ralph Wilson Plastics Co.

Porcelain Enamel

Alliance Wall® Corp.

Mirror*

National Association of Mirror Manufacturers

Metal*

Pinecrest, Inc.

Acoustic Panels

Soundsoak®, Armstrong World Industries, Inc.

Vicracoustic®, L.E. Carpenter

Owens-Corning Fiberglas Corp.

Cork

Dodge Cork Company Inc.

Chapter 4

Wood*

Any of the wood flooring manufacturers

Trysil, Bangkok Industries

Acoustic Ceiling—Residential

Armstrong World Industries, Inc.

Hunter Douglas Inc.

Acoustic Ceiling—Commercial

Soft Look, Armstrong World Industries, Inc.

Celotex Corp.

Conwed International Products

Donn Corp.

Gold Bond

U.S. Gypsum

Mirror*

Mirrored Effect

Antique Glass, Armstrong World Industries, Inc.

VISTA SONIC®, Mirror access panels, U.S. Gypsum

Banners and Others

Lean-To™, Pipe & Junction™, Integrated Ceilings

Vicracoustic® baffles, L.E. Carpenter & Co.

Stamped Metal Ceiling

AA Abbingdon Ceiling

Chelsea Decorative Metals Co.

Pinecrest, Inc.

W.F. Norman Corp.

Strip Metal Ceilings

Alcan Building Products

Donn Corp.

Hunter Douglas, Inc.

Chapter 5

The Door and Hardware Institute promotes those two industries.

Mouldings

Driwood Moulding Co.

Focal Point Inc.

Old World Moulding & Finishing, Inc.

Doors*

Customwood

Morgan, Combustion Engineering, Inc.

Hinges

Baldwin Hardware Corp.

Grass America

Hager Hinge Co.

Soss Invisible Hinge, Universal Industrial Products

Hardware*

The Broadway Collection

Hewi Inc.

Sargent, Division of Kidde, Inc.

Schlage

Stanley Hardware

Valli & Colombo (USA), Inc.

Closers*

Corbin Division, Emhart Hardware Group

LCN Closers

Rixso-n-Firemark

Keyless Locks

Simplex Security Systems, Inc.

Shelving

Knape & Vogt Manufacturing Co.

Chapter 6

Architectural Woodwork Institute

Chapter 7

Kitchen Cabinets

Allmilmo

Poggenpohl USA, Inc.

Quaker Maid

St. Charles Manufacturing Co.

Kitchen Appliances

Amana*

Chambers*

Frigidaire*

General Electric*

Jenn-Air

Sub-Zero

Thermador/Waste King

Kitchen Sinks

Corian®, E.I. duPont de Nemours & Co.

Elkay Manufacturing Co. (Stainless steel)

Kitchen Faucets

Chicago Faucet Co.

Kroin Architectural Complements

Riser™, Moen Division, Stanadyne Corp.

U.S. Brass

Kitchen Cabinets

Allmilmö Corp.

Poggenpohl USA Corp.
St. Charles Manufacturing Co.

Kitchen Counters

Corian®, E.I. duPont de Nemours & Co.
COLOR CORE®, Formica Corp.
SOLICOR®, Ralph Wilson Plastics Co.

Chapter 8

Plumbing Fixture Manufacturers
American Standard
Eljer Plumbingware
Jacuzzi Whirlpool Bath Inc.

Environment™, Habitat™, Kohler Co.
Villeroy & Boch USA, Inc.

Specialty Lavatories

Sherle Wagner International

Faucets

The Broadway Collection
Sherle Wagner International
U.S. Brass

Stall Partitions

Marblestal
Bobrick Washroom Equipment, Inc.

Bathroom Accessories—Commercial

Bobrick
Bradley Corp.
Charles Parker

B

RESOURCES

AA Abingdon Affiliates, Inc.
2149 Utica Avenue
Brooklyn NY 11234

Alcan Building Products
280 North Park Avenue
Warren OH 44481

Alliance Wall Corp.
P.O.Box 48545
Atlanta GA 30362

Allmilmö Corp.
P.O.Box 629
Fairfield NJ 07006

Amana Refrigeration, Inc.
Amana IA 52204

American National Standards Institute
1430 Broadway
New York NY 10018

American Olean Tile Co.
P.O.Box 271
Lansdale PA 19446

American Parquet Association
1650 Union National Plaza
Little Rock AR 72201

American Society for Testing and Materials
1916 Rose Street
Philadelphia PA 19103

American-Standard
P.O.Box 2003
New Brunswick NJ 08903

Anderson Hardwood Floors
P.O.Box 1155
Clinton SC 29325

Applied Radiant Energy Co.
2432 Lakeside Drive
Lynchburg VA 24501

Architectural Brasada Embellishments
17045 El Camino Real
Houston TX 77058

Architectural Woodwork Institute
2310 S. Walter Reed Drive
Arlington VA 22206

Armstrong World Industries
P.O.Box 3001
Lancaster PA 17604

Azrock Floor Products
P.O.Box 34030
San Antonio TX 78265

Baldwin Hardware Corp.
P.O.Box 82
Reading PA 19603

Bangkok Industries Inc.
Gillingham & Worth Street
Philadelphia PA 19124

Bobrick Industries, Inc.
60 E. 42nd Street
New York NY 10165

Bolta Wallcoverings
401 Hackensack Avenue
Hackensack NJ 07601

The Briare Company, Inc.
51 Tec Street
Hicksville NY 11801

The Broadway Collection
250 N. Troost Street
Olathe KS 66061

Bruce Hardwood Floors
16803 Dallas Parkway
Dallas TX 75248

Buchtal Inc.
5780 Peachtree-Dunwoody Rd., N.E.
Atlanta GA 30342

Buckingham-Virginia Slate Corp.
P.O.Box 11002
Richmond VA 23230

Burke Flooring Products
2250 South Tenth Street
San Jose CA 95112

California Redwood Association
591 Redwood Highway, Suite 3100
Mill Valley CA 94941

L.E. Carpenter & Co.
170 N. Main Street
Wharton NJ 07885

Carthage Marble Corp.
Carthage MO 64836

Celotex Corp.
1500 N. Dale Mabry
Tampa FL 33607

Champion International Corp.
One Champion Plaza
Stamford CT 06921

Chelsea Decorative Metals Co.
6115 Cheena Drive
Houston TX 77096

Chicago Faucet
2100 South Nuclear Drive
Des Plaines IL 60018

Congoleum Corp.
195 Belgrove Drive
Kearny NJ 07032

Conwed Interior Products Division
P.O.Box 43237
St Paul MN 55164

Corbin Division, Emhart Hardware Group
225 Episcopal Road
Berlin CT 06037

Customwood
Box 26208
Albuquerque NM 87125

Dal-Tile
7834 C.F. Hawn Freeway
Dallas TX 95217

The Diller Corp.
P.O.Box 997
Morton Grove IL 60053

Dodge Cork Co. Inc.
P.O.Box 989
Lancaster PA 17603

Donn Corp.
1000 Crocker Road
Westlake OH 44145

Door & Hardware Institute
7711 Old Springhouse Road
McLean VA 22102

Driwood Moulding Co.
P.O.Box 1729
Florence SC 29503

Du Bose Architectural Floors
905 San Pedro
San Antonio TX 78212

E.I. DuPont de Nemours & Co., Corian Products
Market Street Room X39196
Wilmington DE 19898

Dynasty Corp.
100 Peachtree, N.W.
Atlanta GA 30303

Eljer Plumbingware
Three Gateway Center
Pittsburgh PA 15222

Elkay Manufacturing Co.
2222 Camden Court
Oak Brook IL 60521

Eurotex
2400 Market Street
Philadelphia PA 19103

Flexco Co.
P.O.Box 553
Tuscumbia AL 35674

Flexible Materials
2921 South Floyd Street
Louisville KY 40213

Florida Tile, Division of Sikes Corp.
P.O.Box 447
Lakeland FL 33802

Focal Point Inc.
2005 Marietta Road, N.W.
Atlanta GA 30318

Formica Corp.
One Cyanamid Plaza
Wayne NJ 07470

Fritz Chemical Corp.
P.O.Drawer 17040
Dallas TX 75217

Georgia Marble Co.
Structural Division
Nelson GA 30151

Georgia-Pacific
133 Peachtree, N.E.
Atlanta GA 30303

Glidden Coatings Systems, Division of SCM Corp.
900 Union Commerce Building
Cleveland OH 44115

Gold Bond Building Products
2001 Rexford Road
Charlotte NC 28211

B.F. Goodrich Wallcoverings Products, Dept. 1911
500 South Main Street
Akron OH 44318

Grass America, Inc.
P.O.Box 1019
Kernersville NC 27284

Hager Hinge Co.
St. Louis MO 63104

Harris-Tarkett
P.O.Box 300
Johnson City TN 37601

Hewi, Inc.
6 Pearl Court
Allendale NJ 07401

Hillyard Chemical Co.
302 N. 4th Street
St. Joseph MO 64502

Hunter Douglas Inc., Architectural Products
87 Route 17
Maywood NJ 07607

Integrated Ceilings
11500 Tennessee Avenue
Los Angeles CA 90064

Jacuzzi Whirlpool Bath, Inc.
P.O.Drawer J
Walnut Creek CA 94596

Jason Industries, Inc.
340 Kaplan Drive
Fairfield NJ 07006

Johnson Rubber Co.
Middlefield OH 44062

Katzenbach & Warren
950 3rd Avenue
New York NY 10022

Kentile Floors
979 Third Avenue
New York NY 10022

Kentucky Wood Floors, Inc.
P.O.Box 33276
Louisville KY 40212

Knape & Vogt Manufacturing Co.
2700 Oak Industrial Drive, N.E.
Grand Rapids MI 49505

Kohler Company
Kohler WI 53044

Kroin Architectural Complements
14 Story Street
Cambridge MA 02138

LCN Closers
Princeton IL 61656

Mannington Mills, Inc.
P.O.Box 30
Salem NJ 08079

Marazzi USA, Inc.
55 Clay & Scyene Road
Sunnyvale TX 75182

Marble Institute of America
33505 State Street
Farmington MI 48024

Marble Technics Ltd.
150 E. 58 Street
New York NY 10155

Masonite Commercial Division
P.O.Box 250
Dover OH 44622

Memphis Hardwood Flooring
P.O.Box 7253
Memphis TN 38107

Miami Carey
203 Garver Road
Monroe OH 45050

Moen Division, Stanadyne Corp.
377 Woodland Avenue
Elyria OH 44035

National Association of Mirror Manufacturers
9005 Congressional Court
Potomac MD 20854

National Oak Flooring Manufacturing Association
804 Strick Building
Memphis TN 38103

National Products
2921 South Floyd Street
Louisville KY 40213

National Terrazzo & Mosaic Association, Inc.
3166 Des Plaines Avenue
Des Plaines IL 60018

Nora Flooring
4201 Wilson Avenue
Madison IN 47250

W.F. Norman Corp.
P.O.Box 323
Nevada MO 64772

The October Co.
Box 71
Easthampton MA 01027

Old World Moulding & Finishing, Inc.
115 Allen Boulevard
Farmington NY 11735

Olympic Stain
2233 112th Avenue, N.E.
Bellevue WA 98004

Oregon Lumber Co.
P.O.Box 711
Lake Oswego OR 97034

Osterman & Scheiwe USA
4109 192nd Street
Tacoma WA 98446

Owens-Corning Fiberglas Corp.
Fiberglas Tower
Toledo OH 43659

Charles Parker Co.
P.O.Box 916
Meriden CT 06450

Peace Flooring Co., Inc.
Dept. B., Box 87
Magnolia AK 70754

PermaGrain Products, Inc.
22 West State Street
Media PA 19063

Pinecrest, Inc.
2118 Blaisdell Avenue
Minneapolis MN 55404

Pittsburgh Corning Corp.
800 Presque Isle Drive
Pittsburgh PA 15239

Poggenpohl USA Corp.
222 Cedar Lane
Teaneck NJ 07666

Potlatch Corp., Townsend Unit
P.O.Box 916
Stuttgart AK 72160

PPG Industries
One PPG Place
Pittsburgh PA 15272

Quaker Maid
Rt 61
Leesport PA 19533

R.C.A. Rubber Co., an Ohio Corp. of Akron, Ohio
1833 E. Market Street
Akron OH 44305

Rixson-Firemark
9100 W. Belmont Avenue
Franklin Park IL 60131

Roppe Rubber Co.
1602 N. Union Street
Fostoria OH 44830

St. Charles Manufacturing Co.
1611 E. Main Street
St. Charles IL 60174

Sargent, Division of Kidde, Inc.
P.O.Box 9725
New Haven CT 06536

Schlage Lock Co.
P.O.Box 3324
San Francisco CA 94119

Schumacher
919 3rd Avenue
New York NY 10022

Sherle Wagner International, Inc.
60 East 57th Street
New York NY 10022

Sherwin-Williams Co.
101 Prospect Avenue, N.W.
Cleveland OH 44115

Simplex Security Systems, Inc.
P.O.Box 377
Collinsville CT 06022

Stanley Hardware Division
195 Lake Street
New Britain CT 06050

Structural Slate Co.
222 East Main Street
Pen Argyl PA 18072

Summitville Tiles, Inc.
Summitville OH 43962

Tarkett, Inc.
P.O.Box 264
Parsippany NJ 07054

Tejas Architectural Products, Inc.
1725 Sandy Lake Road
Carrollton TX 75006

Terrazzo and Marble Supply Co.
5700 South Hamilton Avenue
Chicago IL 60636

Thermador/Waste King
5119 District Blvd.
Los Angeles CA 90040

Tibbals Flooring Co.
P.O. Drawer A
Oneida TN 37841

Tile Council of America
P.O. Box 326
Princeton NJ 08542

U.S. Brass
901 Tenth Street
Plano TX 75074

U.S. Gypsum Co.
101 South Wacker Drive
Chicago IL 60606

Universal Industrial Products
P.O.Box 628
Pioneer OH 43554

Valli & Colombo (USA) Inc.
1540 Highland Avenue
Duarte CA 91010

Albert Van Luit & Co.
4000 Chevy Chase Drive
Los Angeles CA 90039

Villeroy & Boch USA, Inc.
I-80 at New Maple Avenue
Pine Brook NJ 07058

Watco Dennis Corp.
Santa Monica CA 90404

Ralph Wilson Plastics Co.
600 General Bruce Drive
Temple TX 76501

Bibliography

Architectural Woodwork Institute. *Architectural Woodwork Quality Standard, Guide Specifications and Quality Certification Program*. Alexandria VA: Architectural Woodwork Institute, 1978.

Harris, Cyril M. *Dictionary of Architecture and Construction*. New York: McGraw-Hill, 1975.

Hornbostel, Caleb. *Materials for Architecture*. New York: Reinhold, 1961.

McGraw-Hill. *1984 Sweet's Catalogue File*. New York: Sweet's Division, McGraw-Hill Information Systems Co., 1984.

Merritt, Frederick S. *Building Construction Handbook*. New York: McGraw-Hill, 1975.

Olin, Harold B., Schmidt, John L., & Lewis, Walter H. *Construction Principles, Materials and Methods* (4th Ed.). Chicago IL: The Institute of Financial Education, and Danville IL: Interstate Printers and Publishers, 1980.

Putnam, R.E., & Carlson, G.E. *Architectural & Building Trades Dictionary* (3rd Ed.). New York: Van Nostrand Reinhold, 1982.

Reader's Digest. *Complete Do-it-yourself Manual*. Pleasantville NY: The Reader's Digest Association, 1973.

Reiner, Lawrence E. *Methods and Materials of Construction*. Englewood Cliffs NJ: Prentice-Hall Inc., 1970.

Reznikoff, S.C. *Specifications for Commercial Interiors*. New York: Whitney Library of Design, an imprint of Watson-Guptil Publications, 1979.

Wakita, Osamu A., & Linde, Richard. *The Professional Practice of Architectural Detailing*. New York: John Wiley & Sons, 1977.

Wise, Herbert H. *Attention to Detail*. New York: G.P. Putnam's Sons, 1982.

INDEX

*Numbers in parentheses can be found in the glossaries.